Sustainable Development Goals Series

The **Sustainable Development Goals Series** is Springer Nature's inaugural cross-imprint book series that addresses and supports the United Nations' seventeen Sustainable Development Goals. The series fosters comprehensive research focused on these global targets and endeavours to address some of society's greatest grand challenges. The SDGs are inherently multidisciplinary, and they bring people working across different fields together and working towards a common goal. In this spirit, the Sustainable Development Goals series is the first at Springer Nature to publish books under both the Springer and Palgrave Macmillan imprints, bringing the strengths of our imprints together.

The Sustainable Development Goals Series is organized into eighteen subseries: one subseries based around each of the seventeen respective Sustainable Development Goals, and an eighteenth subseries, "Connecting the Goals", which serves as a home for volumes addressing multiple goals or studying the SDGs as a whole. Each subseries is guided by an expert Subseries Advisor with years or decades of experience studying and addressing core components of their respective Goal.

The SDG Series has a remit as broad as the SDGs themselves, and contributions are welcome from scientists, academics, policymakers, and researchers working in fields related to any of the seventeen goals. If you are interested in contributing a monograph or curated volume to the series, please contact the Publishers: Zachary Romano [Springer; zachary.romano@springer.com] and Rachael Ballard [Palgrave Macmillan; rachael.ballard@palgrave.com].

Mariana Valente

Online Misogyny in Brazil

Law, Internet Governance, and the Struggle for Gender Justice

IDRC · CRDI
International Development Research Centre
Centre de recherches pour le développement international

Springer

Canada

Mariana Valente
Institute for Law and Economics
University of St. Gallen
St. Gallen, St. Gallen, Switzerland

InternetLab - Law and Technology Research Centre
São Paulo, Brazil

ISSN 2523-3084 ISSN 2523-3092 (electronic)
Sustainable Development Goals Series
ISBN 978-3-032-07726-4 ISBN 978-3-032-07727-1 (eBook)
https://doi.org/10.1007/978-3-032-07727-1

The original submitted manuscript has been translated into English. The translation was done using artificial intelligence. A subsequent revision was performed by the author(s) to further refine the work and to ensure that the translation is appropriate concerning content and scientific correctness. It may, however, read stylistically different from a conventional translation.

This work was carried out with the aid of a grant from the International Development Research Centre, Ottawa, Canada. The views expressed herein do not necessarily represent those of IDRC or its Board of Governors.

This Springer imprint is published by the registered company Springer Nature Switzerland AG
The registered company address is: Gewerbestrasse 11, 6330 Cham, Switzerland

Preface

This book is an adapted and expanded version of *Misoginia na Internet*, a book published in Brazil in 2023, in Portuguese, by Editora Fósforo. The book has been updated to address new research that came out in the period and cover novelties such as the passing of a law to criminalise deepfakes and the Brazilian Supreme Court decision that changes the Internet Service Providers' liability framework. It has also been adapted to contextualise political and social facts for an international audience, incorporating new literature to support and facilitate comparisons with other realities. Part of these adaptations has come in answer to peer reviews conducted by Springer. The International Development Research Centre, Ottawa, Canada, funded both the research and publishing of the Brazilian book and the open-access costs for this English version.

St. Gallen, Switzerland — Mariana Valente

Acknowledgements

This book is the result of more than ten years of research conducted at InternetLab and, more recently, at the University of St. Gallen. I am especially grateful to my current and former co-directors, partners, and friends from InternetLab, Francisco Brito Cruz, Heloísa Massaro, Fernanda Martins, Fernanda Campagnucci, and Clarice Tavares for their support throughout the writing process and their daily intellectual exchanges. It would not have been possible without the financial support of the International Development Research Center (IDRC), under the project #Recognize-*Resist-Remedy: a research project to combat gender-based hate speech against women in Brazil and India*, which funded research, activities related to online misogyny at InternetLab between 2019 and 2023, and the open access to this book. Special thanks go to senior program manager Ruhiya Seward. To the Indian organisation IT for Change for their partnership in the project and all the dialogue, particularly our dear friends Anita Gurumurthy and Nandini Chami. For partnerships in conducting field research in Brazil, to Rede Conhecimento Social, IBEAC, *Revista AzMina*, Núcleo Jornalismo, Casa1, MariaLab, Núcleo de Inteligência Eleitoral, Lux Ferreira, and L4BHD-UFB4. To the University of St. Gallen, for supporting my research activities in the past three years.

Over the past ten years, many researchers at InternetLab have actively contributed to the effort of collecting data, preparing publications, and formulating questions that are part of this work. I want to thank Natália Neris, with whom I worked closely for many years at a time when these paths were opening up, and the other people who were directly involved in the research: Juliana Ruiz, Lucas Bulgarelli, Clarice Tambelli, Beatriz Kira, Nathalie Fragoso, Thiago Oliva, Alessandra Gomes, Fernanda Martins, Clarice Tavares, Ester Borges, Catharina Pereira, Blenda Santos, Jade Becari, and Juliana Fonteles. For their careful reading and exchanges, Stephanie Lima, Alice Lana, Iná Jost, and Barbara Simão. And to the entire team, past and present, who make InternetLab a unique and exciting space for the production of knowledge engaged with digital rights and technologies in Brazil.

The space for exchange over the last few years at Cebrap's Law and Democracy Centre, particularly in the Counterpublics subgroup, was essential. For their generous and attentive reading of the manuscript and their pertinent critiques and special requests, Fernando Túlio, Isabela Del Monde, Bianca Tavolari, Marcos Nobre, Clara Iglesias Keller, Natália Paiva, Nina Santos, Fabiola Fanti, and Jonas Medeiros. For reading and bringing essential insights to the book launches in Brazil, I would like to thank Juliana Borges, Patrícia Campos Mello, Heloísa Buarque de Almeida, Luanda Pires, Manoela Miklos, Bianca Bortoloni, Flávia Biroli, Regina Facchini, Anna Bentes, and Iara Beleli. For help with research for this English adaptation, Max Mayer from the research group "Technology, Power and Domination" at the Weizenbaum Institute, and help with editing, Hana Musljiu at the University of St. Gallen. Of course, any errors or omissions are my responsibility.

For her encouragement, Rita Mattar of Fósforo, who first got excited about me writing this book. For her careful and enthusiastic reading and all her support, to the editor Eloah Pina, and for their work bringing it to a broader public in Brazil, Bia Reigenheim, Thais Naiara, and the team at Fósforo. For the excitement, support, work, and engaged ideas in producing this English version, the editor Bruno Fiuza at Springer.

For their dialogue and inspiration, to the many women from so many fields who have been building the debate on misogyny on the internet in Brazil and internationally, from academia, civil society, political parties, public agencies, and companies. I hope this book does justice to our exchanges and opens new paths between us. To the many girls and women who have been making their voices heard on the internet in Brazil, for their struggle. For accompanying the first discussions of the Portuguese edition from inside my belly, changing how I see the world and giving new meanings to my research, life, and activism, my little daughter, Serena.

Contents

1 Misogyny, Law, and Technology

Abstract

This chapter presents an introduction to the book, which explores nearly 15 years of Brazil's evolving discursive and legal response to online misogyny. It introduces the Brazilian trajectory from early emblematic cases (e.g. the 2002 "Giovanna" episode and journalist Rose Leonel in 2005), which first highlighted the devastating personal and professional consequences of non-consensual image sharing. Conceptually, it distinguishes misogyny from sexism (after Kate Manne), defends the online–offline continuum, interdisciplinary and intersectional approaches, and situates online (or technology-facilitated) violence amid international human rights definitions and the politics of naming. Empirically, it outlines the scale and unequal effects of technology-facilitated gender-based violence and the role of architectures (speed, reach, permanence, anonymity, context collapse); legally, it lays out the theoretical basis for how the law is mobilised by society and goes on to name the legislative landmarks that recur throughout the book and structure the analysis, from the Carolina Dieckmann Law in 2012 against device hacking to recent developments around deepfakes and platform duties. The chapter also situates Brazil's unique context (high internet use, connection asymmetries, gender and racial inequality, and experience in global internet governance spaces), showing how backlash and feminist organising have co-produced both the vocabulary and the normative terrain of regulation.

Keywords

Misogyny · Intersectionality · Internet Governance: Technology-Facilitated Gender-Based Violence (3TFGBV) · Juridification

In 2002, emails began circulating among students and teachers at the Getúlio Vargas Foundation (FGV), a prestigious higher education institution in São Paulo, Brazil, with photographs taken at "Giovanna", a party organised by the institution's student union. The photos were also published on websites of unknown authorship and sent to bank employees, where the people pictured could potentially work one day. They were images taken by hidden cameras located in "*cafofos*", private and closed areas of the party space where couples exchanged intimacies (Padilla, 2002).

The story circulated among the "internauts"—who, that year, were only 7% of the Brazilian population (Folha de S.Paulo, 2022)—while they were downloading MP3s and chatting on ICQ (Tecmundo, 2017). In 2005, journalist Rose Leonel began a years-long saga after having intimate images—some real, others montages—sent

M. Valente, *Online Misogyny in Brazil*, Sustainable Development Goals Series,
https://doi.org/10.1007/978-3-032-07727-1_1

to her by her ex-fiancé, Eduardo Gonçalves da Silva, to friends, family, and work contacts. After the photographs were taken, she began to receive calls from men, who either mocked her or asked how much she charged for sex: Eduardo had included her phone numbers in his emails. Leonel was very well known because she ran a television programme in the city of Maringá, in the state of Paraná, south of Brazil. The radio station where she worked started receiving calls asking for her resignation. Within two months, she was unemployed and would never rise to the same professional level; sometime later, her son moved with his father to Europe, fleeing persecution. The journalist filed four lawsuits, and in 2010, Eduardo was sentenced to prison for almost two years (González, 2011).

Twelve years after the Giovanna party, in 2014, the São Paulo State Court of Appeals ordered the Getúlio Vargas Foundation's Student Union to pay 50,000 reais in compensation to one of the students, who had been photographed without consent in intimate scenes with her boyfriend. The boyfriend was not part of the proceedings, which were held in secret.

When I started researching gender-based violence on the internet in 2014, sexual images were still the first thing that appeared in a simple internet search for Rose Leonel's name. This is no longer the case today, although it is still possible to find them. What has changed since then?

To answer this question, this book aims to reconstruct nearly 15 years of discussion on addressing misogyny on the internet in Brazil. Over this period, we have moved from the public's failure to recognise the problem to a wider debate that considers the gender dimension of much online violence, which has extended to groups and organisations from various social fields and localities. Throughout the chapters, I engage with other disciplines within the human sciences and humanities, but it is the laws enacted since 2012 that guide the path. These laws both signify the evolution of concerns that have entered public debate over time and serve as tangible tools to create new meanings and constraints. As a researcher specialising in law and a feminist activist, I have closely followed this development throughout.

However, the legal aspect is only one of the approaches to addressing misogyny, and it contains many contradictions. I hope that reading this book will help deepen the understanding of the complexity of misogyny online, the social conflicts pursued through law, and the Brazilian experience at this crossroads. This book links internet policy and regulation, gender law, and critical social and technology studies; as a continental country with a colonial history, relatively high internet penetration, and substantial internet use by those with access, Brazil has innovative internet governance institutions and laws. With both significant gender inequalities and a historically active civil society and feminist movement, lessons from Brazil in these areas offer important insights to the world, challenging the dominant perspectives of industrialised nations.

Much of the data I bring here is the result of research carried out collectively with various researchers at InternetLab, the independent research organisation I have been working with since it was founded in 2014, and of which I am a member and director; other data is produced by Brazilian and other researchers who have been building a truly vibrant and diverse field of research and action on gender and technology. The dialogue with women from different backgrounds, identities, and forms of action has been the most fundamental aspect of our research over all these years. Personally, as a White Brazilian woman[1] co-leading a law and technology research organisation for ten years, I have countless stories to tell about how sexism permeates our field, from day-to-day work to the difficulty of positioning gender agendas within discussions of regulation and internet governance. I am also aware of my limitations in terms of understanding racism and other forms of discrimination that I don't experience in Brazil, and which are equally structural, and, as an assistant professor in Law in Switzerland, more recently, I am beginning to understand in depth other challenges and contradictions of position and identity. Any writ-

[1] According to the Brazilian racial and ethnic distinctions.

ing is written in the first person, and in these pages, I am seeking sincerity and fidelity with both the collective constructions and the differences. I hope this reconstruction does justice to the powerful exchanges we have established along the way.

Over time, we have engaged with concepts such as online or technology-facilitated gender-based violence (TFGBV),[2] hate speech, image-based violence, and political violence. Therefore, the choice of approaching the issue through the lens of the concept of misogyny is not a trivial one. Misogyny is not yet defined in the Brazilian legislation, although many acts that can be considered misogynistic are. So, what is misogyny? And why choose this guiding concept?

The social and legal debates on misogyny have been catalysed by the internet, and the conflicts surrounding it have been catalysts for this debate. Even so, an initial conceptual exploration is helpful. In her book *Down* Girl*: The Logic of Misogyny*, philosophy professor Kate Manne (2019, p. 32) offers some valuable insights. She rejects a common, "naïve" view of misogyny as a characteristic of individual agents who tend to feel hatred, hostility, or similar emotions (associated, for example, with disgust, fear, and contempt) towards women simply because they are women. Her rejection stems from the fact that, firstly, this attitude towards *all* women, rather than *a few* in particular, is very difficult to identify. The motives behind a person's attitudes are inaccessible (except to their therapist, if that), which limits the understanding of the phenomenon and ultimately silences the victims. Secondly, it is a purely psychologising way of seeing things, which neglects the political nature of the phenomenon. Manne's concept of misogyny is that of "the system that operates within a patriarchal social order to police and enforce women's subordination and to uphold male dominance" (Manne, 2019, p. 32).

There are two fundamental aspects to this definition: misogyny as a characteristic of social systems, i.e. those in which the subordination of women, or most of them, is widely accepted in culture, values, and institutions, and as hostility suffered by women who, in a world that favours men, do not meet expected standards, for example, by not being subordinate, attentive, or loving. The violation of this role by women perceived as insubordinate, negligent, and "out of order" (Manne, 2019, p. 50) can generate this selective hostility.

Therefore, to talk about misogyny is to choose the lens of this expression of difference, being aware that it is necessary to understand how it occurs in the most varied contexts. This has to do with something that Kate Manne (2019, p. 46) also recognises: subordination does not necessarily *succeed* in producing subordinate positions; it is rather a *tendency*. For example, some women do not feel insecure and are very successful, even though people tend to question women more than men, and this often leads to self-questioning, even though both culture and failed institutions and support networks make the professional lives of women, particularly those who are mothers, more difficult. It may also be that misogynistic attitudes are unsuccessful in a concrete way—for example, a woman does not feel affected by comments that diminish her intellect. Finally, at the intersections of power involving other differences—race, ethnicity, class, sexuality, sexual identity—subordinations can be more complex. In many situations, a wealthy White Brazilian woman from the country's southeast, who is an heiress or a successful professional, will have more power than a poorer Black man from the northeast, who carries out a less socially presti-

[2] The field has traditionally worked with the concept of online gender-based violence, but *technology-facilitated gender-based violence* (TFGBV) has more recently been favored for being broader and more precise. It marks a continuum with previously existing forms of violence and includes those not happening exclusively online but involving digital technology in some way. For instance, stalking—defined as a set of repeated and unwanted behaviors that cause fear in the victim, and which disproportionately affects women (Logan & Walker, 2009)—is not new but has been significantly facilitated by digital technologies, including spyware and stalkerware (Khoo et al., 2019). These developments underscore the broader scope and impact of TFGBV (Dunn, 2020).

gious professional activity.[3] None of this eliminates the fact that misogyny exists as a tendency and produces concrete consequences. Otherwise, we could only talk about misogyny if we found a homogeneous reality, a simplicity that does not match the way social relations develop.

This also points to the principle from which I start this book: that there is not just one way of being a woman and that the way different women are affected by violence varies according to certain characteristics, which in turn are affected by different systems of power. This is particularly important as I will discuss misogyny practised in Brazil—where sexism has its own contours but where there are also many other cleavages that define different experiences of being a woman. As Sueli Carneiro (2017) and Patricia Hill Collins (2017) point out, "freedom is indivisible". Ideas of intersectionality (albeit without this conceptualisation) were born in the practices of social movements and women's political struggle in Brazil and the United States and have been imperfectly translated in academia in descriptive projects that have lost the dimension of emancipatory politics (Collins, 2017; Rodrigues, 2013). A project that claims to be intersectional, as this one strives to be, must adopt an analytical strategy that provides new angles of vision on a social phenomenon and a critical praxis, with the horizon of dismantling social injustices of race, class, gender, and sexuality (Collins, 2015).

There is still an essential conceptual distinction to be made. Kate Manne separates misogyny from sexism: if misogyny is a system of monitoring and enforcing the subordination of women, sexism would be the justificatory branch of this hierarchisation, a way of rationalising it: "sexism wears a lab coat; misogyny goes on a witch hunt" (Manne, 2019, pp. 79–80; Ukockis, 2019).

In the Western world, one of the very contrasting characteristics of sexism is the naturalisation of the difference between gender and sex, i.e. making it appear that social differences are part of nature, part of the biology of things, through claims that are not and cannot be proven, or even that contradict scientific arguments. In their book *History of Misogyny*, the Spanish psychologists Esperanza Bosch Fiol et al. (1999) argue that, over European history (and going back to Aristotle), beliefs in women's inferiority have revolved around biology, intellect, and morals, and been supported by a series of religious, anatomic-biological, and pseudo-scientific claims. And while it would be incorrect to frame Brazil as part of the Western world, we can follow Brazilian anthropologist Lélia Gonzalez in recognising that, as a colonised country, various Western symbolic regimes of European origin operate in our context, denying but at the same time being challenged and transformed by the knowledge of original and African peoples—the *amefricanity* (Gonzalez, 2020). In this context, misogyny operates firmly—enforcing these Western gender social norms or expectations, even where reality challenges stereotypes.[4] Conceptually, however, it has found its ground more recently, as I will explore in depth in this book.

Another crucial conceptual clarification from the outset is that I will not be engaging with the concept of *machismo* as understood in the English language. *Machismo*, in Portuguese, stands simply for sexism. It is my understanding that most of the descriptive and theoretical endeavours about *machismo* in English are foreign views of Latin American culture that frequently exoticise, simplify, generalise, and single out aspects of sexism which exist just as well in other cultures. As a Brazilian engaging with local gender literature, I refuse this external stereotyping and choose to offer local accounts and interpretations of sexism and misogyny throughout this book.[5]

[3] There are marked socioeconomic differences between the different regions in Brazil, and the Southeast and South concentrate states with higher levels of income and socioeconomic indexes such as the HDI (IBGE, 2024).

[4] I will discuss further how, for example, the association between women and private sphere corresponds to only a narrow parcel of Brazilian women.

[5] A good account of the problems associated with adopting *machismo* as an uncontested term is offered by Benjamin Arthur Cowan, who reconstructs its use as an English-language term. "Linked anxieties about overpopulation,

Misogyny, therefore, as a system that enforces sexism, has various methods, including gender-based violence. Gender-based violence is a slice of misogyny, but whether offline or online, it has gained more space in the public debate because misogyny itself has not yet fully integrated social discussions and legal vocabulary—many people, in Brazil and elsewhere, are still unfamiliar with the term. In addition, it is easier to relate violence to the law, as we will also discuss in this book. Reducing the problem of misogyny to violence, however, can be limiting. I will address violence before we return to misogyny. After all, as I will discuss, violence is more controversial than it seems on the surface.

And why restrict the approach to violence on the internet? Until at least the mid-2010s, it wasn't even considered that an online act could be qualified as violence. In November 2015, a team of Brazilian university students making a documentary interviewed me and researcher Natália Neris at InternetLab, when we were investigating the legal confrontation with the non-consensual online dissemination of intimate images—so-called *revenge porn*.[6] At the time, the students were surprised that we used the word violence repeatedly—something they said the other interviewees had not done. On receiving this feedback, it became clear to us that naming these practices as violence is itself a kind of *statement*–a strong and, as we shall see, performative statement (Valente et al., 2016).

At a time when the internet and its activities are a central concern for global societies, especially in debates about the role of digital technologies in democracy, public debate, social integration, and the exercise of rights, it is crucial to understand how gender differences manifest in this space and what the struggles for women's equality and freedom have entailed. As we will observe throughout this book, the social and legal notions of misogyny have been shaped in Brazil based on context and significant disputes. We never arrive at a definitive answer; ultimately, I demonstrate where this construct has already led us and where it might still guide us.

1.1 Gender-Based Violence and Internet Governance Debates

If naming an online act as violence was questionable between 2013 and 2015, addressing gender and race issues in spaces where internet policies are debated was even more difficult. There have always been those who have done so: a notable example is the Association for Progressive Communications (APC), an international network of civil society organisations founded in 1990 with a mission linked to justice issues in the field of communication and information technologies. The APC has had programmes in support of women's rights since the beginning of that decade and even took part in the Beijing World Conference on Women in 1995. It is an institution focusing on gender issues in the spaces where the internet is discussed, and its history is, therefore, intertwined with the broader history of the subject.

At the UN Internet Governance Forum (IGF), a meeting that has been held annually since 2006 to develop recommendations based on multisectoral discussions (government, private sector, civil society, and the technical community) (UN, ITU, & WSIS, 2005), debates on gender have slowly gained some ground. As early as the 2009 meeting, APC and other organisations demanded the following meetings to promote a rights approach explicitly and the presence and training of women in the spaces using a "dynamic gender coalition" (Internet Governance Forum, 2009).

poverty, communist subversion, and increased immigration lent urgency to sociological, public health, and psychological research on these places and on associated communities. Propagating the academic use of the term *machismo*, such studies assumed and concurrently reinstantiated the term's validity. Presuming, in contradictory fashion, their own empiricism, they found what they set out to find: not whether Latin Americans' gender systems were problematic, but how they were. The resultant social science did not firmly ground *machismo*'s meaning but it did grant the word traction as a means of stigmatizing and pathologizing Latin American masculinities" (Cowan, 2017).

[6] In this book, it will be referred to as NCII (non-consensual intimate images).

The presence of the subject has expanded over the years but with many setbacks. In 2014, online gender-based violence was a topic chosen to be worked on between sessions in a mechanism called the Best Practices Forum. In 2015, at the IGF held in João Pessoa, Brazil, the Best Practices Forum presented a survey based on multiple methodologies.[7] Before the meeting, the organisers, several of whom were linked to the APC, prepared a Twitter campaign with the hashtag #TakeBacktheTech. It was linked to a much older APC project, founded in 2006, to connect the issue of online violence with anti-violence actions already carried out by women's organisations. The reference is explicitly to the Take Back the Night marches on violence against women in the streets (Friedman, 2016, p. 81). The 2016 online campaign received much attention—more than 25,000 tweets—but not for the intended purpose: the campaign suffered a coordinated attack by opponents with critical messages and, what was much more worrying, images of women being physically and sexually assaulted, as well as public threats or threats in the personal emails of the organisers (APC, 2015). Some opponents claimed to be associated with the #Gamergate episode, a well-known campaign of virtual harassment that took place between 2014 and 2015 in the video game community ("*gamer* world").

A YouTube video from the *settle4truth* channel, with several thousand views, did an in-depth investigation of the campaign and the organisation around the Best Practices Forum, with excerpts from the meetings, their chats, the reports, and information about the APC and the biographies of the women involved in the process. A conspiratorial voice claims to know everything about the next steps of the initiative, which supposedly aims to "end freedom of expression on the internet to protect feminists". And it goes further: analysing excerpts from the report, it criticises explicitly the choice of the expression "*online violence*" instead of "*abuse*" (Seattle4truth, 2015). There emerged the argument that equating what happened on the internet with what happened off it—violence—would be disproportionate and dangerous.

Does this argument make sense? Violence can only be understood in relational terms. It is not easy to define what violence is, and there are many attempts to do so. Perhaps a minimum cross-culturally valid concept would be that of *non-legitimate or contestable physical harm* (Harvey & Gow, 1994). But authors such as the Brazilian anthropologist Maria Filomena Gregori (2008) point out how, particularly in the field of sexual violence, there can be blurred boundaries in the definition of violence, "connoted as abusive acts subject to moral or social condemnation or criminalisation"—beyond physical harm, even. The normal and the abusive are often resignified—what the author calls the *boundaries of sexuality* (Gregori, 2008). When the digital environment comes into play, it is to be expected that these boundaries will be renegotiated.

Anthropological approaches that see violence as an enunciation, a performative act, are also helpful. Argentinian Rita Segato describes gender violence not only as an act directed at a subject but also as an expression that occurs in the relationship between the aggressor and their peers. The vertical dimension of violence would be that of difference, of hierarchical power—expressed through the hierarchies of gender, race, and sex. The horizontal dimension would be that of alliance, mutual recognition, and competition—a signal to peers of belonging. As the balance between these two axes is unstable, belonging is reinforced by violence (Segato, 2003, p. 253; Natansohn & Morales, 2022). British social anthropologist Henrietta Moore (1994), in dialogue with psychology, sees interpersonal violence, especially that related to gender, race, and class differences, not as the breakdown of the social order but as its maintenance (in the form of fantasies of power and identity involving these differences). In other words, in these interpretations, violence has an intimate relationship with power and difference.

Of course, there are the "official"—legal—concepts of violence and gender-based violence

[7] Part of this account is a first-person experience, as I took part in the panel that debated the results of this initiative and gender-based violence on the Internet in general.

in particular. In the international legal sphere, it has long been recognised that discrimination and violence against women must be addressed. The CEDAW (Convention on the Elimination of All Forms of Discrimination against Women) was adopted at the UN in 1979 and enacted in Brazil in 2002, and obliges the 189 signatory states—by 2022—to incorporate the principle of equality and ensure the elimination of acts of discrimination against women; in the 1993 UN DEVAW (Declaration on the Elimination of Violence Against Women), violence against women is defined as any act of gender-based violence that results in or is likely to result in physical, sexual, or psychological harm or suffering to women, including threats of such acts, coercion, or arbitrary deprivation of liberty, whether occurring in public or private life. In the Americas, the 1994 Convention of Belém do Pará (Inter-American Convention on the Prevention, Punishment and Eradication of Violence against Women), promulgated by Brazil in 1996, reaffirms non-discrimination and obliges states to prevent, punish, and eradicate violence against women, defined as "any act or conduct based on gender that causes death, physical, sexual or psychological harm or suffering to women, whether in the public or private sphere". As you would expect from a 1996 convention, there is no mention of the virtual or digital sphere. However, the concept of violence set out in the convention applies to these cases, too—if the act or behaviour causes physical, sexual, or psychological harm or suffering.

This is the theoretical and international debate, and it has a legal expression. We will see how it played out internally in Brazil. The message from the opponents of the João Pessoa event was clear: online acts should not be treated as violence. The panel at the IGF ended without further incident. Today, it is hard to imagine there being any controversy over whether or not online violence is, in fact, violence. We still see a great legacy of it when one raises the simplistic contrast between online violence and freedom of expression and when the work of gender justice is systematically attacked in spaces where internet policy is debated. However, it is worth remembering that this vision of a digital world separate from the real one comes from a more prolonged heritage and was very popular in the 1990s. At that time, techno-deterministic ideas about how the internet was a world apart—and a superior one—dominated an important part of discussions on technology, from theorisations on cyberculture (as in Pierre Lévy, 1997) to blunt ideas on the independence and lack of possibility of regulation of cyberspace (such as John Perry Barlow's famous 1996 manifesto) (Barlow, 1996). This view still finds expression in explanations of the virtual world, but it is becoming less and less sustained.

1.2 The Gender of Technology and the Technology of Gender

In various fields of knowledge, it is understood that social relations, online and offline, form a continuum.[8] Also in 2015, together with Natália Neris and Lucas Bulgarelli, I was part of a case study on a phenomenon called Top 10: the "sluttiest lists", made by teenagers and circulated on social networks and messaging apps. These lists aimed to assess the sexual behaviour of young women in their schools and neighbourhoods (Valente et al., 2015). The media began to write about the phenomenon when two suicide attempts were reported in São Paulo, in the peripheral neighbourhoods of Parelheiros and Grajaú (Albuquerque, 2015). The lists circulated online (and were, therefore, an online event in themselves). However, they went beyond the online environment, and curses against teenage girls

[8] Already in the 2010s, works such as those by anthropologist Larissa Pelúcio and sociologist Richard Miskolci, both studying different social networking platforms, pointed in this direction: "The fact that we are immersed in online environments does not exempt us from having a body, on the contrary. The creation of an avatar, our iconographic identity, involves embodying ourselves" (Pelúcio, 2015). See also: "My research experience over the last five years has proved to me that the field does not have its borders delimited by a website, nor does it need to understand the articulation between online and offline, a continuum in which we insert ourselves as well as our research subjects" (Miskolci, 2011).

began to appear on walls near schools. Some of the incidents began to circulate among teachers and families. Teenagers began to suffer from problems that went far beyond online: difficulties integrating, depression, and even cases of attempted suicide. Reactions of resistance also took place along this continuum: collectives such as *Mulheres na Luta* (Women in Struggle) in Grajaú, organised actions such as a graffiti project to cover the walls graffitied with feminist messages, and groups such as *Sementeiras de Direitos* (Rights Seeders), in Parelheiros, organised educational activities with young people about the representation of women in the media—all of which also had some expression on the internet (Valente et al., 2015). For the teenagers going through the problem, it made little sense to make a watertight distinction between what happened on the internet and what happened off it.

Although the nature of the relationship between technology and society is the subject of much discussion, based on cases like this, it seems fair to say, along with many other authors, that technology and society are constituted in a reciprocal way.[9] In other words, on the one hand, technology impacts society—as long as it is recognised that people have agency and appropriate technologies based on their experiences and the social places in which they are inserted. On the other hand, the characteristics of a given society also play a role in the design and choices involved in creating technologies; in this way, they reflect society.

Professor and gender and technology studies researcher Judy Wajcman (2004) writes about how, even when this co-construction is recognised, gender inequalities are not always taken into account: for example, the gender (and other characteristics, such as race and sexuality) of the individuals who develop a particular technology and what impact this has on the choices that shape the technology back. In Brazilian sociologist Elizabeth Bortolaia Silva's (1998) words, scientific and technological change involves social, political, and economic interests, which incorporate particular gender politics.

An emblematic study with a gender lens that helps to understand how this happens is the microwave oven. In the book *Gender and Technology in the Making,* Cynthia Cockburn and Susan Ormrod show how a domestic appliance in the 1980s in the UK was an exemplar for thinking about the relationship between gender and technology. By studying the life cycle of technology from Electro UK, a major Japanese manufacturer, through to the major retailer Home-Tec, and finally, to the perceptions and uses of end users, the authors showed that, throughout the process, the binary opposition of male and female was reinforced (along with the technological and non-technological dichotomy). During production, the vast majority of male engineers initially thought of the microwave as a male technology; in retail, other actors tested and produced meanings, for example, by separating high-tech products (brown line) from functional products for the family (white line), into which the microwave ("for women") was eventually inserted. In the domestic environment, gender roles began to govern who would actually use the appliance—and the authors concluded that it did not necessarily reduce women's workload (e.g. one interviewee stated that she now had to heat several different versions of the same meal) (Cockburn & Ormrod, 1993). These conceptions—involving who uses technologies, who is the recipient of technologies, whether they are simple or complex technologies, among others—guide each stage of the cycle, and in the end, there are appropriations that relate to conceptions and negotiations around gender roles.

[9]In the article *"To talk about online gender violence: a theoretical and methodological proposal"*, Natália Neris and I analysed some of the literature that deals with this, discussing "technological determinism" approaches—which see technology as a given, with a decisive and predetermined role in social change (e.g. McLuhan & Lapham, 1994)—and the "social construction of technology", which focuses on uses and appropriations to explain that different social groups understand technologies in different ways (Pinch & Bijker, 1984). In doing so, they perhaps also underestimate the specificities of technology. We argue that "reciprocal conditioning" approaches (Simões et al., 2011) and "mutual construction" perspectives (Wajcman, 2004) are more fruitful (Valente & Neris, 2019).

The understanding of technology as a terrain of masculinity and Whiteness has been historically constructed. Some technologies, such as military artefacts and industrial machinery, have often been associated with Western activities and understood as masculine. In contrast, others used in everyday aspects of life, professions in which women are more present, such as machine operation or telemarketing (Wajcman, 2004, 2010), or even ancestral technologies, not linked to the industrial age or to White people, are underrepresented. Another book highlights this construction: *Recoding Gender: Women's Changing Participation in Computing,* by Janet Abbate (2012), on the changing role of women in the history of computing in the United States and England shows that women went from being the leaders among programmers during the Second World War to being relegated to the background with the social reconfiguration (and increased prestige) of the profession of "engineer", also localised in specific parts of the world. As a result, differences were naturalised and biologised, i.e. understood as part of people's "biological nature"—and as structuring gendered subjectivities, as Donna Haraway (1987) observes.

All these debates have very concrete effects. For example, understanding the online and offline environments as a continuum enables us to better comprehend reality and act upon it, but this is not the only benefit. In the sphere of law, having this understanding means giving online events the same legal consequences as analogous offline events. For example, a threat by messaging app should be analogous in law to a verbal threat in the street. Of course, there are actions related to the digital world that do not find legal expression, so this book reconstructs some disputes over changes that would address so-called gaps in the law. But it is not always the case. In Brazil, an act of online violence can be understood as domestic violence under the terms of the 2006 Maria da Penha Law—at least psychological, but possibly sexual, property, and physical. However, doubts about the continuity between online and offline have meant that the domestic violence legislation has not been used by lawyers and other actors in the justice system in cases of non-consensual dissemination of intimate images.[10] To avoid such doubts, in 2018, the law that criminalised unauthorised recording of sexual intimacy—the Rose Leonel Law—included "violation of your intimacy" among the forms of psychological violence against women (Law 13,772/2019—Rose Leonel Law).

These discussions are vital for us to glimpse the root of the issue, the fundamental reason for the concerns of this book: online misogyny stands as an obstacle between women and the potential of communication, information distribution, and expression via the internet. This raises the question of the internet's impact on women's lives, particularly on feminism and other emancipatory movements. How does the internet change these movements? How do they change it—and how does this happen in the case of Brazil? Let us immediately rule out techno-solutionist views that great transformations happen when we "throw technology at them".[11] The relationship between the development of the internet and activism, especially feminist activism, will be explored more deeply in the second chapter. However, understanding technology as something mutually constructed by society is fundamental for the analyses that follow. The feminist socio-material perspective considers the unstable and changing interconnection between digital technologies marked by inequalities and also by utopian projections, and individuals marked by gender, sexuality, race, and class characteristics.

[10] This perception comes from my own experience in research and participation in events, as well as analysing case law in different studies. It was in 2016 that I realised a significant difference and a merging of the fields and discussions of gender and feminism with internet policies and online violence.

[11] The expression was used by activists Faith Wilding and María Hernández, from the cyberfeminist collective sub-Rosa, in an interview with researcher Elisabeth Jay Friedman: "It is foolish to believe that major social, economic, and political issues can be addressed by throwing technology at them" (Friedman, 2016, p. 4).

1.3 Online Violence

Recognising an online/offline continuum does not mean ignoring that the online environment poses specific challenges. For example, the internet increases the speed with which information is disseminated, and with it, the seriousness of the non-consensual dissemination of intimate images, which already existed but was not on a large scale. Conditions have also arisen for new forms of violence, such as hacking into a computer device. In addition to rapid reproduction, the internet makes it possible to reach large audiences and carry out crowd actions (with small, coordinated actions). On the internet, there are new conditions for exercising anonymity or pseudo-anonymity; effects can become permanent or lasting, and the crossing of previously separate audiences—work, neighbourhood, friends, football—can occur, which is also called context collapse (Dunn, 2020; boyd, 2008; Natansohn & Morales, 2022; Šimonović, 2018). All of this is linked to *architectures*, which are the choices, designs, and functions of online spaces. If they are private, as most of the spaces in which we interact today are, they are guided by the decisions of private agents, who can encourage or amplify certain behaviours—and I will go back to this further in this book. The continuum means, above all, that the effects of online violence are not restricted to these environments but can spread offline and even become increasingly indistinguishable.

As discussed, the notion of violence itself is contextual, relational, and mutable. Nevertheless, online (and technology-facilitated) violence has become a category widely used by victims, activists, research institutions, networks of activist lawyers, international organisations, and legislation. Moreover, there is a performative effect in naming something as violence: attention is drawn to the act, and the event is connected to other acts, notions of wrongdoing and transgression.

It has become quite common to talk about online violence without this causing any great surprises per se. Nevertheless, on day zero of the IGF 2022, which took place in Addis Ababa, Ethiopia, when self-organised activities occurred, one of the first tables was Future of a Female Web. As the post-pandemic event took place in a hybrid format, it was possible to participate via Zoom. And again, more than seven years later, the feminist event on IGF was attacked (Internet Governance Forum, 2022)—now with new contours. It was a *zoombombing* attack, a concept developed during the COVID-19 pandemic when online meetings were normalised, which consists of acts of disruption of a meeting by unidentified people, who usually start sharing their screen and audio with violent content (Lorenz, 2020). In this case, there were images of extreme physical violence against women—until the invaders were mutated and removed from the room.

1.4 The Size and Faces of the Problem

There are not enough official statistics to understand the scale of the problem of technology-facilitated gender-based violence. As is the case with many forms of violence, particularly sexual violence,[12] underreporting is prevalent, and it is common that data such as race and sexual orientation are not recorded. However, research centres and institutes have been providing important data. Some organisations receive reports of online violence—in Brazil, the best known is Safernet (n.d.), which runs a reporting centre and a *helpline* and has been releasing data since 2007. For example, in 2021, 273 people turned to the *helpline* to report problems with the exposure of intimate images, compared to 304 in 2020. Although the figures may provide some insight into the different "violations for which Brazilian internet users ask for help" and how the preva-

[12] The National Victimisation Survey, carried out by the National Secretariat of Public Security with Datafolha in 2013, indicated that the crime notification rate in Brazil was 19.9% in general—but 90% in the case of car theft and only 7.5% in the case of sex crimes (Datafolha, Crisp, & SENASP, 2013). A more recent survey by Datafolha and the Brazilian Public Security Forum also indicated that, in 2021, 24.7% of Brazilian women who suffered violence sought out official bodies (police, women's protection organisations, police stations, Women's Call Centre no. 180) (FBSP, 2019).

lence changes over time, the number lacks statistical significance and does not aid in understanding the spectrum of victimisation.

Important surveys have shown the prevalence of online violence in different social groups. The Brazilian TIC Kids Online survey showed that 33 per cent of children and adolescents (users aged 9–17) reported having experienced offensive situations that they didn't like or that upset them on the internet—36 per cent of girls (Cetic.br, 2022). Plan International interviewed 14,000 girls and women between the ages of 15 and 25 in 22 countries, and the result was that 58 per cent had faced some form of harassment on social networks. In Brazil, it was 77 per cent. The definition of harassment in these reports included "abusive and insulting language", "purposeful humiliation", "racist comments", and "body shaming". According to the survey, as a result of this harassment, victims suffer from low self-esteem or confidence, mental and emotional stress, a sense of physical insecurity, and problems with family, friends, school, or employment (Plan International, 2020). In a survey of women aged between 19 and 23 in southern India, the organisation IT for Change found that more than a third had experienced some form of harassment or abuse or had been the victim of unwanted behaviour online, and in 83% of cases, the act was sexual. The survey also pointed to high psychological and academic consequence rates and low rates of seeking or adequate institutional support and response mechanisms (Gurumurthy et al., 2019). In 2021, CIGI (Centre for International Governance Innovation), a Canadian *think tank*, carried out a survey called "Supporting a Safer Internet" in 18 countries, with a prevalence in the Global South, representing the population aged between 16 and 74 (Valente, 2023). By way of comparison with the previous one, in this survey, when considering only women under 35, the prevalence in the eighteen countries surveyed is 68.7 per cent—and 67.9 per cent in Brazil. The questions asked were different—they asked about experience with *harms* on the internet, involving coercion and harassment, identity and reputation, privacy and security, and sexuality.

In addition, the CIGI survey involved both men and women. It showed that, although there were no considerable differences when asked generically about suffering harm, many more women and LGBTQIAP+ people reported that the violence occurred as a result of their gender (Valente, 2023),[13] as well as severe effects on their personal lives. For example, 49 per cent of women spoke of severe impacts on their mental health, compared to 45 per cent of men; 57 per cent of people who said they had suffered from the non-consensual dissemination of intimate images reported such severe consequences. A Pew Research study carried out in the United States in 2021 brought results in the same direction: American men say they receive more *harassment* than women (43 per cent to 38 per cent), but 47 per cent of women say that the harassment occurred because of their gender, compared to only 18 per cent of men; in the specific field of sexual abuse, the difference was also felt: it was reported by 33 per cent of women under 35, compared to 11 per cent of men of the same age (Vogels, 2021). Even if the prevalence of violence in women's lives is higher than in men's, these figures show that the effects are felt by women more, which seems to point to the consequences of sexist cultures.

Although TFGBV is identified as a problem of significant proportions around the world, some comparisons show specificities in Brazil. I have already pointed out the extremely high numbers of girls affected by harassment on social networks in the Plan International survey in the global comparison. CIGI's research also provides

[13]There were no statistically significant differences between women and men—59.1 per cent of people worldwide and 54.2 per cent in Brazil reported having suffered online harm. It's worth noting that the figures are much higher when only LGBTQIAP+ people are considered (75 per cent in the global case, 80.4 per cent in Brazil). But globally, 39.2% of females say that, in the most relevant case, they have been victimised because of their gender, compared to 26.7% of males. In Brazil, it's 37.9 per cent and 29.5 per cent. Thirty-six per cent of Brazilians respond that online violence is a big problem for men (33% globally), but 67% think it's a big problem for women; when only women respond, the figure rises to 72%.

much evidence in this regard: Brazilians, and especially Brazilian women, are among the victims who report adverse consequences related to these harms. For example, 60 per cent of Brazilian women report having the freedom to express political opinions affected (the global aggregate is 38 per cent). In general, these figures are much lower in the countries of the so-called Global North—in the survey, Germany, the United States, Canada, and France—signalling very close links between online violence, cultural context, other inequalities, and institutional issues, such as investigative or redress capacities. In addition, more people in Brazil point to race as the cause of the most significant harm they have suffered—16.2 per cent in total compared to 14.5 per cent globally. The difference is even more significant in the case of women and LGBTQIAP+ people as a whole (Valente, 2023).

As these studies show, there are very different ways of characterising TFGBV. Analysing recent literature, Suzie Dunn, a professor at the University of Ottawa and a researcher on the subject, categorises nine broad forms of TFGBV: harassment, mass attacks, image-based sexual abuse, publication of private information (or *doxxing*), defamation, *stalking*, impersonation, threatening, and hate speech. This is a good starting categorisation as long as we are committed to the notion that the boundaries are mobile, the forms of violence are constantly updated, and there are many possible subcategories and overlaps. For example, the category "image-based sexual abuse" includes the non-consensual dissemination of intimate images, *sextortion* (demanding some advantage from someone based on the possession of intimate images), and synthetic media (manipulation of images, often to place someone's image in erotic or sexual scenes, including *deepfakes*). The overlaps between these acts are abundant: someone threatens a person with a *deepfake* or actually disseminates intimate images and with them private information, such as a telephone number—as was the case with Rose Leonel. Giving concrete form to this is a way of not letting the numbers, essential to give dimension to the phenomenon, appear as cold, disembodied statistics. The stories and struggles dealt with in this book involve real people who experience fear and suffering but find strategies of resistance.

And these people are usually girls, women, and transgender, non-binary, and gender non-conforming people, who are unfortunately affected in a reasonably indiscriminate way. Moreover, empirical studies show three aggravating factors of TFGBV: intersections with other social markers of difference, such as race, sexuality, and disability; abusive intimate relationships; and a vocal, leading position or spaces traditionally occupied by men, as is the case with women in politics, human rights activists and defenders, journalists (Dunn, 2020). For example, CIGI's research showed extremely high numbers of violence against LGBTQIAP+ people in Brazil and also higher than average in the case of high-profile women. In the latter case, the consequences in the country led to the passing of the Law on Political Violence Against Women, to be discussed below.

The unfolding visibility of these cases and their consequences has generated a cross-pollination between issues of TFGBV and other policy debates involving digital technologies. There is a vast field of research and many organisations dedicated to TFGBV, and the issue is increasingly being debated more diffusely—for example, in its relationship to disinformation (so-called gendered disinformation), to economic and political participation, and to women's rights in general.

One final note on the scope of the problem: it is impossible to discuss gender inequality and the digital environment in Brazil without referencing that there is a contingent of unconnected people in the country or people who, although connected, still lack what is known as significant connectivity, which presupposes a certain frequency and autonomy in use, access to devices, and connection speed (Senne, 2022; A4AI, n.d.). The *digital divide* refers to unequal access to digital technologies and the internet, reflecting local and global inequalities and creating new ones. There are a few different classifications, but a good way to refer to these differences is to divide them into three levels (Van Deursen & Van Dijk,

2019): the first refers to the internet connection and the device used. For example, many people only use the internet via their mobile phones. The second level concerns skills and the actual use of the internet. The frequency and types of activities carried out online are assessed. The third level is the concrete results or tangible benefits of using the internet (Van Deursen & Van Dijk, 2019). This stratification of the digital divide exists to account for more than just access since many other factors are related to how the internet impacts a person's life.

In 2023, 89 per cent of the Brazilian population were internet users; i.e. they had used the internet on any device in the previous three months (Cetic.br, 2024). This user definition follows international patterns adopted many years ago and is vital for comparing countries and historical series (ITU, 2020), but it certainly is not enough to understand the totality of contemporary practices, and it does not fit well with the access and uses that characterise digital inclusion today. However, in 2023, 96% of these internet users were daily users. According to this data, more than 10% of the Brazilian population is not connected (Cetic.br, 2024).

Following the track of inequalities, we have that in what is defined as economic class A (the highest income strata), 98% of people are users, compared to only 79% in classes D and E; 90% of people in cities are connected, compared to 82% in rural areas; 82% of indigenous people are connected. And although there are no significant differences between women and men or Black and White people in terms of whether or not they are users, there are differences in the type of access and the type of activity carried out. For example, in 2021, 45% of male users played online games, compared to only 32% of women; considerably more women (66%) than men (64%) and more Black people (56%) than white people (51%) *only* have access to mobile devices, which limits the diversity of activities carried out. This is also the case for 70 per cent of indigenous people and 86 per cent of people in classes D and E (Cetic.br, 2024).

Another layer of internet use in Brazil can help contextualize the debate: in 2022, 99.3 per cent of Brazilians used the messaging app WhatsApp to communicate daily and maintain social links, according to research by InternetLab and *Rede Conhecimento Social* (2023) (Social Knowledge Network). 47% per cent used Telegram, focusing more on access to content than communication. Add to this the fact that the mobile internet offer in Brazil is tied to data volume (franchise) and the practice of *zero rating*, i.e. making it possible to use certain apps without deducting from the monthly franchise and maintaining access to these apps even after the franchise ends and other activities are blocked. In 2019, the Consumer Defence Institute (Idec) analysed 45 plans from four operators in Brazil and found that 43 offered *zero rating*: 93% included WhatsApp (Simão et al., 2020). There is much debate about how these commercial practices have contributed to the adoption of this particular app.

When we think about violence and resistance, connectivity plays an important role, for example, in access to information and the capacity for autonomous reaction, articulation in protection networks, and the creation of counter-discourses. This is another dimension of the *online/offline* continuum. The normalisation of online misogyny in Brazil is an amalgam of technical and cultural factors—for example, when it comes to WhatsApp groups used by men to share intimate images of women without their consent. Considering all this is important, above all, to differentiate the debate in Brazil from other contexts, considering its violent colonial history, which permeates the problem from start to finish and requires a critical look at generalising foreign interpretations of why misogyny is so prevalent on the internet in the country.[14]

[14] Some American and European authors have written about misogyny as a response either to women's activism online or to a culture of "political correctness" that would have dominated certain online spaces (Siapera, 2019; Nagle, 2017). The interpretation of misogyny as a response to something also finds space in qualified discussions in Brazil; the caution here is not to abstract the problem, as if it were not inscribed in historical-social roots. Let us not forget that, in Brazil, sexual violence against enslaved Black women was a colonial instrument (Gonzalez, 2020).

1.5 Crime, Violence, and Misogyny

So far, I have talked about misogyny and violence, as well as mentioning laws that refer to them without explicitly dealing with crime. There is a reason for this. Since law results from social disputes, power, and interests, it filters reality according to its categories and institutions. Although law transforms the social expressions and understandings that actualise it, it does not fully account for them.

Criminalisation is the criminal classification of the conflict and addresses some aspects, blurring others. This depends on the power of the voice of those participating in the democratic game. Guita Debert and Maria Filomena Gregori argued in a 2008 text that the same happens with concepts of violence (Debert & Gregori, 2008). In other words, criminalisation is just one of the ways in which the law refers to reality, although it is usual to identify the law with criminal law.

Some concepts are not part of the grammar of law or are filtered by it in different ways, and others exist in both law and the field of social disputes but not necessarily with the same meanings. Rather, misogyny and violence come from the field of social recognition and, as such, must be thought of in relational terms, in terms of social relations. Even so, as we saw at the beginning of the book, violence is part of the grammar of law—in Brazil, for example, in domestic violence law (Maria da Penha Law), while misogyny is not. This point will be important below.

In Brazil, violence against women was a term coined in the 1980s, based on the political experiences of activists who worked with women who suffered from violence in the SOS-Mulher and discussions on the international scene (Debert & Gregori, 2008).[15] One thing that the literature on the 1980s and 1990s shows is that in the practice of the Police Department for Violence Against Women created in 1985 in Brazil, violence against women, which was not defined in the legislation, was understood as crimes and offences committed in the domestic sphere, in marital relations (Debert & Gregori, 2008).[16] The Maria da Penha Law of 2006 defined and qualified domestic and family violence against women without creating new crimes since they already existed, but by creating a framework for recognition and protection, which, in turn, qualifies the existing ones.[17]

Part of the discussion on violence and crime is based on a critique of the concept of "judicialisation of social relations" as an "invasion" of the law into them. This criticism sees the fact that the law expands into the social field as inherently harmful. I agree here with the criticism made by Marcos Nobre and José Rodrigo Rodriguez in a 2011 paper that it only makes sense to talk about this so-called expansion of the law (or even "judicial activism") from a normative viewpoint, which does not consider either the code of the law itself or the transformative potential it carries. Who determined that rights are only realised by the legislature?

When social groups develop discourses and demands about their rights—for example, women who demand the legal creation of protective measures for domestic violence, thus prosecuting cases—they are also negotiating with the law and transforming it. More appropriate, then, is to

[15]In the following decade, the debate on gender violence began to address how this notion had generated a certain essentialisation.

[16]The authors also show that, with the creation of the Special Courts in 1995, they came to be widely used for cases of domestic violence and that their characteristic of prioritising conciliation and alternative sentences led from the "defence of women to the defence of the family".

[17]The Maria da Penha Law defines violence against women in general as "any action or omission based on gender that causes death, injury, physical, sexual or psychological suffering and moral or property damage", but its central concern is the definition of what domestic and family violence against women is. It's worth remembering that talking about gender violence, and not just violence against women, also includes violence against transgender, non-binary, and gender non-conforming people who suffer from violence related to sexism—recognising that sexism is a system that doesn't just affect cis women. Neither does misogyny. Despite the celebration, there is the critical perspective that the law focused on the judicial solution (and the police stations) and not on stopping aggression and listening, which would not serve the interests of Black and poorer women (Flauzina, 2015).

think of the concept of *juridification*, which presupposes that the structuring logic of law shapes and excludes options, alternatives, and demands and also takes into account the translation of the aspirations of individuals, groups, and social movements, so that legal terms can also result in the renewal of institutional grammar (Nobre & Rodriguez, 2011; Maciel & Koerner, 2002). A similar thesis is that of the *mobilisation of law*, which focuses on the intersubjective power of law in the meanings constructed by and between subjects within society. The diagnosis is that laws and courts are an essential arena of dispute for social movements and that there is a symbolic dimension to the language of rights (McCann, 2006).

From a strategic point of view, as Fabiola Fanti (2016) reminds us in her study on the mobilisation of rights by feminist movement organisations in the city of São Paulo, Brazil, social movements adopt a diverse range of actions, which include filing lawsuits in the courts, but also educational actions, campaigns aimed at society or the judiciary, mobilisation of international courts, and participation as amicus curiae, among others.[18] In Brazil, the 1988 Federal Constitution was a significant milestone in the legal regulation of social relations, as it began to organise demands for the rights of social groups that Brazilian law and institutions tend to marginalise, disrespect, and violate. In particular, the feminist movement and caucus mobilised strongly in the Constituent Assembly, with significant gains, as did the Black movement (Teles, 2017; Neris, 2018).

Therefore, law is not static nor does it have a predetermined meaning; it is rather disputed by society. This translation of the grammar of violence into the grammar of law, and particularly of crime, is strongly criticised by other sectors of social movements and critics. Part of Brazilian feminism, specifically Black feminism, has been highlighting how the application of criminal law and the penal system as a whole discriminates against Black men and women, both from the perspective of those who are convicted and the length of prison sentences, as well as the violence produced in prison. In her book *Criminalisation of Racism*, PUC-Rio professor Thula Pires (2016) provides an in-depth critique of the legal instrument as incapable of serving emancipation and recognition, as I will discuss later. From another critical perspective, feminists celebrate specific achievements in struggles directed at the judiciary—to cite a few examples covered in this book: the 1991 (Federal) Superior Court of Justice decision that rejected the "legitimate defence of honour" thesis, a decision confirmed by the Supreme Court in 2021, and Supreme Court decisions declaring the interpretation of abortion of anencephalic babies as a crime to be unconstitutional (2012), or on the constitutionality of aspects of the Maria da Penha Law (also in 2012).

In any case, concerning misogyny on the internet, a social concept of misogyny has been refined over the years and has taken on new features, and the law has been mobilised by social movements and institutions using different strategies, which I will discuss systematically and chronologically.

1.6 Over a Decade of Legal Responses

During the period covered in this book, the legal disputes surrounding online misogyny reflected how the issue was presented in the public debate at different times. How was the problem filtered through the laws, and what was omitted? The disputes also highlight the prevalence of choosing penal, criminalising solutions to the problem of misogyny. The Carolina Dieckmann Law of 2012 was a legislative response to the perceived dangers of unauthorised access to devices and the violation of women's privacy. The Marco Civil da

[18] Returning to the field of gender violence, Guita Debert and Maria Filomena Gregori respond to the criticism of "judicialisation"—that the special police stations aimed at defending minorities would transform citizenship problems into a "legal system"—by arguing that these mechanisms are the fruit of social demands, an "intervention in the political sphere capable of translating the interests of groups subject to the status of personal dependence into rights" (Debert & Gregori, 2008).

Internet 2014 addressed the view that platforms need to act swiftly in cases of the unauthorised dissemination of intimate images, which at the time was making headlines nationwide. The Lola Law, which in 2018 determined that the Federal Police are responsible for investigating online crimes involving misogyny ("defined as those that promote hatred or aversion towards women"), arose from the recognition that police need to be properly equipped to investigate individuals and organisations attacking women. In the same year, two laws—the Sexual Harassment Act and the Rose Leonel Act—amended the Criminal Code to specifically criminalise acts of producing, editing, or disseminating scenes of nudity and sex without the consent of the parties. These acts were previously classified as insults or defamation.

In 2021, the Stalking Law was a criminal law response to the concern about the persistent harassment of women, even if the small acts involved were not considered illicit. In the same year, following the brutal murder of Rio de Janeiro councillor Marielle Franco and her driver Anderson Gomes (in 2018), the Political Violence Against Women Law was the legislative response to a growing recognition that misogyny is the invisible barrier to women's participation in politics, both outside and inside the internet. The memory of Marielle, a Black woman from the Maré favela in Rio de Janeiro, mother, feminist, and bisexual, lives on in the struggles for the effective and safe participation of women, especially Black women, in Brazilian politics. Allied to this recognition is the fact that vocal women in other fields, such as journalists and activists, are also unequally affected by violence, and in particular, intensified ways when they are Black, indigenous, or LGBTQIAP+. Even so, as this set of laws with women's names and the most well-known, reported, and debated cases of online misogyny show, it is common for violence against women from a particular social class, usually White, very commonly from the southeast, to gain more visibility and mobilise social and legal debate. The Political Violence Against Women Law is not called the Marielle Franco Law, although her murder was the trigger for this discussion. My selection of notorious violence cases in this book reflects this inequality, which I try to fill with other data and reports when available.

In 2025, new concerns over the misogynistic use of AI led to the approval of the Deepfakes Law, specifically addressing using women's likeness to generate nudity and sexual content, and the Supreme Court issued a decision obliging platforms to adopt a *duty of care* in cases of misogyny.

While all this was happening in Brazil, the international debate was also moving. In addition to the history of disputes in internet policy debate spaces, of which the IGF is just one example, there was a transversalisation of the agenda of online violence. For example, the UN rapporteurs on violence against women and freedom of expression have dedicated recent reports to the problem of misogyny, particularly online, for women's participation in civic life and the exercise of rights (Šimonović, 2018; Khan, 2021). In the following chapters, I will systematically reconstruct the demands and contradictions in the relationship between gender and the internet in Brazil around major cases and the legal frameworks that have built a framework for legally confronting online misogyny, translating these issues into the sphere of law and institutions, and the relationship between national debates and those taking place in other places and spheres.

References

A4AI - Alliance for Affordable Internet. (n.d.). *Meaningful connectivity: Unlocking the full power of internet access*. Retrieved March 18, 2025, from https://a4ai.org/meaningful-connectivity

Abbate, J. (2012). *Inventing the internet* (5th ed.). MIT Press.

Albuquerque, S. (2015, May 27). Meninas abandonam estudos e tentam suicídio após entrar para lista das 'mais vadias'. R7. https://noticias.r7.com/saopaulo/meninas-abandonam-estudos-e-tentam-suicidio-apos-entrar-para-lista-das-mais-vadias-27052015.

Association for Progressive Communications (APC). (2015, October 12). *Facts on #TakeBacktheTech*. Retrieved March 18, 2025, from https://www.apc.org/en/pubs/facts-takebackthetech

Barlow, J. P. (1996, February 8). *A declaration of the independence of cyberspace*. Retrieved March 18, 2025, from https://projects.eff.org/~barlow/Declaration-Final.html

Bosch Fiol, E., Ferrer Pérez, V., & Gili Planas, M. (1999). *Historia de la misoginia*. Anthropos Editorial.

boyd, d. (2008). *Taken out of context: American teen sociality in networked publics* [Doctoral dissertation, University of California, Berkeley].

Brasil. (2019). *Lei 13.772/2019 (Lei Rose Leonel)*. Retrieved March 18, 2025, from http://www.planalto.gov.br/ccivil_03/_Ato2015-2018/2018/Lei/L13772.htm#art2

Carneiro, S. (2017). Raça, estrutura, classe no Brasil [Interview]. *Cult, 223*, 13–20.

CETIC.BR. (2022). *Pesquisa sobre o uso da internet por crianças e adolescentes no Brasil: TIC Kids Online Brasil 2021*. Comitê Gestor da Internet no Brasil. https://cetic.br/media/docs/publicacoes/2/20221121120124/tic_kids_online_2021_livro_eletronico.pdf

CETIC.BR. (2024). *TIC Domicílios 2023*. Comitê Gestor da Internet no Brasil. https://cetic.br/pesquisa/domicilios/

Cockburn, C., & Ormrod, S. (1993). *Gender and technology in the making*. Sage.

Collins, P. H. (2015). Intersectionality's definitional dilemmas. *Annual Review of Sociology, 41*(1), 1–20.

Collins, P. H. (2017). Lost in translation? Black feminism, intersectionality, and emancipatory politics. *Paragraph, 5*(1), 6–17.

Cowan, B. A. (2017). How machismo got its spurs—In English: Social science, cold war imperialism, and the ethnicization of hypermasculinity. *Latin American Research Review, 52*(4), 606–622.

Datafolha, CRISP, & SENASP. (2013). *Pesquisa Nacional de Vitimização*. https://www.crisp.ufmg.br/documentos/pesquisa_nacional_vitimizacao.pdf

de Almeida Teles, M. A. (2017). *Breve história do feminismo no Brasil e outros ensaios*. Alameda.

Debert, G. G., & Gregori, M. F. (2008). Violência e gênero: Novas propostas, velhos dilemas. *Revista Brasileira de Ciências Sociais, 23*, 165–185.

Dunn, S. (2020). *Technology-facilitated gender-based violence: An overview*. Centre for International Governance Innovation.

Fanti, F. (2016). *Mobilização social e luta por direitos: Um estudo sobre o movimento feminista* [Doctoral dissertation, Universidade Estadual de Campinas]. https://www.academia.edu/30046720/Mobilização_social_e_luta_por_direitos_movimento_feminista_e_a_campanha_pela_descriminalização_e_legalização_do_aborto_no_Brasil

FBSP. (2019). *Visível e invisível: A vitimização de mulheres no Brasil*. Fórum Brasileiro de Segurança Pública. https://www.forumseguranca.org.br/wp-content/uploads/2019/02/relatorio-pesquisa-2019-v5.pdf

Flauzina, A. L. P. (2015). Lei Maria da Penha: entre os anseios da resistência e as posturas da militância. *In Discursos negros: legislação penal, política criminal e racismo*. (pp. 115–144). Brasília: Brado Negro.

Folha de S.Paulo. (2022, June 10). Internet cresce no Brasil; audiência de esporte salta 60%. Folha de S.Paulo. https://www1.folha.uol.com.br/folha/informatica/ult124u10226.shtml.

Friedman, E. J. (2016). *Interpreting the internet: Feminist and queer counterpublics in Latin America*. University of California Press.

González, L. (2011). *Sexo, vingança e vergonha na rede: Expostas por seus ex, elas dão o troco na justiça*. Marie Claire. https://revistamarieclaire.globo.com/Revista/Common/0,,EMI259500-17737-1,00-SEXO+VINGANCA+E+VERGONHA+NA+REDE+EXPOSTAS+POR+SEUS+EX+ELAS+DAO+O+TROCO+NA+J.html

Gonzalez, L. (2020). *Por um feminismo afro-latino-americano*. Zahar.

Gregori, M. F. (2008). Limites da sexualidade: Violência, gênero e erotismo. *Revista de Antropologia, 51*(2), 575–606.

Gurumurthy, A., Vasudevan, A., & Chami, N. (2019). *Born digital, born free? A socio-legal study on young women's experiences of online violence in South India*. IT for Change.

Haraway, D. (1987). A manifesto for cyborgs: Science, technology, and socialist feminism in the 1980s. *Australian Feminist Studies, 2*(4), 1–42.

Harvey, P., & Gow, P. (Eds.). (1994). *Sex and violence: The psychology of violence and risk assessment*. Routledge.

IBGE. (2024). *New geographic divisions detail inequalities in the country in 2023*. https://agenciadenoticias.ibge.gov.br/en/agencia-news/2184-news-agency/news/42111-ibge-s-new-geographic-divisions-detail-inequalities-in-the-country-in-2023

International Telecommunication Union (ITU). (2020). *Manual for measuring ICT access and use by households and individuals*. https://www.itu.int/en/ITU-D/Statistics/Pages/publications/manual.aspx

Internet Governance Forum. (2009). *Dynamic coalition on gender and internet governance*. https://www.intgovforum.org

Internet Governance Forum. (2022). *IGF 2022 Day 0 Event #75*. https://www.intgovforum.org

InternetLab, & Rede Conhecimento Social. (2023). *Os vetores da comunicação política em aplicativos de mensagens: Hábitos e percepções*. https://internetlab.org.br/pt/pesquisa/em-ambiente-de-receio-confianca-individual-no-emissor-e-no-retransmissor-e-central-no-consumo-de-informacoes-politicas-aponta-nova-pesquisa/

Khan, I. (2021). Report on gender justice and the right to freedom of opinion and expression. Geneva: *United Nations OHCHR*. https://www.ohchr.org/en/calls-for-input/2021/report-gender-justice-and-right-freedom-opinion-and-expression.

Khoo, C., Robertson, K., & Deibert, R. (2019). *Installing fear: A Canadian legal and policy analysis of using, developing, and selling smartphone spyware and stalkerware applications*. https://tspace.library.utoronto.ca/handle/1807/96321

Lévy, P. (1997). *Cibercultura*. Editora 34.

Logan, T. K., & Walker, R. (2009). Partner stalking: Psychological dominance or "business as usual"? *Trauma, Violence, & Abuse, 10*(3), 247–270.

Lorenz, T. (2020, March 20). 'Zoombombing': When video conferences go wrong. *The New York Times*. https://www.nytimes.com
Maciel, D. A., & Koerner, A. (2002). Sentidos da judicialização da política: Duas análises. *Lua Nova: Revista de Cultura e Política, 55*, 113–133.
Manne, K. (2019). *Down girl: The logic of misogyny*. Penguin.
McCann, M. (2006). Law and social movements: Contemporary perspectives. *Annual Review of Law and Social Science, 2*(1), 17–38.
McLuhan, M., & Lapham, L. H. (1994). *Understanding media: The extensions of man*. MIT Press.
Miskolci, R. (2011). Novas conexões: Notas teórico-metodológicas para pesquisas sobre o uso de mídias digitais. *Cronos, 12*(2) https://periodicos.ufrn.br/cronos/article/view/3160
Moore, H. (1994). The problem of explaining violence in the social sciences. In P. Harvey & P. Gow (Eds.), *Sex and violence: The psychology of violence and risk assessment* (pp. 138–156). Routledge.
Nagle, A. (2017). Kill all normies: Online culture wars from 4chan and Tumblr to Trump and the alt-right. Winchester/Washington: Zero Books.
Natansohn, G., & Morales, S. (2022). As estruturas elementares da violência digital de gênero. In B. Barbosa, L. Tresca, & T. Lauschner (Eds.), *TIC, governança da internet e gênero 2* (pp. 1–12). CGI.br.
Neris, N. (2018). *A voz e a palavra do movimento negro na Constituinte de 1988*. Letramento.
Nobre, M., & Rodriguez, J. R. (2011). "Judicialização da política": Déficits explicativos e bloqueios normativistas. *Novos Estudos Cebrap, 91*, 5–20.
Padilla, I. (2002). *Cafofo on-line*. Época.
Pelúcio, L. (2015). O amor em tempo de aplicativos: Notas afetivas e metodológicas sobre pesquisas com mídias digitais. In L. Pelúcio, H. Pait, & T. Sabatine (Eds.), *No emaranhado da rede: Gênero, sexualidade e mídia — desafios teóricos e metodológicos do presente*. Annablume.
Pinch, T. J., & Bijker, W. E. (1984). The social construction of facts and artefacts: Or how the sociology of science and the sociology of technology might benefit each other. *Social Studies of Science, 14*(3), 399–441.
Pires, T. (2016). *Criminalização do racismo: Entre política de reconhecimento e meio de legitimação do controle social sobre os negros*. Editora PUC-Rio.
Plan International. (2020). *Free to be online? A report on girls' and young women's experiences of online harassment*. https://plan-international.org/publications/free-to-be-online
Rodrigues, C. (2013). The relevance of the concept of intersectionality to research and practice in Brazil. *Fazendo Gênero, 10*, 1–12.
SaferNet. (n.d.). *Indicadores helpline*. https://indicadores.safernet.org.br/helpline/helplineviz/helpchart-page.html
Seattle4truth. (2015, November 10). *Another UN report on net censorship coming* [Video]. YouTube. https://www.youtube.com/watch?v=lK7nnL11dIE
Segato, R. (2003). *Las estructuras elementales da violencia*. Universidad Nacional de Quilmes.
Senne, F. J. N. de. (2022). A inclusão digital importa?: Origens, efeitos e geografia das desigualdades na internet no Brasil (Doctoral dissertation). *Universidade de São Paulo*. https://www.teses.usp.br/teses/disponiveis/8/8131/tde-05102022-183134.
Siapera, E. (2019). Online misogyny as witch hunt: Primitive accumulation in the age of techno-capitalism. In D. Ging & E. Siapera (Eds.), *Gender hate online: Understanding the new anti-feminism*. Palgrave Macmillan.
Silva, E. B. (1998). Des-construindo gênero em ciência e tecnologia. *Cadernos Pagu, 10*.
Simão, B., Moysés, D., Oliveira, R., Santos, F., Gomes, T., & Lima, A. (2020). *Acesso móvel à internet: Franquia de dados e bloqueio do acesso dos consumidores. TIC Domicílios 2019*. Comitê Gestor da Internet no Brasil.
Simões, M., Las Heras, S., & Augusto, A. (2011). Gênero e tecnologias da informação e da comunicação no espaço doméstico: Não chega ter, é preciso saber, querer e poder usar. *Cultura, Tecnologia e Identidade, 8*, 155–172.
Šimonović, D. (2018). *Report of the special rapporteur on violence against women, its causes and consequences on online violence against women and girls from a human rights perspective*. United Nations OHCHR. https://digitallibrary.un.org/record/1641160
Tecmundo (2017). 5 anos do Penta: como era o mundo da tecnologia em 2002. https://www.tecmundo.com.br/tecnologia/118575-15-anos-penta-mundotecnologia-2002.htm
Ukockis, G. (2019). *Misogyny: The new activism*. Oxford University Press.
United Nations (UN), International Telecommunication Union (ITU), & World Summit on the Information Society (WSIS). (2005). *Tunis agenda for the information society*.
Valente, M. (2023). *Online gender-based violence in Brazil: New data insights*. Centre for International Governance Innovation.
Valente, M., & Neris, N. (2019). Para falar de violência de gênero na internet: Uma proposta teórica e metodológica. In G. Natansohn & F. Rovetto (Eds.), *Internet e feminismos*. Edufba.
Valente, M., Neris, N., & Bulgarelli, L. (2015). *Not revenge, not porn: Analysing the exposure of teenage girls online in Brazil*. GISWatch. https://genderit.org/sites/default/files/giswatch2015-brazil_0.pdf
Valente, M., Neris, N., Ruiz, J., & Bulgarelli, L. (2016). *O corpo é o código*. InternetLab.
Van Deursen, A. J. A. M., & Van Dijk, J. A. G. M. (2019). The first-level digital divide shifts from inequalities in physical access to inequalities in material access. *New Media & Society, 21*(2), 354–375.
Vogels, E. A. (2021, January 13). *The state of online harassment*. Pew Research Center. https://www.pewresearch.org/internet/2021/01/13/the-state-of-online-harassment/
Wajcman, J. (2004). *Technofeminism*. Polity Press.
Wajcman, J. (2010). Feminist theories of technology. *Cambridge Journal of Economics, 34*(1), 143–152.

The Internet of Activism and the First Laws

2

Abstract

This chapter traces how feminist counterpublics and allied fields leveraged the internet for protection, pedagogy, and mobilisation—while confronting platform architectures and rising conservatism, in clashes that are typically traced back to the 2013 mass protests that took over Brazil. It maps practical TFGBV victim support infrastructures, such as acoso.online (regional legal guidance for NCII), and the repertoire of resistance (digital security, evidence preservation, networked solidarity, reporting to platforms and authorities), alongside reflections on their limits. Historically, it asks whether "the internet is feminist", contrasting early cyberfeminist hopes with Latin American organising and feminist media traditions that long predated social media. It returns to the Carolina Dieckmann Law (2012) to show how a celebrity case catalysed device-intrusion crimes yet left gendered harms unaddressed. Finally, it shows how feminist counterpublics grew amid Brazil's new right and the crisis of a young democracy, context collapse, and attention-economy affordances (e.g. Orkut/ Facebook, WhatsApp), culminating in mass feminist street mobilisations (#MarchaDasVadias, #EleNão) that braided online and offline tactics.

Keywords

Feminist Counterpublics · Slut Walks · Mutual construction of technology · Feminist media · Algorithms

In 2018, Chileans Paz Peña and Francisco Vera, two researchers and activists with experience in human rights and technology, created the project *acoso.online* (online harassment) (Peña & Vera, 2018) with guidelines for victims of the dissemination of intimate images in 14 Latin American countries—specifically with cis heterosexual women and LGBTQIAP+ people in mind. Partner organisations with legal knowledge of each country—InternetLab in the case of Brazil—provided information on what laws exist in different areas, such as what to do if the violence is domestic. What if it happens in the workplace? How do we keep evidence to take to the authorities? How do we report it to the platforms? Thus, providing victims with knowledge about their rights is a central dimension of the project. The earlier mentioned CIGI survey on safe internet identified that in Brazil, only 7% of victims go to the police, and 14% believe that the police are effective in the case of online harm (9% in Chile) (Valente, 2023); at the same time, 81% of people believe that information on protection, education in schools, and laws are very or extremely important.

M. Valente, *Online Misogyny in Brazil*, Sustainable Development Goals Series,
https://doi.org/10.1007/978-3-032-07727-1_2

In the book *How to Be a Woman Online? Surviving Abuse and Harassment, and How to Fight Back*, Nina Jankowicz (2022), a US disinformation researcher who has suffered misogynistic attacks because of her work, organises strategies to respond to and combat these cases. Most of the examples she gives of combating TFGBV are from the United States and reflect the cultural and political characteristics of that country. Still, the categorisation of forms of resistance she creates aligns with what Brazilian and Latin American organisations have been debating. Firstly, digital security solutions, such as protecting passwords, double-checking social media and email accounts, and encrypting communications and files (especially for those who are more visible or deal with sensitive content). Then there are strategies and ways of dealing with different types of attacks without amplifying them—one example is to *print screen* a misogynistic attack and post it without identifying the attacker so as not to give the person the visibility they so desperately want; another is to silence or block the person ("your profile is your kingdom, not democracy"). Jankowicz addresses the importance of support and solidarity networks, something that the *acoso.online* project also says is central beyond the legal confrontation, and she recognises the possibilities of notifying platforms in the event of violations of their terms of use and the existing laws and their application. She discusses how frustrating legal protection is for victims of TFGBV—and, probably for this reason, devotes only three pages to legal and institutional strategies. Danielle Citron and Carrie Goldberg have been writing about the limitations of the law and the institutions that apply it in the US case and about the importance of disputing it, nonetheless.

Is Brazilian law working for women? What demands is Brazilian feminism formulating? What has been achieved and how? What are the contradictions? And what gaps are there? Like the questions, there are many answers. Let us start with the first of the laws passed specifically after a case of gender-based violence on the internet in Brazil.

2.1 The Carolina Dieckmann Law

At the beginning of May 2012, 36 nude photos of actress Carolina Dieckmann began circulating on the internet.[1] Carolina took a firm and combative stance: she filed a police report, did not succumb to the threats, and spoke to the press about it on several occasions. She said in interviews that she had been subjected to extortion for about two months—she received anonymous contacts, by phone or by email, asking for 10,000 reais not to publish the photos (G1, 2012a). A report on the TV Globo *Fantástico* (2012), a well-known TV show with extensive viewing that airs every Sunday for decades, on 14 May 2012, shows the moment when the police arrived at the home of one of the "hackers".

A brief aside: this use of the word "hacker" reflects a backwards and prejudiced view of technology. Anthropologist and Harvard professor Gabriella Coleman (2012, p. 16) has undertaken extensive research into what is known as the "hacker ethic" among developers—a self-image that includes specific values, mainly libertarian, and aesthetics linked to enthusiasm for technology, but also displaying significant variations and tensions. Some self-described hackers even use the term *cracker* to distinguish (and differentiate from) those who commit crimes and illicit acts through hacking, although others argue that this division between good and evil is unhelpful in understanding that some techniques can be employed for both lawful and unlawful purposes, legitimate or not. When discussing technology, it is important to engage seriously with the debates among those who develop it.

In the reports at the time, a common crime—extortion—was treated as something exceptional, mysterious, and practised by obscure hackers. In 2012, Carolina's first suspicion was that the photos had been accessed when she left her computer

[1] Carolina Dieckmann was and is still an actress working for the Brazilian larger TV content producer and broadcaster, Rede Globo de Televisão. She is extremely popular in the country, which made her case all the more remarkable.

for repair. The service providers were even investigated, but the Police Department for Cybercrime used counterintelligence programmes to find another group responsible for disseminating the photos. They discovered that, in fact, the undue access had been to her email. The Civilian Police (the name of the investigative state-level police unit in Brazil) even had access to conversations between people in the group and claimed to have obtained one of their IP addresses. Police Chief Rodrigo de Souza Valle told *Fantástico*: "The police will get there [to the person responsible], yes. It may take a little longer, a little less time, but the police will get there".

Theft, qualified extortion, and defamation: these were the offences for which "the hackers" were indicted. In one of the message exchanges shown on *Fantástico*, one expresses fear since the reports talked about extortion—"that's the serious penalty". Then they make fun of the fact that the case is being investigated—"last instance, go to jail and pay me a visit". "Come on, brother. Nothing's going to happen," replies the other. In addition to the belief that nothing would happen—it was 2012, and it was very common to hear that the internet was a "lawless land"—the investigated parties' statements expressed another fact: there was no provision for criminal punishment for unauthorised access to computers and emails nor for the dissemination of intimate images without authorisation (which was framed as insult or defamation).

It is worth taking a moment to discuss the terms used in this case. "Leakage" of intimate images or, as is usual to say, *nudes,* is a term that is very widespread to this day, which is quite revealing of the fears and also the myths that this problem has brought up since the case involving Carolina Dieckmann: it seems like an event without a subject, inevitable and difficult to deal with, like a pipe that has burst or a tap that will not turn off. Throughout this book, I will talk about the *non-consensual* dissemination of *intimate* images, or the acronym NCII.[2] If "leak" erases the conflict and the dimension of power that exists in the act and the perceptions and consequences of NCII, the term "*revenge porn*" misses the mark twice. "Revenge porn" gained traction in the media in the early 2010s as a result of highly publicised cases of ex-boyfriends disseminating intimate images after break-ups or betrayals.

"Revenge" refers to the victim's behaviour and presupposes that there is a causal relationship between a previous action and the dissemination of the images. In reality, the cases involve very different stories, which often have nothing to do with this narrative, and even when they do, the use of the word "revenge" seems to establish an equivalence, a certain justification for the act, which, in the context of gender violence, reinforces misogynistic values. "Pornography" also gets in the way because it refers to something that the victims do not necessarily recognise (use for commercial purposes or sexual arousal of others) and removes the cases from the field of violence and non-consent to the field of what serves the pleasure of the other (although pornography is another controversial subject that I won't go into here).[3] In addition, many of the documented cases of NCII or related violence do not necessarily involve explicit sex or even explicit nudity: this is the case of the Top 10, which we documented in a 2015 InternetLab case study among teenagers in the south zone of São Paulo, and which involved sensual or even social media profile images seen together with phrases describing the sexual behaviour of the young women (Valente et al., 2015).

Returning to the outcome of the Carolina Dieckmann case, justified by the lack of a legal

[2]There is also A critical importance attached to the term intimacy in this context. As researcher Beatriz Accioly Lins puts it, "intimate" carries sexuality but also shame, modesty and secrecy and involves the taboo practice of sexuality. "Within this 'hegemonic sexual morality', the dignity of women would be all the more unblemished the more it is performed in terms of discretion, modesty and seclusion" (Lins, 2021, p. 147).

[3]In the feminist field, there are different positions on pornography, which also refer to positions on sexuality—from associations with oppression to associations with liberation. On the terms of the dispute in the United States that became known as the *sex wars*, in the 1970s and 1980s, see Wendy Chapkis, *Live Sex Acts: Women Performing Erotic Labor.* Nova York: Routledge, 1996.

framework for what had happened, in that same year, the National Congress passed Law No. 12,737/2012, known as the Carolina Dieckmann Law. The law included Article 154-A in the Brazilian Criminal Code, which describes the crime of "hacking a computer device" with the following wording:

> Breaking into someone else's computer device, whether or not connected to a computer network, *by improperly breaching a security mechanism*[4] and with the aim of obtaining, tampering with or destroying data or information without the express or tacit authorisation of the device's owner or installing vulnerabilities to obtain an illicit advantage.
> Penalty—detention, from 3 (three) months to 1 (one) year, and a fine.

The article has five subsections, which provide details and derivations. For example, the penalty is increased from one-sixth to one-third to the extent of the economic loss, from one to two-thirds if the data and information obtained are disclosed, and from one-third to one-half if the offence is committed against the President of the Republic, the Supreme Court, and other state bodies. We will come back to that in a moment. In addition to the offence of hacking a computer device, the law also amended two other articles of the Criminal Code to include the offence of interrupting a "telematics or public utility information service" and forging a credit or debit card.

Thus, although the Carolina Dieckmann Law is a political response to the case involving the actress, legally, it is not the case—and the law does not even touch on the gender dimension of the problem. This is because, firstly, the crime of hacking into a computer device would not account for the email hacking that occurred with Carolina Dieckmann—since what was criminalised was the hacking of "desktop computers, notebooks, tablets (iPads and others), laptops, as well as smartphones, which today constitute real microcomputers, among others to be created for the same purpose" (Nucci, 2021). Secondly, because the law shows specific concern about the invasion of devices belonging to powerful figures, such as the President, and the occurrence of economic damage (including the articles dealing with credit and debit card forgery), which shows that the time was taken to deal with other concerns that were already on the table and had nothing to do with the case.

And how did this happen? The Carolina Dieckmann Law was actually the passing of a bill that had already been proposed in the House of Representatives in 2011 to criminalise conduct in cybercrime. Presented by MPs Paulo Teixeira, Luiza Erundina, Manuela D'Ávila, João Arruda, Brizola Neto, and Emiliano José, the bill was intended to be an alternative to another bill, Bill 84/1999, which had already been approved in the Senate and was being debated in the House of Representatives in 2008.

Bill 84/1999, initially proposed by MP Luiz Piauhylino (Brazilian Social Democrats Party, PSDB), had been highly criticised by the press and Brazilian civil society. Because of a substitute (a new text) proposed by Senator Eduardo Azeredo (Brazilian Democratic Movement Party, PMDB) in 2008, which brought together Piauhylino's bill and others that were being processed together, it became known as the Azeredo Bill—and was baptised by "internet activists", then a fairly new category, as the "digital AI-5". AI-5 or Institutional Act n. 5 is the infamous decree that suspended political rights in 1968, during the Brazilian military dictatorship. According to researcher Paulo Rená Santarém's reconstruction of the first years of internet policy discussion in Brazil, the bill was penalising and made no provision for guarantees for internet users (Santarém, 2022). This was a trend in the bills proposed at the time: as Rená notes, although Brazil was relatively early in its initiatives to regulate the internet, the approach was predominantly criminal. The MPs who proposed the alternative made similar criticisms, saying that very open criminalisation proposals would crimi-

[4] In 2021, the law underwent a reform (through Law No. 14,155/2021), which removed this requirement and increased the penalty. This means that any unauthorised access can be punished. This change was intended to punish cases where malicious access occurs on devices that are not protected with additional layers of security, but it is also criticised for the openness it introduced. For example, access by journalists and researchers could be punished, depending on political flavours.

nalise ordinary citizens, so they proposed criminalising a more limited set of behaviours. It was this bill that was quickly rebranded after the Carolina Dieckmann case and passed.

The Azeredo Bill ended up passing a little later, completely reduced in scope, basically providing for specialised cybercrime police stations. The mobilisation had worked, and the MPs who proposed the alternative, which ended up in the Carolina Dieckmann Law, achieved their aim. The demonstrations against the Azeredo Bill, such as the #MegaNo campaign, became known for having paved the way for legislation protecting fundamental rights on the internet in Brazil, which I will talk about later in this chapter. The point here is that there was a previous context and that the dissemination of intimate images of Carolina Dieckmann—and her nonconformist and resistant reaction—was the trigger for the finalisation of that process, without the new legislation even directly recognising the problem, which was beginning to become explicit, at that time.

An important point has yet to be uncovered. Carolina Dieckmann's case also involved another problem overshadowed by the events and the law's passing. The actress's intimate images had been hosted on various websites and could easily be found by searching for her name on search engines such as Google. After Dieckmann's lawyer, Antônio Carlos de Almeida Castro, famously known in Brazil as Kakay, announced that he would file a lawsuit asking that the results no longer be shown, Google said so in a statement:

> Google has clarified that it does not interfere with its search results. Google's search engine is an indexer, i.e., a tool that searches for content available on the internet. If you do not want the content to appear in Google's search results, you need to contact the website hosting the content and ask for it removed. (G1, 2012b)

After receiving an informative letter from Google itself detailing technical difficulties in removing content from search results, Kakay announced a few days later that he would drop his lawsuit against the company since it had shown a willingness to engage in dialogue (Tabak, 2012). Google's statement that it does not interfere with its search results and that the removal should be done at the original source would be repeated for some time to come. As we shall see, the company decided to revise its stance a few years later.

2.2 Is the Internet Feminist?

The way Carolina Dieckmann's case was portrayed in the press at the time and the fact that the bill was passed without much debate on gender make it seem as if the violence that was perpetrated against her happened in a vacuum or that there was no concern for the law to address violence against women on the internet. This is not true. In the previous chapter, I looked at how feminist organisations had discussed internet policies at least since the 1990s. The issue of TFGBV has also been on the agenda since then, although it was only in the mid-2010s that it gained a structured debate.

By structured debate, I mean publications, organisations dedicated to it, academic papers, media space, and parliamentarians' discussions. However, the issue had already been simmering in other spaces without breaking the bubble, so the press reports on Dieckmann's case didn't even reference the gender dimension of what had happened, and the legislative response was disconnected from any of these discussions. For example, an article in the national outlet G1[5] talks about "virtual crimes", "a gang of hackers specialising in breaking into computers", linking the case much more to panic about the many forms of crime that would be possible with the internet than to the gender dimension, which is connected to a story that does not begin on the internet.

> *Fantástico* exclusively shows how the photos from actress Carolina Dieckmann's personal archive were stolen and ended up on the internet. Reporters Tyndaro Menezes and Paulo Renato Soares take you behind the scenes of the police investigation

[5]Belonging to the same media group, Globo, as the Fantástico TV Show—which is the group that Carolina Dieckmann worked for.

> that dismantled a gang of hackers specialising in breaking into computers.
> [...]
> Brazil does not have a specific law for computer-related offences. But that does not mean that those who commit cybercrime go unpunished. Justice is based on the Criminal Code, and in the case of the actress, those involved will be indicted for theft, qualified extortion and defamation. (Rede Globo, 2012)

It is worth looking at the context where the case was discussed and where the conversation stood. The theory of counterpublics can explain the fact that it wasn't then a common-sense subject—but I will come back to that later. In the 1990s, a movement came to be known as *cyberfeminism*: a set of artistic, academic, and activist interventions that celebrated the internet as a space to overcome gender inequality. The feminist collective VNS Matrix, formed in Adelaide, Australia, in 1991, claims to be the first to have used the term in its *A Cyberfeminist Manifesto for the twenty-first Century*, distributed in an art gallery and then published on a giant billboard in Sydney. The manifesto is combative and enthusiastic, openly influenced by Donna Haraway's *Cyborg Manifesto*: "we are the virus of the new world disorder/rupturing the symbolic from within/saboteurs of big daddy mainframe / the clitoris is a direct line to the matrix / the VNS Matrix" (VNS Matrix, 1991). In 1995, Sadie Plant, a British philosopher and cultural theorist, proposed that the internet's fluidity, horizontality, and relationality made it inherently suitable for women's agency (Plant, 1995). A 1997 text by Anna Sampaio and Janni Aragón (1997), both professors in the United States, argued that communication in cyberspace was devoid of cultural indicators such as age, race, and gender and thus challenged traditional constructions of rationality and masculinity—as long as anonymity prevailed. In 1999, Nancy Paterson, a Canadian artist and university professor, published a text called "Cyberfeminism", in which she said:

> The body, in virtual space, is no mere user interface; VR offers the chance to trade-in, remodel, or even leave behind the physical nature with which we are, in reality, burdened. Outside forces which act upon us, impose restrictions, are gone. Gravity, and the laws of physics, gone. Entropy and the passage of time become meaningless concepts. Women have always, by virtue of necessity, been adept at free fall, grounding themselves in personal physical experience. This skill will serve well as we venture into other dimensions and back home again. However skilled we become at navigating these spaces and temporarily leaving our bodies behind, it is doubtful that we will ever achieve immortality. Virtuality is patriarchy's blind spot. (Paterson, 1996)

There is a lot of zeitgeist in these expressions: 1996 was the year in which John Perry Barlow, a central figure in the American hippie movement who had then become an enthusiast of digital technologies of a libertarian nature (Turner, 2008), published his famous *A Declaration* of *the Independence of Cyberspace* (Barlow, 1996), advocating the abstention of any state interference in the virtual because it would be superior, a "land of the mind", free from the ties of the material world. *Wired* magazine published many other opinions with similar views, which at the time were already being criticised for being somewhat partial, utopian, and ideological in terms of the relations of production and consumption of new technologies (Barbrook & Cameron, n.d.). Barlow's manifesto did not have the overcoming of gender inequality on the horizon. Cyberfeminism did. And looking back makes so much enthusiasm seem innocent. There was, in fact, an epistemological issue, a problem with approaching technology as an almost neutral container disconnected from the ills of the world of bodies.

On the other hand, to avoid anachronisms, it is worth remembering that the internet of the 1990s had very little to do with the internet we know today. It wasn't populated with images, let alone videos; the inhabitants of that space were few: only those who had access to a computer and a telephone line and knew how the World Wide Web worked. In 1998, Brazil had only 2.1 million users (NIC.br & R7, 2009). It is not difficult to conclude that many inequalities expressed themselves. At the same time, it is easier to understand why this perception of an internet without a body was seductive. But to tell only the cyberfeminist side of the story is also to give a partial version. Other feminist articulations were being made about the internet, especially in Latin America. And online misogyny also existed at the time. Australian professor Emma Jane (2016, p. 18), in her book *Misogyny Online,* recalls receiving emails with rape threats since 1998.

So, we can see that feminist movements have used the internet from the outset—just as they used the other communication technologies that preceded it and were also transformed by it. Referring to this is central for two reasons: firstly, because the internet is not just misogynistic. It has undoubtedly become a space of new expressive possibilities for women and LGBTQIAP+, Black, and ndigenous people. Secondly, if misogyny is a system for monitoring and enforcing the subordination of women, as we defined earlier, an intentional or indirect product of misogyny on the internet is to act in the bowels of these spaces of articulation and agency.

In her book *Interpreting the Internet: Feminist and Queer Counterpublics in Latin America,* Elisabeth Jay Friedman presents an extensive survey of feminist organisations in Latin America which shows that not only were some organisations and collectives aware from the outset of how the internet could facilitate their goals but that the very popularisation of the internet in the 1990s enabled these articulations. Based on her research trajectory, Friedman adopts a vision of mutual construction, understanding that the internet has impacted feminist movements and that they have also impacted technology. "Eventually, I realised that the importance of the internet is determined by its use; in this case, the many ways in which activists in Latin America have incorporated the internet over time"—and the Latin American region has been prominent in the Global South in efforts to connect counterpublics to the internet (Friedman, 2016, own translation).

Why talk about feminist counterpublics? Historically, in Latin America and elsewhere in the world, women have created various forms of organisation to confront the many forms of repression and marginalisation, from inequality in political power (even the right to vote) to the absence of sexual and reproductive rights, violence in the home and public spaces, precarious work and reproductive work overload, discriminatory representation in the media, and public debate. This history can be characterised by phases and, faced with a growing complexification of actors and actresses, the Brazilian political scientist Sonia Alvarez (1997) proposes the use of *discursive fields of action* to account for the references shared by both more formalised feminist practices, such as NGOs, and less formalised ones, such as autonomous collectives, recognising the inequalities between these spaces and the differences in approaches to feminism.

The concept of a *feminist counterpublic* or, more broadly, *subaltern counterpublic* has also been progressively used by Brazilian authors (Medeiros & Fanti, 2019; Rocha & Medeiros, 2020; Medeiros, 2019): these are alternative discursive spheres or spaces in which marginalised people develop their identities, build communities, and formulate strategies to have an impact on broader publics. It goes back to Nancy Fraser's critique of Jürgen Habermas' formulation of the concept of the public sphere: there is not and never has been, nor could there ever be, a single public sphere for all discursive exchanges in a society. In the original formulation, Habermas' public sphere would be a space for White, middle-class, conventional men to reinforce their power. In subaltern counterpublics, subaltern groups formulate oppositional interpretations based on their places, identities, interests, needs, and counter-discourses. One example Fraser (1990) brings up is the US feminists who, at the end of the twentieth century, organised media outlets, publishing houses, conferences, meetings, academic programmes, and even a specific vocabulary to deal with problems that were not sufficiently addressed by the public sphere—such as "rape culture" or "double journey". Patricia Hill Collins formulates something similar when she talks about the *safe spaces* in which US Black women construct independent self-definitions, manufacturing themselves according to the roles of historically dominant Black women in their own communities—in relationships, but also in writing and music, such as the blues (Friedman, 2016, p. 31).

Therefore, the choice to talk about counterpublics and not social movements is to focus on the discursive moment, on spaces of development that often pre-date social movements, understood here as organisations for social transformation sustained over time or concurrent with it. A proposed dialogue between the concept of counterpublics and that of the discursive field is that the discursive field focuses on the growing imbrication between dominant publics and subaltern counterpublics. In contrast, counterpublics focus on producing the latter as their own sphere, even if their discourses aim outwards (Medeiros, 2019). Between the two focuses, that of counterpublics has been mobilised productively by research in the field of communication, giving an adequate account, it seems to me, of strategies, spaces, and forms of appropriation of the media.

2.3 Feminist Counterpublics

When the internet began to become popular in Latin America, feminist counterpublics had been organising for over a century. And they were using media. In Brazil, before the 1870s, the few so-called women's newspapers were run by men, avoided controversial topics, and, if they mentioned emancipation, it was to show opposition (Duarte, 2019). From then on, several feminist newspapers began to appear in Rio de Janeiro and other cities. The launch of *O Sexo Feminino* (The Feminine Sex), by Francisca Senhorinha da Motta Diniz, was notable in 1873. The periodical had three phases, changed its name to *O Quinze de Novembro do Sexo Feminino* (The November 15 of the Feminine Sex)[6] after the proclamation of the Republic, and lasted until 1890, with a considerable readership (at one point they printed 4000 copies of the first ten issues to cater for an audience that even included Emperor Pedro II and Princess Isabel). Written only by women and for women, its editorial line aimed at proving that women could be intellectually equal if they had opportunities and that the great enemy of women was ignorance of their rights. In the last phase, Diniz' newspaper began to defend the right to education and work more emphatically (Duarte, 2019). Other examples were *A Família* (The Family), which circulated between 1888 and 1897, first in São Paulo and then in Rio, run by journalist Josefina Álvares de Azevedo, fighting for female emancipation in higher education, divorce, paid work, and the vote; *O Corimbo*, by sisters Revocata Heloísa de Melo and Julieta de Melo Monteiro, between 1884 and 1944 in Porto Alegre; and *A Mensageira* (The Messenger), between 1897 and 1900, by Presciliana Duarte de Almeida, in São Paulo. In 1952, Joana Paula Manso de Noronha, an Argentinian living in Rio de Janeiro, launched the *Jornal das Senhoras* (Ladies' Newspaper), which, in the first editorial, presented the aim to encourage women's education for their emancipation. These and many other publications echoed the news of each woman graduating in Brazil and abroad and were vehicles for raising awareness and creating mutual support.

It seems that these were all newspapers led by elite White women. In a reconstruction by researcher Natália Neris, there are records of a Black press at least as far back as the 1820s, with the newspaper *O Bahiano*, which circulated between 1828 and 1831—and there was a significant proliferation of the Black press between 1910 and 1960 in São Paulo, stifled by the military dictatorship, only to make a strong comeback later. I have not found any records of Black women's or feminist newspapers from this period—this may be due to the lack of data or because the differentiation of a Black women's movement from both the Black and the feminist movement (which then had White and Eurocentric characteristics) took place mainly from the 1980s onwards (Carneiro, 2003), as I will point out below.

Similar experiments were taking place in the region simultaneously, such as the newspaper *La Mujer* (The Woman) in Chile and *El Aguila Mexicana* (The Mexican Eagle) in Mexico. These were initial platforms for communicating and

[6] 15 November 1889 was the day of a military coup d'état against the constitutional monarchy that established the First Brazilian Republic.

publishing ideas that did not make it into the media dominated by White men. Before 1979, there were records of more than 200 women's magazines in Latin America—publications that dealt with rights issues related to domestic and public life and connected with political agendas, from the abolitionist movement to anarchism, socialism, and conservatism (Greenberg, 1990). Face-to-face, national and regional meetings fuelled the production of communications.

After the suffragette movement, the 1970s were widely recognised as years of feminist exuberance in the world and Brazil. It was the year the UN defined as the International Women's Year, which generated a series of exchanges between local and international activists. In Brazil and other parts of Latin America, women were submerged in a repressive dictatorial context and were fighting for equal rights and against sexual discrimination, but also for democracy, against censorship, and for better living conditions. The right to pleasure and abortion gained some ground (Duarte, 2019). The positioning of feminist issues among other left-wing struggles was not without conflict. However, this was the time when important feminist media emerged: *Brasil Mulher* (Brazil Woman, 1975), *Nós Mulheres* (We Women, 1976), and *Mulherio* (1981), which dealt with issues such as racial discrimination, women in literature, sexual and reproductive rights, violence, women's work, and the lives of female workers. It was also the time of the founding of the Unified Black Movement (1978) and the Black women's movement, which stated that identity on gender issues did not mean solidarity on racial issues, and vice versa—the Black movement did not automatically cover the gender issue (Carneiro, 2003).

Between 1980 and 1990, the number of publications in Latin America practically doubled. They were now more long-lasting, such as the influential *Fem* in Mexico, *Mujer/fempress*, which circulated in several countries in the region, as well as initiatives like Mexico's *CIMAC*, which supported other women's groups in their communication efforts. The Xerox machine was widely used by different sectors of feminism, just as were community radios (Greenberg, 1990). They were already used not only for communication but also for identity development, such as the conversations that took place in the letters to the editor section and the debates opposing ideas that *Fem* magazine published.

Even when, faced with the transition to democracy and neoliberal economic policy from the 1980s onwards, part of the Latin American feminist movement began to become "institutionalised" in non-profit organisations, and conflicts between the "autonomous" and the "institutionalised" absorbed part of the movement's disputes, organisations maintained contact by forming part of national and regional counterpublics, such as the *Encuentros Latinoamericanos y Caribeños* (Latin American and Caribbean Meetings), which began to organise from 1981, forming local committees in nine countries, including Brazil. Feminist media continued to be central to the discussion before and after the Encuentros. Despite internal disagreements, regional coalition-building efforts were central to the passing of legislation against violence against women, anti-discrimination laws based on sexuality and gender expression or identity, and same-sex marriage (Friedman, 2016). It was also in the late 1970s and early 1980s that important research centres on women's studies were established at universities (Costa et al., 2019).

The internet began to be popularised after the feminist resurgence of the 1970s. Many utopian visions of the internet's potential argued that it would provide the conditions for forming a vibrant public sphere in Habermasian terms. However, the internet has moved to very different places since the utopias of the 1990s, especially because of the construction of walled spaces with their own logic, controlled by large corporations called *big tech,* and the renewed forms of state control over online communications. Social inequalities appear in the technologies themselves, their access, and how they are used. Even in the face of this, online counterpublics have formed.[7] Although they are present on the internet, this does not mean that the internet is entirely feminist. What is interesting and makes sense to investigate is how feminist counterpublics have made use of this space.

There are at least two critical perspectives in understanding the relationship between the internet and feminist counterpublics: one that adopts a more historical perspective, centring already existing counterpublics and how the internet, as yet another form of communication, transforms and is transformed by them, and another that looks specifically at digital counterpublics, those that are formed predominantly through networks, even though they are linked to movements and issues that go far beyond them.

Even though the start of the internet was a military venture in the United States and remained under its control for around three decades, there have always been programmers and users working to democratise the technology and create alternative uses (Abbate, 2000), including grassroots movements. Latin American civil society organisations, taking advantage of the opportunity to offer people the chance to participate in the UN's Eco-92, could connect to the internet when it was not yet commercially available, providing connection through "civil servers" for organisations. This was the case with AlterNex in Brazil, coordinated by Carlos Afonso. At the time, the Brazilian internet connected universities and research centres via the National Research Network (RNP), but it was not possible to connect to it individually or contract independent access (Nepomuceno & Pereira, 1997).

In the wake of regional feminist organising from the 1980s, which relied heavily on alternative media, feminist activists working in technology played a significant role in connecting activists and groups. The Association for Progressive Communications (APC), which I mentioned in the previous chapter as an organisation discussing gender at technology policy meetings since ancient times, was central at this time (Friedman, 2016). The APC is an amalgamation of organisations; i.e. it articulates an infrastructure of existing communities. One of its most successful programmes was the Women's Networking Support Programme (WNSP), which in 1993 began working with Latin American organisations to train women's groups to use the internet and media policy *advocacy* so that Mexican women could prepare for the UN Beijing Conference. For example, activists Beatriz Cavazos and Erika Smith, through the Mexican organisation LaNeta, founded ModemMujer, which connected women's entities to use email and participate in the conference. They helped create four hundred email accounts, to which information about the conference was sent and then forwarded by fax, local newspapers, and community radio. The replies were dispatched to the ModemMujer in Beijing, where they were used to put pressure on the Mexican delegation there. The WNSP opened a civilian server (at the NGO Forum, which took place parallel to the conference) and worked locally and remotely to open 1700 email accounts, through which 62,000 messages passed (Friedman, 2016, p. 73). In this way, alternative information to official sources was shared. As a result, the APC was putting into practice the vision that the internet should not just be a space for men in the West—and it was doing so from the bottom up, starting with the women's counterpublics that already existed (Friedman, 2016, p. 71). Meanwhile, it also worked with the results that came out of the meeting, managing to include demands for training in internet technologies for south–south and south–north communication to promote rights and gender equality in the conference recommendations. It was a crucial moment for the use of the internet to become part of the fabric of feminist demands.

In the late 1990s and early 2000s, email distribution lists were extremely popular among Latin American organisations. The Brazilian ones circulated less among the other countries due to language differences (Friedman, 2016, p. 93). But

[7] For media theorist Lincoln Dahlberg, the internet favours three central characteristics of counterpublic building: the creation of identities, of community based on new ways of thinking, and the strategising of change—but it is the appropriation and transformation of these characteristics by a community that shape the counterpublics. Lincoln Dahlberg,

even so, a lot of internal articulation took place. For example, on the occasion of the UN World Conference against Racism, Racial Discrimination, Xenophobia and Intolerance, a group led by organisations across the country (Criola in Rio de Janeiro, Geledés Institute of the Black Woman in São Paulo, and Maria Mulher in Rio Grande do Sul) organised the Coalition of Brazilian Black Women (*Articulação de Mulheres Negras Brasileiras*) and coordinated the participation of Black women and their agendas at the conference—especially via an email list (Friedman, 2016, p. 118).

In the Latin American region, internet use for organisations' end-activities, such as contact with communities, has always been limited by inequalities in access, which create new forms of exclusion. Therefore, ways of tackling this exclusion have also been devised: in 2001, Cimac in Mexico integrated the internet into a broader communications chain, for example, by designating a person to read news received by email on a local radio station. *Mulheres do Alto das Pombas* (Alto das Pombas Women), an organisation of Black women in Salvador, relied on a network of university students to send and receive emails (Friedman, 2016, p. 98). In 1999, Geledés produced an internet and media *advocacy* workshop for women in Salvador, and communications coordinator Nilza Iraci recounted how difficult it was to convince funders that the internet was not just a "luxury" when faced with problems such as health and education. Around 20 women were trained by four Black women, not only in technological skills but also in gender and racial inequalities and how to address them with digital technologies in their respective organisations to make technology relevant to those women (Friedman, 2016, p. 99).

By the 2010s, organisations were already getting to grips with social networks and the challenges of communicating on them: older organisations often had to hire younger people and reported difficulties in finding network specialists who also had knowledge of gender inequalities and the organisation's language (Friedman, 2016, p. 104). This is when what I have called *digital* counterpublics came on the scene, referring to spaces that, even if they are not exclusively based on social networks, have their genesis closely linked to these new forms of communication. These are feminisms with new contours that, in many ways, clash with previous ones.[8]

Researchers Jonas Medeiros and Fabiola Fanti have built a database of more than four hundred protests in Brazil between 2003 and 2017. Analysing them, they concluded that there was a significant increase from 2011 onwards, which coincides with the start of what has been called the "cycle of protests" in Brazil (which peaked in 2013 but continued until President Dilma Rousseff's impeachment) (Medeiros & Fanti, 2019). It is a common analysis that, in the 1990s and 2000s in Brazil, the institutionalisation of NGOs, which were funded by and had access to international networks, and the opportunity for historical activists to become government officials from the first Lula government (2002–2006) onwards, would have kept women off the streets (Alvarez, 1997). This return, in 2011, was initially linked to a particular event: the Slut Walk.

The Slut Walk was born in Canada in response to a lecture at the University of Toronto, where a police officer said that in order to avoid violence, women needed to stop "dressing as sluts". The first Slut Walk, on 3 April 2011, was a protest that incorporated the word *slut* and called for freedom and autonomy over the body and sexuality. From then on, several marches began to be organised worldwide; the first in Brazil took place in São Paulo on 4 June that year. The following year, a unified date was set, and on 26 May 2012, demonstrations took place in more than 30 cities in the country—and more in the following years (Gomes & Sorj, 2014). The marches began to be organised decentrally and through social net-

[8]One aspect that sociologists Flávia Rios and Regimeire Maciel emphasise is that the generations of "new activists" after the 2000s articulate their demands mainly in terms of their individuality and their own experience, while previous generations articulated more collective and organisational experiences. Activists of the new generation are also working to rescue Black feminist authors and to centre Black feminism in opposition to White feminism (Rios & Maciel, 2021).

works. Their rapid spread and the repertoires used—"flag-bodies", with short clothes, topless, slogans on the skin—were linked to disseminating information and images via the internet. In addition to the chain of protests, the importance of the SlutWalks has survived: feminist collectives were formed from them and have continued to gain expression. But their significance has not been unanimous in the feminist movements: some Black women's collectives, such as the *Pretas Candangas* (Candanga Blacks), referring to a predominance of White, university-educated women at the Marchas das Vadias, criticised the very banners, stating that for Black women sexualisation happens regardless of certain types of clothes, and that "we do not want to claim the right to be sluts, but to be doctors, lawyers, doctors" (Magalhães Pinto, 2013).

Although they are a hallmark, not least because the media have prominently covered them, the marches were part of a moment of enthusiasm far beyond them: there was what political scientist Sonia Alvarez calls a multiplication of fields and popularisation of feminism, whether in the city, in the countryside, among domestic workers, quilombolas, indigenous women, lesbians, trans women, hip-hoppers and graffiti artists, and among all Black feminists. In 2015, the Black Women's March against Racism and Violence and for the Good Living (*Bem Viver*) also evoked the colonial struggle, as in other parts of Latin America. Throughout this movement, the internet and social networks have played a significant role, including in organising street marches. Jonas Medeiros and Fabiola Fanti (2019) note, however, how women's presence on the streets shifted in 2013 to "defensive" agendas—initially against the Statute of the Unborn Child, which, despite being from 2007, was back on the table in the Congress at the time and jeopardised the already reduced possibilities for legal abortion in the country. In 2015, women marched against congressman Eduardo Cunha, who was leading conservative movements against women's rights and Dilma Rousseff's presidency; in 2018, outside the period of Medeiros and Fanti's study, women organised the massive *#EleNão* (#NotHim) marches against the election of Jair Bolsonaro, which attests to the links between this process of sprawling connections through the internet and the strengthening of the right wing in the country.

Although the focus here has been on the streets, the networks have also been effervescent. It was in the 2010s that the large social networking platforms began to gain scale in Brazil and around the world. Orkut, created in 2004, became immensely popular in Brazil between 2005 and 2007—among internet users, of course, who were concentrated in the richer populations (Rocha, 2021). From the late 1990s to the early 2000s , the blogosphere gained enormous popularity. As early as 2010, Facebook took centre stage, and private mobile messaging applications such as WhatsApp also began to become popular.

Feminist counterpublics were formed out of the construction of these multiple spaces. Blogs such as *Escreva Lola Escreva* (Write Lola Write), which I will deal with later, but also *Blogueiras Feministas* (Feminist Bloggers), *Blogueiras Negras* (Black Female Bloggers), and *Lugar de Mulher* (Women's Place), Facebook pages such as *Feminismo sem Demagogia* (Feminism without Demagogy) and *Moça, Você é Machista* (Lady, You are Sexist), and many others, were spaces for the formation of new discourses and new practices, such as a culture of calling out sexism, racism, and other situations of violence (Rodrigues, 2016; Seridório et al., 2016; Santos & Barros, 2015; Malta & de Oliveira, 2016). In her doctoral research, anthropologist Fernanda Kalianny Martins Sousa (2017) studied how the dynamics of discussion between the internet and other environments for political action have created and re-signified the category of abusive relationships within the feminist repertoire. In another piece of research, this time a PhD that Jonas Medeiros defended in 2016 on the formation of peripheral collectives in the city of São Paulo, it becomes clear how the use of the internet, and Facebook groups in particular, was central to the articulation of women from one end of the city to the other, to the dissemination of cultural soirées, and to the development of debates with their own new grammars.[9]

Since the 2010s, the networks have also had the role of aggregating audiences, agendas, and vocabularies in so-called hashtag campaigns, such as *#MeuPrimeiroAssédio* (#MyFirstHarass ment), *#MeuAmigoSecreto* (#MySecretFriend), *#EuNãoMereçoSerEstuprada* (#IDon'tDeserve ToBeRaped), and so many others with a wide or niche reach, as was the case with *#NãoPoetize OMachismo* (#DontPoeticiseSexism), about sexist practices in peripheral poetry soirées (Rodrigues, 2016; Seridório et al., 2016; Santos & Barros, 2015; Malta & de Oliveira, 2016). We saw #MeToo and #NiUnaMenos gaining transnational visibility. Many of these campaigns transcended the networks and took over the traditional media and the debate outside the networks, breaking through the bubble of counterpublics. They are also expressions of what I previously called mutual construction, i.e. a demonstration of how technologies impact social relations and how social relations make use of technologies, moulding them.

2.4 Architectures, Conservatism, and Violence

As much as women were online and articulating themselves on the web, the internet was far from being a bed of roses for them or for LGBTQIAP+ and Black people to express themselves. This period also saw the rise of the new right, conservative anti-corruption protests, the impeachment of President Dilma Rousseff and the election and government of Jair Bolsonaro, and therefore significant anti-feminist victories. Looking at how feminist counterpublics are impacted or constituted by the internet is inescapable when talking about misogyny for two reasons. The first is because it is necessary to emphasise the women's agency and prominence in this space to understand how violence directly affects it. The second is that, although neither violence nor the rise of conservatism can be attributed without mediation to the successes of these mobilisations and discursive disputes by feminisms, there is a connection between one thing and the other.

For context, in 2016, President Dilma Rousseff from the centre-left-wing Workers' Party (PT) was impeached following a big turmoil that traces back to the 2013 mass protests and beyond. Right-wing social groups and parliamentarians gained rising power in the process, supported by discourses around anti-corruption and anti-progressive politics. Her vice-president, Michel Temer, was pivotal in her impeachment and took office until the end of 2018, with the election of extreme right-wing President Jair Bolsonaro, who governed between 2019 and 2022. In this process, the country was deeply divided by opposing political preferences.

In an experiment we carried out at InternetLab in 2018, researcher Natália Neris and I looked at the posts made by Facebook pages during the week of International Women's Day to map the different debates the pages carried out, with the assumption that some feminist themes were more prominent than others (Valente & Neris, 2018). We analysed the pages mapped by the University of São Paulo's Digital Political Debate Monitor, which categorised them according to a reading of the political debate at the time: between the Anti-Workers' Party axes (libertarians, conservatives, military apology groups, parties from the allied base of then-President Michel Temer, and anti-corruption groups) and "anti-anti-Workers Party" groups (not necessarily supporters of the Workers' Party: they were NGOs, opposition parties, left-wing groups, and social movements—including pages from the feminist, antiracist, and LGBTQIAP+ movements).

The result was completely different from what we expected: the most shared posts and news items were all from the conservative camp,

[9] For example, the women's graffiti collective m.A.N.A. (Mulher Atitude Negritude e Arte) Crew began with the meeting of two (future) leaders on Instagram, physically separated by almost twenty kilometres in the city of São Paulo: one in Ermelino Matarazzo and the other in Cidade Tiradentes (Medeiros, 2019).

ironising women politicians from the progressive field (and, in turn, ironising the struggles of International Women's Day). We also saw that the posts from the progressive field were much more numerous but much less shared. This showed, on the one hand, the degree of conflict in the women's rights debate. On the other hand, how immersed we are in homogenous digital spaces, since as authors, we had our expectations frustrated, and this predominance of the conservative camp did not even appear in our hypotheses.

There is a commonplace about the existence of "filter bubbles"—or "echo chambers" or "*rabbit* holes"—as a result of the personalisation of the experience promoted by algorithms on digital platforms, which means that people are mostly subjected to content that is close to their preferences and opinions. There is considerable discussion and research about whether people are really subjected to more homogeneous opinions on the networks than off them and whether they are subjected to more personalised content. This depends on many factors, such as social context and the person's media diet (Sunstein, 2017).[10] In her book *The World Inside Out: Truth and Politics in the Digital Age*, the Brazilian anthropologist Letícia Cesarino (2022) states that it is fruitless to try to identify whether or not an algorithm such as YouTube's causes radicalisation since algorithms are programmed in advance to perform tasks, but they relate to real users, who bring "extra-algorithmic factors". This amalgam matters: how algorithmic processes relate to users, extracting their data to deliver a result, but based on their behaviour. It is, however, a brutally asymmetrical relationship due to technical alienation: there is a lack of clarity about how the algorithms of social media platforms operate. For example, in the reasons why something gains prominence or is shown to us to the detriment of another, or in the differences in meaning and use of a specific action: a *like* seems to be used to demonstrate that I am happy with someone's post, but the social network uses it to cluster users and target them with ads. Although personalisation in content delivery can give a sense of empowerment, users are becoming increasingly passive.

In the case of the 8 March experiment, we were surprised to find posts that were very different from those we were seeing in our use of social networks based on our own homophilic segmentations, i.e. those that connect like with like, based both on the choices of those we follow and on algorithms. However, what matters more to online misogyny is what lies *between* these segmentations: clashes and violence often occur at the intersection of audiences that the same networks allow. Danah boyd's (2010) concept of *context collapse* gives a critical dimension to the problem: she studied how young people on the first social networks had difficulties managing the separation of social roles and expectations, which is more controllable in the offline environment. A post to friends would end up with teachers and grandparents—just as we now see unmediated opinions from people we have no relationship with or with whom we have relationships of other kinds (e.g. your neighbour's political opinion). For Cesarino (2022, p. 104), the context collapse characterises the way digital media is organised as a whole today.

Nor would this prominence of posts on conservative pages have surprised us if Camila Rocha's book, *Less Marx, more Mises*, had already been published (and we had already read it). In it, Rocha analysed the emergence of the new right in Brazil in the 2010s, based on its much longer history, and identified a moment of great enthusiasm in Orkut communities in the 2000s—based on pages dedicated to discussing the work of the right-wing philosopher Olavo de Carvalho, deceased in 2022. The story goes through an internal differentiation between libertarians, who ended up joining a not necessarily libertarian conservatism in organising the protests for Dilma Rousseff's impeachment in 2016, forming the "ultra-liberal-conservative" amalgam. In this process, both the intensive (and competent) use of social networks and the professed

[10] There are also those who propose that we use feedback loops to refer more precisely to the cycles of feedback between humans and machines. See Thorburn et al. (2023).

"shock politics" adopted by many of their representatives as a way of gaining attention for their agendas led to the immense popularity of these profiles and pages—Rocha speaks of tens of millions of people reached by Facebook alone in 2014 (Rocha, 2021).

Another central point in reconstructing the history of clashes between these publics is that, while conservative groups in the 1960s impacted civil society and politics using anti-communist discourse, after re-democratisation in Brazil, older and more recent conservative groups turned their attention to the feminist, LGBTQIAP+, antiracist, and indigenous agendas. Especially during President Dilma Rousseff's mandate, conservatives felt the "progressive shock": just in four years, they were faced with the legalisation of homosexual civil marriage, affirmative action in universities, the abortion legalisation in the case of anencephaly,[11] and a ban on child physical punishment, which they felt threatened by. In 2003, Jair Bolsonaro told MP Maria do Rosário that he "wouldn't rape her because she did not deserve it" (after she had called him a rapist, according to him); in 2011, he started a crusade against what he called the "gay kit" (fake news about supposed anti-homophobia material distributed by the Ministry of Education). "Gender ideology", a term that had been used worldwide by the Catholic Church since the 1990s, came to be strongly repudiated: for political scientist Flávia Biroli and her co-authors (2020), the concept was central to the organisation of the conservative, particularly religious, camp.

This context has not only complicated the progress of the feminist movements and their agendas but has also imposed concrete and daily challenges. As might be expected, online violence against activists, journalists, and women in politics has gained prominence since 2016, as I will discuss in the following chapters. Denouncing and debating online violence against women, LGBTQIAP+ people, and Black people has become more risky, full of confrontations, and has taken on very limited contours, i.e. negotiated with those that this conservatism accepts in the debate on gender violence. The confrontation between online expressions of feminism, antiracism, queer activism, and manifestations by representatives of the new right, in these broad strokes, is not exclusive to Brazil. Authors who write about the United States, such as Whitney Phillips (2015) and Angela Nagle (2017), comment on similar disputes. But the Brazilian context, within the broader Latin American context, brings the many particularities pointed out here. It is also worth recognising the multiplicity of the new right—following Camila Rocha and philosopher Marcos Nobre, who argue that reducing the new right to the extreme right and the extreme right to a mere reaction to emancipatory agendas gaining ground makes it difficult to understand its complexity as an anti-system and anti-establishment force (Nobre, 2022). This argument should be taken seriously: the issues that led to the strengthening of the extreme right and the crisis of democracy in Brazil must be approached to their full social, political, and economic extent. Even so, the opposition to emancipatory agendas and achievements is a relevant part of the story, which, given our subject, makes sense to emphasise.

This is because it was from 2013 onwards (the year of the mass demonstrations and the strengthening of conservatism) that cases of TFGBV began to appear more systematically in the press and to gain more concrete expression in legislative debates. Let us remember how the story between Carolina Dieckmann's lawyer and Google, which claimed not to remove links from its search results for essentially technical reasons, ended a year earlier. So, although the debates on TFGBV— which had been going on since long before by the APC, taken up by the Geledés training programme, and debated (perhaps initially) by digital feminist counter-publics—had not yet left their niches and gained a broader public debate at that time, big tech was paying attention. The proliferation of the non-consensual dissemination of intimate images and its consequences for girls and women would put more pressure on these companies in the aftermath.

[11] By law, abortion is only legal in Brazil in two circumstances: when the procedure is done to save the life of the pregnant woman and when the pregnancy is the result of rape.

References

Abbate, J. (2000). *Inventing the internet* (5th ed.). MIT Press.

Alvarez, S. E. (1997). Articulación y transnacionalización de los feminismos latinoamericanos. *Debate Feminista, 15*. https://seminarioteoriasocialfeministaunpsjb.wordpress.com/wp-content/uploads/2016/04/alvarez-feminismo-transnacionalizaicion.pdf

Barbrook, R., & Cameron, A. (n.d.). *The Californian ideology*. http://www.imaginaryfutures.net/2007/04/17/the-californian-ideology-2/

Barlow, J. P. (1996, February 8). A Declaration of the Independence of Cyberspace. https://projects.eff.org/~barlow/Declaration-Final.html.

Biroli, F., Vaggione, J. M., & Campos Machado, M. D. D. (2020). *Gênero, neoconservadorismo e democracia: Disputas e retrocessos na América Latina*. Boitempo.

boyd, d. (2010). Social network sites as networked publics: Affordances, dynamics, and implications. In Z. Papacharissi (Ed.), *A networked self: Identity, community, and culture on social network sites* (pp. 39–58). Routledge.

Carneiro, S. (2003). Mulheres em movimento. *Estudos Avançados, 17*, 117–133.

Cesarino, L. (2022). *O mundo do avesso: Verdade e política na era digital*. Ubu.

Chapkis, W. (1996). *Live sex acts: Women performing erotic labor*. Routledge.

Coleman, E. G. (2012). *Coding freedom: The ethics and aesthetics of hacking*. Princeton University Press.

Costa, A. d. O., Barroso, C., & Sarti, C. (2019). Pesquisa sobre a mulher no Brasil: Do limbo ao gueto? In H. B. Hollanda (Ed.), *Pensamento feminista brasileiro: Formação e contexto*. Bazar do Tempo.

de Nucci, G. S. (2021). *Código penal comentado* (21st ed.). Forense.

Duarte, C. L. (2019). Feminismo: Uma história a ser contada. In H. B. Hollanda (Ed.), *Pensamento feminista brasileiro: Formação e contexto*. Bazar do Tempo.

Fantástico. (2012). *Polícia encontra hackers que roubaram fotos de Carolina Dieckmann [Television broadcast]*. Rede Globo. https://globoplay.globo.com/v/1945667/

Fraser, N. (1990). Rethinking the public sphere: A contribution to the critique of actually existing democracy. *Social Text, 25/26*, 56–80.

Friedman, E. J. (2016). *Interpreting the internet: Feminist and queer counterpublics in Latin America*. University of California Press.

G1. (2012a). *Carolina Dieckmann fala pela 1ª vez sobre fotos e diz que espera 'justiça'*. http://g1.globo.com/pop-arte/noticia/2012/05/carolina-dieckmann-fala-pela-1-vez-sobre-roubo-de-fotos-intimas.html

G1. (2012b). *Google tem responsabilidade por fotos, diz advogado de Dieckmann*. http://g1.globo.com/rio-de-janeiro/noticia/2012/05/google-tem-responsabilidade-por-fotos-diz-defesa-de-dieckmann.html

Gomes, C., & Sorj, B. (2014). Corpo, geração e identidade: A Marcha das Vadias no Brasil. *Sociedade e Estado, 29*, 433–447.

Greenberg, J. (1990). Toward a history of women's periodicals in Latin America: A working bibliography. In E. Dore, M. Molyneux, & E. J. Friedman (Eds.), *Women, culture, and politics in Latin America* (pp. 181–231). University of California Press.

Jane, E. (2016). *Misogyny online: A short (and brutish) history*. Sage.

Jankowicz, N. (2022). *How to be a woman online: Surviving abuse and harassment, and how to fight back*. Bloomsbury Academic.

Lins, B. A. (2021). *Caiu na net: Nudes e exposição de mulheres na internet*. Telha.

Magalhães Pinto, A. F. (2013, June 27). *Do trágico ao épico: A Marcha das Vadias e os desafios políticos das mulheres negras*. Blogueiras Negras. https://blogueirasnegras.org/desafios-politicos-feminismo-negro/

Malta, R. B., & de Oliveira, L. T. B. (2016). Enegrecendo as redes: O ativismo de mulheres negras no espaço virtual. *Gênero, 16*(2) https://periodicos.uff.br/revistagenero/article/view/31234

Martins, F. K. (2017). Narrativas sobre relacionamentos abusivos e mudança de sensibilidades do que é violência. In *Seminário FESPSP: Incertezas do Trabalho*.

Medeiros, J. (2019). Do "feminismo popular" ao "feminismo periférico": Mudanças estruturais em contrapúblicos da Zona Leste de São Paulo. *Novos Rumos Sociológicos, 7*(11), 300–335.

Medeiros, J., & Fanti, F. (2019). Recent changes in the Brazilian feminist movement: The emergence of new collective actors. In P. Ferrero, A. Natalucci, & L. Tatagiba (Eds.), *Socio-political dynamics within the crisis of the left: Argentina and Brazil*. Rowman & Littlefield.

Nagle, A. (2017). *Kill all normies: Online culture wars from 4chan and Tumblr to Trump and the alt-right*. Zero Books.

Nepomuceno, C., & Pereira, M. D N. F. (1997). *Na távola da internet: O Centro de Informação Alternex-RNP*. Universidade Federal do Rio de Janeiro (UFRJ).

NIC.br, & R7. (2009, September 27). *'População comum' ganhou acesso à internet em 1995*. https://nic.br/noticia/na-midia/populacao-comum-ganhou-acesso-a-internet-em-1995

Nobre, M. (2022). *Limits of democracy: From the June 2013 uprisings in Brazil to the Bolsonaro government*. Springer.

Paterson, N. (1996). Cyberfeminism. In *Fireweed: A feminist quarterly of writing, politics, art and culture* (Vol. 54). https://vacuumwoman.senecacollege.ca/About/Main/Fireweed-Cyberfeminism-1996orig.pdf

Peña, P., & Vera, F. (2018). *Acoso.online* [Online platform]. https://acoso.online

Phillips, W. (2015). *This is why we can't have nice things: Mapping the relationship between online trolling and mainstream culture*. MIT Press.

Plant, S. (1995). The future looms: Weaving women and cybernetics. *Body & Society, 1*(3–4), 45–64.

Rede Globo. (2012). *Polícia encontra hackers que roubaram fotos de Carolina Dieckmann [Television broadcast].* Fantástico. https://globoplay.globo.com/v/1945667/

Rios, F., & Maciel, R. (2021). Brazilian Black feminism in rural and urban spaces. *Agrarian South: Journal of Political Economy, 10*(1), 59–85.

Rocha, C. (2021). *Menos Marx, mais Mises: O liberalismo e a nova direita no Brasil.* Todavia.

Rocha, C., & Medeiros, J. (2020, April 27). *"Vão todos tomar no...": A política do choque e a esfera pública.* Horizontes ao Sul. https://www.horizontesaosul.com/single-post/2020/04/27/vao-todos-tomar-no-a-politica-do-choque-e-a-esfera-publica

Rodrigues, L. M. (2016). *Blogs coletivos feministas: Um estudo sobre o feminismo brasileiro na era das redes sociais na internet* [Master's dissertation, Universidade Estadual Paulista (Unesp)]. https://repositorio.unesp.br/handle/11449/148674.

Sampaio, A., & Aragón, J. (1997). *'To boldly go (where no man has gone before)': Women and politics in cyberspace.* Ethnic Studies. https://scholarcommons.scu.edu/ethnic/32

Santarém, P. R. da S. (2022). *O direito achado na rede: A concepção do Marco Civil da Internet no Brasil.* Dialética.

Santos, N. O., & Barros, J. F. (2015, December). O movimento feminista no Facebook: Uma análise das páginas Moça, Você é Machista e Feminismo sem Demagogia. In *Simpósio Internacional de Tecnologia e Narrativas Digitais, Maranhão.*

Seridório, D. F., Graciano, D. A., Magalhães, E., Vicente, G. H., & Lopes, J. C. (2016). Movimento feminista em rede: Análise do blog e do Facebook 'Lugar de Mulher'. *Pensamento Plural, 17*, 151–172.

Sunstein, C. (2017). *#Republic.* Princeton University Press.

Tabak, B. (2012, May 11). *Após carta do Google, advogado de Dieckmann desiste de processar site.* G1. http://g1.globo.com/rio-de-janeiro/noticia/2012/05/apos-carta-do-google-advogado-de-dieckmann-desiste-de-processar-site.html

Thorburn, L., Stray, J., & Bengani, P. (2023). *When you hear 'filter bubble', 'echo chamber', or 'rabbit hole': Think 'feedback loop'.* Medium. https://medium.com/understanding-recommenders/when-you-hear-filter-bubble-echo-chamber-or-rabbit-hole-think-feedback-loop-7d1c8733d5c

Turner, F. (2008). From counterculture to cyberculture: Stewart Brand, the Whole Earth Catalog, and the rise of digital utopianism. The University of Chicago Press.

Valente, M. (2023). *Online gender-based violence in Brazil: New data insights (Supporting a safer internet paper).* Centre for International Governance Innovation.

Valente, M., & Neris, N. (2018). Elas vão feminizar a internet? O papel e o impacto do ativismo on-line para o feminismo no Brasil. *Sur, 27.* https://sur.conectas.org/wp-content/uploads/2018/07/sur-27-portugues-mariana-valente-natalia-neris.pdf

Valente, M., Neris, N., & Bulgarelli, L. (2015). *Not revenge, not porn: Analysing the exposure of teenage girls online in Brazil.* InternetLab.

VNS Matrix. (1991). *A cyberfeminist manifesto for the 21st century.* https://vnsmatrix.net/projects/the-cyberfeminist-manifesto-for-the-21st-century

3 From the Body to *Nudes*: Sexuality, Gender, and the Internet

Abstract

Focusing on the non-consensual sharing of intimate images (NCII), this chapter connects 2013's widely publicised tragedies and online resistance mobilisations such as #SomosTodasFran to legislative innovation and case-law practice. It reconstructs the participatory process that produced the Marco Civil (2014) and explains why NCII received a bespoke takedown rule (Art. 21) outside the general court-order model (Art. 19), and how, from a criminal law perspective, Brazil then moved beyond a "crimes against honor" framework to protect sexual autonomy: the Rose Leonel Law (2018) adds "violation of intimacy" as psychological violence in the Maria da Penha framework and criminalises unauthorised recording/montage of nude/sexual scenes (Art. 216-B); the Sexual Harassment Law (2018) criminalises dissemination of sex/nudity without consent (Art. 218-C), with penalty aggravators for intimate relationships and revenge/humiliation motives. This chapter critiques how courts and media frame "honor", double standards, and classed/racialised respectability, and unpacks consent's limits under gendered power. Through cases like Encantado's WhatsApp groups, it shows how the media and local institutions can reproduce harm, why many victims avoid the justice system, and why civil, criminal, and educational approaches must be combined. Overall, NCII is read as a lens on sexual morality, platform governance, and the politics of privacy/publicness.

Keywords

Non-consensual intimate images (NCII) · Sexuality · Honour and defamation crimes · Internet service providers (ISP) liability; Marco Civil (Brazilian Civil Rights Framework for the Internet)

On 10 November 2013, Julia Rebeca, a seventeen-year-old teenager, was found dead in her bedroom in Parnaíba, state of Piauí, Northeast Brazil. She left a message on Twitter before taking her life: "It'll all be over soon"/"I love you, I'm sorry I'm not the perfect daughter, but I tried… I'm sorry I love you very much…". On the 14th of the same month, a sixteen-year-old teenager also committed suicide in Rio Grande do Sul. The popular magazine that reported the cases, *IstoÉ*, linked them to previous stories, such as that of Carolina Dieckmann:

> If before the most significant threat came from strangers who hacked into mobile devices and spread intimate photos, more recent cases show that the risk now comes from boyfriends or husbands who, resentful of the end of the relationship, are willing to do anything to get revenge. The phe-

M. Valente, *Online Misogyny in Brazil*, Sustainable Development Goals Series,
https://doi.org/10.1007/978-3-032-07727-1_3

> nomenon has grown so much that it has earned a name, "revenge porn". (Perez, 2013)

That same year, a nineteen-year-old girl from Goiânia, Middle-Western Brazil, had a sex video with her boyfriend spread on the internet. In a statement to the TV show *Fantástico* on 17 November, she said that after the incident, she changed her appearance, stopped working, and avoided leaving the house:

> My mobile phone wouldn't stop. People calling, calling. I filed a police report on Friday. People hadn't taken much notice. When it was Monday, I realised how big it was.
> He took my life; I don't have a life anymore. I can't go out, I can't study, I can't work. (G1/Fantástico, 2013)

Fran became a meme: in the video, she made an O.K. gesture, and people started sharing images mimicking the gesture (Lins, 2021). Feminists organised a counter-communication campaign on social media using the hashtag *#SomosTodasFran* (#WeAreAllFran). Others created a petition calling for a law that would "make it a criminal offence to improperly disseminate intimate material (be it video, photo, audio, etc.) in any media". Alongside the signatures, there were many comments: "Respect the privacy of others"; "Our bodies, our rights!"; "For the end of sexism! For the end of *revenge porn*! *#forçafran* ("#HoldOnFran") (Petição Pública, 2014). Texts were published on various feminist blogs, such as Geledés and Think Olga. The internet was paying attention.

The cases triggered several bills to be proposed in the House of Representatives and the Senate. They dealt with the issue especially from a criminal point of view.[1] But an important thing happened before that. Precisely while the cases were happening, Brazil was discussing the approval of a legal framework to equalise rights in the digital environment. The NCII debate gained a foothold in this process, advancing by years a conversation that at the time was in its infancy: how to make digital platforms do more against TFGBV.

3.1 Gender Violence Meets Digital Rights: Brazilian Civil Rights Framework for the Internet

In 2005, the Federal Prosecutor's Office began to agree on terms of conduct with technology companies such as AOL, UOL, Click 21, Terra, IG, and Abranet (Brazilian Association of Internet Access, Service and Information Providers) against the spread of racism, child sexual exploitation, and other crimes. Thus, in 2006, the country was already showing a tendency to focus on internet intermediaries, in addition to the individual agent who carries out the behaviour in cases of crimes and damage caused in the digital environment. It was in that year that the Federal Prosecutor's Office signed a *Conduct Adjustment Agreement* (TAC or *Termo de Ajustamento de Conduta*, in Portuguese) with Google Brazil, with the participation of the NGO Safernet. A TAC is an agreement that the Prosecutor's Office signs with someone who violates a collective right as an alternative way of making the illegal situation or the damage cease, thereby possibly avoiding legal action.

The Prosecutor's Office had been requesting the identification of criminal profiles on the social network Orkut, then owned by Google; Google had been systematically replying that these requests should be directed to Google Inc. in the United States, asserting that its headquarters in Brazil only dealt with marketing and sales. Foreign internet application companies often used this argument at the time. The Agreement ended a Public Civil Action filed by the Prosecutor's Office against Google Brazil, aiming to make it comply with more than fifty court rulings: Google Brazil would now have to notify the Prosecutor's Office when it identified child sexual exploitation, store or delete data and certain content when ordered by the courts, moderate posts by human or automated means, and be fined for any non-

[1] Before that, several bills attempting to regulate nudity and pornography on the internet had been proposed, especially in the period that Paulo Rená calls the "legislative prehistory" of internet regulation. These were projects that used "obscenity" as a rhetorical resource, with a strong moral character, see Santarém (2022), See also the reconstruction of the history of these projects, in Brazil and in other parts of the world, in Chap. 3 of Valente et al. (2016).

compliance. However, there was no law specifically regulating internet service providers.

If debates on digital platforms seem intense today, they were also quite vigorous in those years—though more in niche areas. It was in 2008 that the Azeredo Bill, dubbed by Brazilian civil society campaigns as "Digital AI-5"—mentioned in the previous chapter—elicited a strong reaction and paved the way for discussions on civil (rather than criminal) legislation, with protections for internet users. Confronted with this movement, in 2009, the Ministry of Justice launched public consultations for an a Civil Rights Framework for the Internet (a Marco Civil da Internet, in Portuguese) through an online platform. Many individuals dedicated themselves to reflecting on the participatory experience of the Marco Civil (de Cruz, 2015; Papp, 2014; Abramovay & Lotta, 2022). It was a rich online debate, conducted in stages, which ultimately resulted in a law of rights and guarantees that establishes rules and limits for access to user data and identification, net neutrality, and the framework for holding internet application providers liable for third-party content they host and make available—such as social networking platforms, search engines, and messaging apps.

The discussion remains and continues to be central. For instance, consider a user who posts a death threat to a woman on a social network. He can face criminal prosecution for the threat and be sued in civil court to compensate her for moral or material damages. If the case involves domestic violence, the woman can also seek a restraining order. But what about the platform where the threat was made? Is it also liable, meaning it may have to compensate the woman for moral and material damages? If so, at what point should it intervene—from the moment the post was made, upon notification by a user, or after a court decision to remove the threat? What incentives does each model create? If responsibilities start from the moment of posting, does that imply platforms must verify the legality of all content? What justifies one approach over another, considering reasonableness, the rights involved, and the economic incentives of this business model?

There were many questions involved, and the model that emerged victorious from the public consultations on the Marco Civil was the one that exempts these services from liability until the moment they receive a court order to remove content. This means that they will only be held liable for the content if they fail to remove it in the face of this order.[2] This does not affect the possibility of these companies developing their own rules on content and applying them—the so-called content moderation. However, in the Marco Civil model, the private activity of content moderation is not regulated (in June 2025, the Supreme Court partially struck down that rule, claiming that it failed to protect fundamental rights and democratic values over time, and establishing some guidelines for content moderation—but this will be discussed in Chap. 6).

It was a victory for internet application companies and digital rights activists who argued that the move favoured freedom of expression because it is the judiciary (not the companies) that determines whether content is illegal in this model. For them, this decision would create a better balance between the rights involved. It would also prevent "superblocking": according to the argument, when application providers are responsible for illegal content from third parties, they tend to censor other posts in advance out of fear of liability. The logic of this argument aligns with the view of Brazilian legal culture as being quite lenient towards censorship, especially of the powerful, and that the internet could become a space dominated by big power, like other media that came before it. As we shall see, controversy surrounds all of these claims.[3] The approved rule was:

[2] The access provider, which "connects the user to the Internet", is not liable under any circumstances: "Art. 18: The Internet connection provider shall not be held civilly liable for damages arising from content generated by third parties".

[3] There were also those who, at that time, advocated alternative models. I address some of these issues in Chapter Five, when discussing content moderation. See, for instance, Clara Iglesias Keller on the shortcomings of the model: Iglesias Keller (2020), pp. 185–203.

> Art. 19: To ensure freedom of expression and prevent censorship, the Internet application provider can only be held civilly liable for damages arising from content generated by third parties if, after a specific court order, it fails to take steps to make the content identified as infringing unavailable within the scope and technical limits of its service and within the specified timeframe, subject to legal provisions to the contrary.

After the public consultation phase in the negotiation of the bill in Congress, the entertainment industry, especially the broadcaster Rede Globo, the Brazilian Association of Radio and Television Broadcasters (ABERT), and the Brazilian Association of Record Producers (ABPD), now Pró-Música Brasil (of which the companies from the Rede Globo group are also members), fought hard for this rule not to apply to content that violates copyright. The clash between these copyright-based industries and the unauthorised availability of works such as music and films on the internet was almost twenty years old at the time. What they wanted was a liability framework that was more favourable to them, that did not oblige them to take every case to court to force providers to remove, for example, musical works shared without authorisation (Papp, 2014). Sewing together agreements for the law's approval, the rapporteur of the bill in the House of Representatives, Alessandro Molon (then Workers Party, PT), created an exception for the case of copyright infringement. The final text reads as follows:

> Art. 19. § Paragraph 2. The application of the provisions of this article to offences against copyright or related rights depends on specific legal provisions, which must respect freedom of expression and other guarantees provided for in Article 5 of the Federal Constitution.

And this is where the dots come together once again: the two suicides, one in the North and the other in the South of the country, after the episodes of NCII, were widely reported during the final stages of the Marco Civil process and even became a story on *Fantástico*. According to a report by journalist Ana Carolina Papp, rapporteur Alessandro Molon attributed the insertion of a specific rule for these cases to the public commotion:

> Art. 21. The Internet application provider that makes third-party content available will be held subsidiarily liable for the violation of privacy resulting from the dissemination, without the authorisation of its participants, of images, videos or other materials containing scenes of nudity or private sexual acts when, after receiving notification from the participant or their legal representative, it fails to promote diligently, within the scope and technical limits of its service, the unavailability of this content.
> Sole Paragraph. The notification mentioned in the caput must contain, under penalty of nullity, elements that allow for the specific identification of the material identified as violating the participant's privacy and verification of the request's legitimacy.

The rule means that in the case of unauthorised images and videos of nudity or sex, the platform is liable after a *valid private notification* from the person depicted. The intention is to make it easier to make platforms liable and, as a result, to make them remove this type of content quickly—without the victim having to go to court. At the beginning of this inclusion, there was some disagreement with digital rights activists because the original wording did not require the removal request to be made by the participant in the image—which could lead to its use for removing any and all nudity content off the internet. The rapporteur listened to the concern and changed the text, landing at this final wording.

With this, Brazil passed an original intermediary liability rule, which appears to be the first in the world to address their liability for NCII specifically (Neris et al., 2017).[4] The rule, however, does not refer to gender: it applies to anyone portrayed in unauthorised intimate images. In any case, according to the data presented below, this behaviour affects significantly more women. If we consider the reasons given for the model of intermediary liability chosen at the time for the Marco Civil, the exclusion of NCII from the "general framework" and the creation of a specific one appears justified: nudity or non-consensual sexual activity are not forms of expression that fall within the scope of freedom of expression, nor do they

[4] See also Neris et al. (2018).

raise doubts or grey areas regarding potential "overblocking" or censorship. Whether the "general framework" would make sense ten years later became a separate (heated) debate, which I will address ahead. The point is that it did not already make sense to NCII in 2013.

Although child sexual exploitation was a catalyst for the Azeredo Bill, at that time no dialogues were established between internet rights activists, who took part in the consultations, and the feminist, LGBTQIAP+, or child and adolescent protection activist communities. According to Sonia Corrêa, Horacio Sívori, and Bruno Zilli, in a 2012 paper, this may have had to do precisely with how these debates entered the legislative field: through sensationalism, sexual moralism, and religious dogmatism, which would have led to vigilantism that did not represent the debates that these communities were having in other spaces (Corrêa et al., 2012).

In a book published in 2016, analysing court rulings on the removal of NCII and conducting interviews with lawyers and other agents of the justice system, I and co-authors concluded that the rule had already made a difference (Valente et al., 2016, p. 12). Lawyers and prosecutors who sought the removal of this content realised that the response to requests for removal was more agile (without the need for a court order). This is also because platforms have started to adopt their own policies for removing content. Even PornHub, a pornographic video platform, made a request for deletion form available in 2015 (Valente et al., 2016, p. 118).

Going back to the Carolina Dieckmann case, in 2012, Google replied to the actress's lawyer, Kakay, that it had critical technical reasons for not meddling with its search results. On 19 August 2015, however, Google announced that due to "disturbing stories of *revenge porn*", it would alter its policies and create a form through which victims could request the de-indexing of content from search results (Singhal, 2015), although the content would continue to be available from the original sources, over which Google has no control. Other companies, particularly those that host the content, have followed the same trend and have generally begun to develop technologies and policies to remove NCII quickly. Still, challenges remain in messaging app groups or even on larger platforms that have removal policies. For example, in 2022, a forum on Reddit began to be used to circulate thousands of intimate photos of women without this being detected or controlled (Plaha et al., 2022). I also tested searching for images from the high-profile cases I described throughout the chapters. Although not on the first page of the search, nor with the same ease, they are still there.

3.2 Gender, Honour, and the Framing of the *Nude*

The non-consensual dissemination of intimate images, or NCII, is a problem that does not use any criteria other than gender to choose its victims. It is enough to be a woman. Age, social class, race and ethnicity, religion and territory are all factors that play a part in the particularities or how cases develop and even how they can be faced and responded to, but all women are subject to experiencing it.

In 2015, when discussing gender and technology, there was a prevailing narrative about a vacuum, an absence of protection for cases of attacks against women, particularly for cases of NCII. At InternetLab, we initiated a study out of the suspicion that the cases would reach the courts and then be dealt with somehow. We did a comprehensive search in the São Paulo State Court of Justice with various keywords combined to find NCII cases and understand how they entered the judiciary—and how they left.

The analysis of these decisions, together with interviews and a case study, was published into a book—The Body is the Code, or *O Corpo é o Código*, in Portuguese (Valente et al., 2016). After a manual screening of the cases—since the search with keywords returned many false positives, such as court rulings that quoted excerpts from other court rulings but were not about what we were looking for—we found ninety directly related cases. And the surprises started there.

Reality challenges categories, and looking across the board at court cases helps understand how they develop beyond the public debate and how the media frames problems, even though the judiciary is a filter per se. It is, however, a filter of a different nature. When looking for NCII cases, we found others involving the possession of intimate images but not (yet) their dissemination: women who suffered threats, extortion or even rape when men demanded sex in exchange for not disseminating those images. Some examples, in the words of the magistrates themselves:[5]

> The defendant had conversations with the victim in an internet chat room. After the victim had been persuaded to show intimate parts of her body, the defendant recorded them and then threatened her by saying he wanted R$1,000.00 not to publicise the video on YouTube.
> The defendant registered as a user on the instant messenger MSN—keeping in touch with the victim for approximately 8 (eight) months under the alias "Gustavo Padovani". He used this programme to record intimate videos of the victim on his computer and threatened to publish them if he did not receive the sum of R$ 2,000.00. He pointed out that his intention was only to disprove the victim and show that she was not the honourable person she claimed to be, denying that he did not intend to receive anything in return for the images.
> The couple had a relationship when they were teenagers, and at first, the victim didn't know that he was the author of the threats.
> The ex-partner threatened to publicise the couple's intimate videos, demanding that they hand over money and movable property, and threatened the ex-partner with death.
> The victim's ex-boyfriend (the defendant), using a fake Facebook profile, contacted the victim and threatened to publish intimate photos of her, which he had stored on his mobile phone, on the World Wide Web (Internet) if she refused to have sex with him. After numerous threats, the victim went to the gym and had sex with him without her consent. Her ex-boyfriend continued to threaten her and demand sex.
> The defendant (ex-boyfriend), dissatisfied with the end of the relationship and the fact that he saw her with another man, posted intimate photos of her on social networks on the internet and even threatened her by text message, saying that if she told her parents, "she would fuck herself up even more because he would do anything, anything at all".
> The defendant threatened the victim, publishing disgusting messages and intimate photos of the couple online and spreading leaflets around the neighbourhood, claiming that she was a call girl—because the victim had made their relationship public while the defendant was married.

Yes, we are speaking of women: of the ninety cases, only four had men as victims, and only two were cases of heterosexual couples who had been exposed and were seeking compensation together. Of the four cases involving men, one was of a man who had an extramarital relationship and was being extorted based on the images; two were public figures, a mayor and a councillor; the other had photos published on a pornographic website. The overwhelming majority of the cases involved harm and damage to girls and women (almost all of whom were cisgender, except one case involving two trans women), even if the cases involved images of a heterosexual couple.[6] The rulings seldom reveal the ethnic-racial belonging of the victims, which makes this layer challenging to analyse.

"Double standards are the standard way of treating the position of men's and women's bodies" (Warken & Helena, 2015). In 2015, Julia Warken and Ligia Helena published an article in the late *Brasil Post*, dealing with a case that became famous: nude photos of Stênio Garcia, a famous Brazilian TV actor, and his wife Marilene Saade, also an actress, were released without their consent. The text recalls that, in an interview with the gossip magazine *Quem*, Garcia had said: "I was with my wife [...] What's wrong with that? I have nothing to be ashamed of. I wouldn't even go [to the police station to press charges], I have nothing to hide [...], but my wife wants to go to court and find out who leaked those photos". Saade, meanwhile, said in an interview that she no longer felt like leaving the house and that they had been "surprised by this. I'm going to put an end to this internet and all of this. I'm going to move heaven and earth against

[5]According to the cases we selected for the article: Valente and Neris (2019).

[6]Two other studies of Brazilian court rulings came up with very similar figures (Bouchardet, 2020; Lisbino & Caridade, 2022).

anyone, I want to create a law". As mentioned in the first chapter, various studies have shown this difference: the 2022 CIGI study, for example, showed that the most marked gender difference is not in the prevalence of violence but in the effect it has. Many more women and LGBTQIAP+ people report mental health problems, professional and their internet usage patterns consequences. A woman's intimate image has the power to destroy a career and family and community relations, while a man's is often forgotten in a few days.

These cases show how NCII is a problem intimately linked to gendered sexual moralities and the negotiation of their boundaries. Exposure and daring, beyond their possible content as an exercise of freedom, are rewarded by social media algorithms, which provide instant reinforcement and help "engaging content" to go viral. In private communications, images are exchanged within intimate relationships reconfigured by digital mediation. But when the images move to another context—because they are disseminated and shared in other spaces—they acquire other meanings, and actions that deviate from dominant gender norms are quickly punished, which has painful and serious consequences for the lives of girls and women.

In a 2021 study with sixteen focus groups of teenagers from different socio-economic classes in the city of São Paulo, CETIC (the Brazilian Regional Center for Studies on the Development of the Information Society) showed how the groups spontaneously reported cases of NCII and revealed these contradictions: girls are under constant pressure to send intimate images, but are immediately judged and blamed when the images are disseminated (without their consent) (Jereissati & Macaya, 2021). Beatriz Accioly Lins (2021, p. 43), an anthropologist whose PhD research was on the practice and meanings of "sharing *nudes*", explores how these contradictions are expressed in the advice commonly given to girls and women: "avoid sharing intimate images". Implicit in this is the idea that male sexual behaviour is predatory and that women should be restrained, cautious and in control. Lins, on the other hand, reports cases and initiatives in which women send *nudes in* a pleasurable and autonomous way and how these limits are at the same time always in place. She gives as examples the booklet *Safer Nudes!*, on safe ways of sharing *nudes* (Coding rights, 2021), by the Brazilian organisation Coding Rights, and the closed Facebook group *Pimentinhas* (Little Peppers), with severe access controls, in which women shared images and tips on good practices for sending *nudes*, and which dispersed when, around 2018, someone from outside had access and shared the secret content.[7]

Despite the marked gender character and how NCII expresses these norms in an exemplary way, in the court rulings we analysed in our research, this issue was not recognised: the magistrates analysed the evidence, how it fits into the law, and the extent of the damage. Only in one of the decisions did we see a proper discussion of the gender character of NCII:

> The acts committed by the defendant have undoubtedly caused the plaintiff a great deal of damage. Unfortunately, we live in a society in which a woman's behaviour, including concerning her intimate life, is criticised and questioned immensely, and any acts attributed to her, especially in sexual terms, have immense consequences. The documents attached to the application, including those that were removed from the case file as a measure to protect the plaintiff's privacy, show that the defendant exceeded all limits, exposing the plaintiff to an immensely embarrassing situation.[8]

Overall, the full extent of the problem was not recognised.[9] But what did the rulings say about

[7] As Lins also points out, it is much more useful to look at the production and exchange of *nudes* as a practice of pleasure and risk, which articulates the so-called limits of sexuality (Gregori, 2008).

[8] Appeal n. 0003141-93.2007.8.26.0224, 1st Chamber of Private Law, TJ/SP, 29/10/13.

[9] Caroline Bouchardet's research again identified something quite similar, looking at the Courts of Appeals of São Paulo and Rio Grande do Sul states in civil cases: compensation is set based on doctrinal standards for fixing moral damages for violations of image and honour, but they do not go into the subjective effects and even less into the gender character. See Bouchardet (2020). On the other hand, Jhon Lisbino and Sónia Caridade's research, looking at other courts and the Superior Court of Justice,

our initial question about whether the internet is a lawless territory? The answer was more complex than yes or no. There were, indeed, paths to frame the cases that came before the courts within the law. However, there were important questions about the appropriateness of the framework and barriers for the cases to reach the courts and be judged. Finally, always the fundamental question behind the surface: Is the law the appropriate or sufficient solution?

Until 2017, a victim of NCII in Brazil could pursue different avenues in court. In the field of civil law, they could sue the platform for the removal of the content or ask for compensation for their inaction in removing it—in accordance with the Marco Civil. They could also seek compensation from the aggressor for the material and moral damage caused. Additionally, if there was or had been an intimate relationship between the aggressor and the victim, it was possible to frame the case under the Maria da Penha Law against domestic violence (especially as psychological violence) and obtain the protective measures that the law prescribes, for example, restraining orders—although, at the time, few legal professionals were aware of this possibility. Finally, there was the path of criminal liability. However, there was no specific provision for NCII against adult women. In cases against children and adolescents, the offences in the Statute of the Child and Adolescent punish even the mere possession of images (crimes known by the inadequate term "child pornography"). These offences were already being enforced, although we found many acquittals, for which we raised some hypotheses at the time. The most important was that the seriousness of these crimes meant that judges acquitted cases that did not correspond to the constructed image of the "paedophile", particularly if the victim was not a child.[10]

If the victim of the dissemination was an adult, in criminal cases, defamation law applied.[11] When the cases went to civil court, i.e., when the victims wanted monetary compensation for the material and moral damage caused or the actions were against the platforms to remove content or obtain compensation, the magistrates also considered honour and dignity to be important factors. When these concepts are used in an evaluative way, dominant gender norms appear in the magistrates' words. For example, in some decisions, the socioeconomic profile of the women in question was considered to define the extent of the damage. Apparently, businesswomen, models, researchers, and lawyers "would have more reputation to live up to". Some examples of the court rulings we read:

> The aggravated party states in her initial application that she is a renowned businesswoman, belonging to a family of artists, and that although she is a publicly recognised figure, she does not lose the right to keep her private life and the details of her intimacy private. She claims, in a nutshell, that photos and personal data were accessed by a third party, who threatened to publish them in the media, which, in fact, happened in August 2013 [...]. The aggravated party has the right not to have her image—she is a stewardess and not a prostitute—publicised on pornography websites, under the auspices of the aggravating party, from its computers that go out in search of information of all kinds.
>
> The victim had photo montages of her face published on the internet with the aim of denigrating [sic] her image. Some of these montages are being published on pornography websites. She is a biologist with a master's degree and holds a Ph.D. from Unifesp. She is going through trials that are destroying her reputation. She has published several works on the web, which leads to her name being searched for on academic search engines.

identified decisions that recognised either the gender violence or domestic violence nature of NCII cases. I think this difference may be connected to the keywords they used to find the judgements, which already bring up results more closely linked to this interpretation: "pornographic *revenge*"; "*revenge porn*"; "gender violence". This is why they analysed eighteen decisions, a much smaller corpus than our research and that of Bouchardet. After all, many cases of NCII are not necessarily labelled as such by magistrates in their decisions. See Lisbino and Caridade (2022).

[10] It seemed that magistrates were reluctant to apply a criminal offence perceived as so serious to cases involving people with little age difference (for example, a man in his twenties and a teenager aged seventeen), or who had a previous relationship (Valente et al., 2015).

[11] As I mentioned, many of the cases involved not the dissemination of the images themselves, but threats, extortion, and rape. These cases all fall under the provisions of the Criminal Code.

> The judge states that the potential damage to the plaintiff, who is a "practising lawyer and partner in a law firm based in the capital", justifies the exceptional granting of injunctive relief.

We found problems with the fact that cases of NCII were categorised in the criminal sphere as insult or defamation. The first is the open-endedness for judges' moral judgements: What is dignity, and what is defamation? In the ninety decisions we read, we did not find anything as blatant as a vote by a judge of the Minas Gerais State Court of Justice in 2014. It was a civil case, not a criminal one, but one that is very expressive of how moralities operate—in general, more implicitly than here. A woman sought compensation for moral and material damages against her attacker and, at a local court, obtained a favourable sentence of BRL 100,000 (roughly USD 18,000). In the appeal, the compensation was reduced to BRL 75,000 because of the "intensity of the moral damage inflicted on the victim and the economic condition of the offender". What is most striking in this case is the vote of one of the judges, fortunately defeated, who wanted the compensation to be reduced to BRL 5000. Untangling his argument, we see that he assessed the photos—he did not judge them to be sensual, but "gynaecological"—and the victim's morals, which he judged to be non-existent, and stated that she was essentially to blame for what happened. Here is a reproduction of extracts:

> There are doubts about the morals to be protected. Morality is an absolute attitude. It's a rule of conduct—it cannot be relativised. Those who have morals have them in their entirety. At no time were the photos sensual. *Photos in gynaecological positions that show a woman's absolute intimacy are not sensual.* Sensual photos are displayable; they don't hurt, and they don't scare. Sensual photos are those that test the imagination of what the female form looks like. In a less bitter, softer judgement, they can be erotic. They are poses that don't allow pictures. They are volatile poses to be considered immediately evaporated. They are for a closed room, in the dark, even if it was for a boyfriend, but a real one. Not to an ex-boyfriend for a short period of a year. They weren't photos taken at an intimate moment of a couple, even if they were lovers. *And it's not worth claiming a breach of trust. The courtship was short and long-distance. Passing. Nothing serious.*
>
> When the author showed herself that way, she was aware of the possibility of publicity because she was in Uberaba and he was in Uberlândia. [...] Anyone who dares to pose in that way and those circumstances has a differentiated, liberal moral concept. She doesn't care. [...] The author's image, in its crude form, shows that she lacks self-respect and self-esteem. [...]
> The plaintiff's attitude, however, weakens the generic concept of morality, which could have been assessed by the defendant in this sense. She contributed in a positive and preponderant way. Modesty is relevant and was far away.[12]

Although this is a civil case, in the criminal sphere, the judges would also consider how much the action has hurt the woman's honour. Honour is a concept that was used for decades by the Brazilian judiciary to absolve men who murdered their wives and lovers. The famous Ângela Diniz's murder by her boyfriend in 1976 is a landmark in how this old-fashioned argument was mobilised by the defence—which generated a huge feminist backlash in the early 1980s. A study by Silvia Pimentel and other researchers (2006) shows that, even compared to other Latin American countries, Brazil has the most traditional, longest, and deepest history of jurisprudential decisions that have accepted the thesis of legitimate defence of honour, even without any provision for this in the Criminal Code, and decisions to this effect have persisted in the courts for decades. It was only in 2021 that the Brazilian Supreme Court ruled the thesis to be unconstitutional. It is also worth remembering that, until 2005, the Criminal Code also used the terms "honest woman" (who could be a victim of the crime of "violent kidnapping" and "indecent assault by fraud") and "virgin woman" for seduction offences. It also stipulated that perpetrators of sexual crimes could not be punished when they married the victim or when she married a third party since it was deemed necessary to preserve the "honour" of the victim and her family. It is these constructed notions of honour that

[12]After the controversy, sparked mainly by an article in *Marie Claire* magazine, which reproduced extracts from this vote (Arrais, 2014), the case was protected by secrecy. I have access to the full text of the votes because I obtained the decision at that time.

carry a long history of misogyny. This makes it evident that seeing NCII as a matter of *honour* can be a problem for women victims.

We detected yet another difficulty, this one of a procedural nature: the fact that the victims of NCII could only sue in the criminal sphere for the offences of libel and slander. These are offences that the Brazilian criminal law considers to be of interest to the victim, not the state. For this reason, unlike the majority of crimes, which are prosecuted by the Public Prosecutor's Office (based on the understanding that it is in society's interest to investigate and punish), in the case of crimes against honour, the victim must take action on their own, appointing a lawyer, if necessary.[13]

In 2016, we identified that this was one of the factors why low-income women did not sue their aggressors. But it was not the only one: studying the Top 10 case, which took place in Parelheiros and Grajaú, peripheral areas of the city of São Paulo, in which the majority of the population is Black, we identified that the conflictive relationship with the police in many territories is a huge factor that leads to under-reporting (and non-accountability). This points to the necessity of a critical look at the strategy of criminalising social problems, which is often the first of the solutions presented for a problem. I will come back to this later.

For now, it should be pointed out that the law in general, and criminal law in particular, does not cater for people on a homogeneous basis. Socioeconomic class and race are inescapable divides in how justice is accessed and who justice targets. Another caveat is that, especially in the case of adolescents, there is a tendency not to seek help from adults in order to avoid further moral judgement and other forms of punishment. The activists and educators we spoke to in those territories saw much more potential in actions in the field of education and community health and even refused to treat the problem as a criminal one.

It was not precise to state that the internet was "lawless territory". However, some feminist groups, researchers, lawyers, and prosecutors who worked with women's rights began to build arguments for creating a specific criminal offence that could deal with some of these problems. For example, they began to call for a criminal offence that did not protect "honour", a problematic concept for women, but rather dignity and sexual autonomy, and that did not require private prosecution.

3.3 The Rose Leonel Law

In 2018, two laws were passed that created new offences and amended the Maria da Penha Law for domestic violence in view of the question of NCII. One of them became known as the Rose Leonel Law in honour of Leonel's years-long fight against her attacker and the public work she began to do to recognise, prevent, and care for victims of NCII. There is a story to tell about these laws.

2013 was a remarkable year for Brazil in many ways. It was, among many other political and social events, the year in which the before-mentioned suicide of two female victims of NCII made it to the media, plus the case involving Fran and the support campaign, and also the case of Thamiris, a university student who had erotic photos disseminated by her ex-boyfriend and who posted a manifesto on Facebook. "My outburst as a victim of *revenge porn*" had more than 2000 shares in two days (Lins, 2021, p. 121, 164). It was also the year in which legislators decided to create a specific framework for NCII in the Internet Civil Framework and in which the first bill aimed at giving criminal expression to the problem was proposed in the House of Representatives: Bill 5555/2013, by João Arruda (Brazilian Democratic Movement Party, PMDB).

[13] In the case of "crimes of lesser offensive potential", such as libel, slander, and defamation, it is possible to sue through the Special Criminal Court if the case does not fall under the Maria da Penha Law for domestic violence (which rules out this possibility). Therefore, it is unnecessary to appoint a private lawyer, but it is common to do so if you have the resources. Even though there is the possibility of conducting the case without legal services, this possibility seems quite distant from the population, as it requires knowledge of how to do it and because of all the material and symbolic barriers to accessing justice.

The bill was known for some time as the *Internet Maria da Penha Law* and only later was baptised its final name, Rose Leonel Law. The MP proposed to amend the Maria da Penha Law for domestic violence to include a "right to communication" among the rights provided for in Article 3, "violation of intimacy" as one of the forms of violence provided for in Article 7 and, finally, to include a protective measure among the others provided for in Article 22, to be determined by the judge, which was nothing more than the removal, by "information propagating service providers", of content that violates women's intimacy, within 24 hours.

Following this bill, others were proposed and "attached" to Bill 5555/2013. Most of them followed a criminal strategy, with the idea that there was a gap or inadequacy in the criminal response to the problem. The best-known of these was Bill 6630/2013, proposed by then MP Romário (Brazilian Social Party, PSB), the former football player, which proposed adding to the Criminal Code the crime of "disseminating photos or videos with scenes of nudity or sexual acts without the victim's authorisation". Beatriz Accioly Lins (2021, p. 164), looking back over the thirteen bills that were debated in Congress between 2013 and 2016, realises that most of them were proposed by male MPs, not belonging to parties with active feminist benches, far removed from demands for women's rights, which, together with a reading of their content, points to patronising moral notions about sexuality, especially of women. This is a similar conclusion to that reached by researcher, lawyer, and activist Marina Ganzarolli (2016), whose research identified that, in the legislative production on gender, parliamentarians use communicative flows coming from civil society but often distort them or create new stereotypes.

Bill 5555/2013 underwent transformation over time, with new proposals added to it. In 2017, deputy Tia Eron (Workers Party, PT) was its rapporteur at the Justice and Citizenship Committee of the Chamber and proposed a new text with elements from several of the bills that had been approved. In addition to the changes to the Maria da Penha Law, she envisaged a new crime: a new form of insult specific to "public exposure of sexual intimacy"—in other words, another defamation crime among those that already existed.[14] The bill was approved in these terms and sent to the Senate.

In the Senate, the text was greatly modified and returned to the House with a wording that provided for two different insertions in the Criminal Code. One of them was Article 216-B, "Unauthorised recording of sexual intimacy". Here, the proposal was to criminalise anyone who produced, photographed, or filmed, without authorisation, "scenes of nudity or libidinous sexual acts of an intimate and private nature", and also those who made montages. The second was Article 216-C, which criminalised the actual dissemination of such scenes. The proposal for a new crime among defamation crimes (the so-called crimes against the honour) was abandoned.

When the bill was re-examined in the House of Representatives in 2018, the deputy rapporteurs in the responsible committees—Cristiane Brasil and Laura Carneiro (both from the Brazilian Labor Party, PTB)—concluded that the new bill was more appropriate, "given that the legal good being protected is the victim's sexual dignity" (and not honour). But then it was realised that, by providing for the crime of unauthorised dissemination of scenes of nudity or sexual acts, the 216-C bill was formulating something that had already been contemplated in another law passed not long before. Here, the story of Bill 5555/2013 takes another turn, once again motivated by cases of media expression of violence against women.

In May 2016, a highly violent video began circulating on Twitter of a 16-year-old girl from Rio de Janeiro, unconscious, being raped by 33 men. The case took over the web for many days: on the one hand, moral judgements were made that blamed the victim's behaviour, including racist

[14] I took part in an initiative with students from the University of São Paulo who, at the time, spoke out against the idea that NCII was something that fell within the field of "honour", in line with the conclusions of the research we had conducted (Tambelli, 2016).

and classist factors, such as the attack having taken place after a funk ball (Brazilian funk being a rhythm that originated in the favelas of Rio); on the other, online campaigns and the organisation of demonstrations in repudiation of the case, the dissemination of the video and how the investigations were conducted (O Globo, 2016). As the victim was under eighteen, the dissemination of the images was already a criminal offence under the Statute of the Child and Adolescent.

In the same month, other cases of gang rape were reported: four teenagers in Piauí and three cases in Rio Grande do Norte. Senator Vanessa Grazziotin (Communist Party of Brazil, PCdoB) proposed, in June 2016, Bill 5452/2016, increasing the penalty for rape in the case of two or more aggressors. The bill was fuelled by other cases of violence that were widely reported. In 2017, a man was arrested after ejaculating on a woman on a bus in the city of São Paulo. When the man was released, the case sparked a heated debate around the possible interpretation of the act within the crime of rape—because the case, although grotesque, did not really qualify as rape (Mendonça, 2017)—and Grazziotin's bill ended up gaining a new criminal provision of "sexual harassment" to account for cases such as that.[15] Finally, a criminalisation provision was included for the dissemination of rape scenes, which also provided for the dissemination of "sex scenes, nudity or pornography" without the victim's consent, that is, NCII. The bill ended up being approved as law no. 13,718/2018, known as the Sexual Harassment Law, together with a "package" of other laws on violence against women that then-president Michel Temer enacted. The final article that included NCII added to the Criminal Code stated:

> *Dissemination of a rape scene or a scene of rape of a vulnerable person, a sex scene or pornography*
> Art. 218-C. Offering, exchanging, making available, transmitting, selling or exhibiting for sale, distributing, publishing or disseminating, by any means—including by means of mass communication or computer or telematic systems—a photograph, video or other audiovisual recording that contains a scene of rape or rape of a vulnerable person, or that advocates or induces its practice, or, *without the victim's consent, a scene of sex, nudity or pornography*:
> Penalty: imprisonment from 1 (one) to 5 (five) years if the fact does not constitute a more serious offence.
> *Penalty increase*
> Paragraph 1. The penalty is increased by 1/3 (one third) to 2/3 (two thirds) if the crime is committed by an agent who maintains or has maintained an intimate relationship of affection with the victim or for the purpose of revenge or humiliation.
> *Exclusion of illegality*
> Paragraph 2. There is no crime when the perpetrator carries out the conduct described in the heading of this article in a journalistic, scientific, cultural or academic publication using a resource that makes it impossible to identify the victim, with their prior authorisation, if they are over 18 (eighteen) years old.

Thus, in 2018, two laws were passed: this one I mentioned last, Law No. 13,718/18, which provides for the criminalisation of NCII (among other things), and Law No. 13,772/1018, the result of the process that began in 2013 with João Arruda's Bill 5,555, which provides for changes to the Maria da Penha Law for domestic violence and the crime of recording scenes without authorisation:

> Maria da Penha Law, Art. 7:
> Paragraph 2—psychological violence, understood as any conduct that causes emotional harm and diminished self-esteem, or that harms and disturbs full development, or that aims to degrade or control their actions, behaviour, beliefs and decisions, by means of threats, embarrassment, humiliation, manipulation, isolation, constant surveillance, persistent persecution, insult, blackmail, *violation of their privacy*, ridicule, exploitation and limitation of the right to come and go, or any other means that cause harm to their psychological health and self-determination;
> *Criminal Code, Unauthorised recording of sexual intimacy*
> Art. 216-B. Producing, photographing, filming or recording by any means, content with a scene of nudity or a sexual or libidinous act of an intimate and private nature without the authorisation of the participants:
> *Penalty—detention, from 6 (six) months to 1 (one) year, and a fine.*

[15] Art. 215-A. Performing a libidinous act against someone without their consent with the aim of satisfying one's own lust or that of a third party: Penalty—imprisonment from 1 (one) to 5 (five) years, if the act does not constitute a more serious crime.

> Sole Paragraph. The same penalty applies to anyone who mounts a photograph, video, audio or any other recording with the purpose of including a person in a scene of nudity or an intimate sexual or libidinous act.

Strictly speaking, the Rose Leonel Law is the latter. However, the history of these two laws shows how they need to be read together. In addition, Law No. 13,718/2018, i.e., the first one, also established that all these offences are to be prosecuted as "unconditional public criminal lawsuits", which means, as I pointed out earlier, that it is the Prosecutor's Office that starts and conducts the criminal lawsuit. They provide a significant change in the legal landscape, and the problems that had been pointed out have been "solved". But to what extent?

The passing of criminal laws is often seen as an endpoint. This is often a big mistake. Firstly, because laws need to pass the test of jurisprudence, i.e. be tested in terms of their interpretation; even before that, they are part of a legal and social system. Who will be able to prosecute, who will be prosecuted, and the preventive effects of these laws will depend on many factors based on Brazil's concrete inequalities, particularly those of race, class, and territory. As we have seen, many victims do not take their cases to the police or the Prosecutor's Office. Many cases will not be pursued, or the investigation will not be finalised. If the aggressors are punished, many victims will not feel compensated. The root causes of the acts now understood as crimes continue to circulate, even though criminalisation can have a symbolic effect and thus some social and cultural impact.

3.4 Intimate Relationships, Public and Private and Consent

The city of Encantado, in the Southern state of Rio Grande do Sul, has 20,000 inhabitants. In 2015, a 13-year-old resident cut her wrists and was admitted to hospital; another left the internet and moved to another town, and yet another filed a police report. They had been targeted by the men's group "*Ousadia e Putaria*" ("*Daring and Whoring*"), which had the stated aim of "sharing photos of girls from Encantado and the surrounding area, preferably underage and naked". The photos provided by the third victim on the occasion of the police report quickly ended up in the group, posted by a trainee from the police station. The group administrator reacted, but not against the sharing of the confidential images: "Everyone in their right mind knows that a 'girl' who does this [takes naked photos] is a whore. I mean SLUT!" (Aronovich, 2022). A social column in a local newspaper reported that the girls had "decided to let loose for the cameras" and published some of the images. The managing partner of the newspaper was outraged—not by the publication of the column—and published on Facebook: "If these young women don't value themselves, then let them feel sorry for their families. Someone told me that they need psychological counselling. There is a remedy, a good buffalo leather strap with a funky metal buckle, that would really help their psychology". In Lola Aronovich's words, "practically all the institutions of patriarchy acted together in the attack on these girls": family members, the police, the local media, and the school.

There was resistance: a group of young people set up a feminist collective (*Coletivo de Mulheres de Encantado e Vale do Taquari*), which organised a discussion followed by a protest in the city, wrote a letter of repudiation and sent the case to larger newspapers. The then-State MP Manuela D'Ávila[16] joined the chorus, writing on social media, taking the problem to the state Legislative Assembly, and calling in the State Prosecutor's Office. With the repercussions, the Civilian Police launched the Operation Daring and Company, which carried out nine searches and seizures and indicted 40 people for the offence of sharing nude images of teenagers, provided for in the Statute of the Child and Adolescent. Along the way, feminists were threatened with prosecution, and Lola Aronovich (2022), who published

[16] Manuela D'Ávila is an active politician with a feminist platform, who ran for vice-President in 2018. She currently works on projects to fight gender-based political violence; at different times, she has been victimized by it.

a photo of one of those involved on her blog, was, in fact, sued for moral damages and image rights. Given the circumstances, she thought it best to settle—the flights to attend the hearings alone would have been more expensive. It was one of eight lawsuits she has suffered to date.

The Encantado case is an example of the layers of complexity involved in violence involving sexuality, gender, and technology. The Marco Civil would not apply since the images were posted on messaging apps, and there is nowhere to "remove" the pictures from, as they are stored on the group members' devices. Encryption often protects communications (which is important for society and particularly for subalternised populations), making content control even more difficult. Another nuance of the case is that before there was an organised public reaction, the institutions that existed to enforce rights *reinforced the violence*. In other words, the problem is complex, and although the law is one of the instruments in the dispute, it is not enough.

Encantado is also exemplary from another perspective: it was one of the countless situations in which violence occurred outside of a family or affectionate relationship. Combining the instruments of the Maria da Penha Law for domestic violence with NCII is essential to cases where intimate relationships are at the root of the violation, but this type of violence is not limited to this sphere. To be sure, gender-based violence in the domestic sphere obviously expresses misogyny in the social sphere; the point is that there is still less of a cultural and legal repertoire for dealing with violence that occurs in the public sphere. This brings us to two important points made by Beatriz Lins in her book about NCII in Brazil. The first is that labelling images as *intimate* inserts sexuality into a whole repertoire of the private—and the ideas of modesty and morality that go with it. I would add here that the definitions of public and private, already much theorised in feminism,[17] political science, democracy, the right to privacy, and others, have become more complex with the internet. The very fluidity of spaces blurs the boundaries between private and public (is a Facebook group public or private?) and also by the way content travels from conversations perceived as private to spaces perceived as public—from a WhatsApp message to the TikTok *feed* and vice versa.

Lins' second point is that the concepts of *consent* and *authorisation*, used in the debate and to create the existing criminal typology (and even in the concept of NCII I employ here), must also be put into perspective. Consent is a category that has been mobilised in the fight against sexual abuse, but it also needs to be thought of from the perspective of the power dimension in gender relations. Is consent always free in unequal relationships? There are many cases recounted in Lins' book (and others that I and other researchers have registered) of consent being given for images to be taken and even sent, but not given willingly. They were responses to a fear, for example, of emotional retaliation. From the opposite perspective, the focus on consent seems to reinforce the gender norm that the male has predatory behaviour, and the female has the role of containing and controlling this impetus, which denies other standards of sexual behaviour. That said, it is known that a huge number of situations of violence take place in conditions where women's sexual autonomy is completely violated, and this is what the law tries to deal with when it filters the problem into rules that apply across the board. I make this point so that we can see beyond the categories of consent and authorisation, which do, however, have practical and political applicability.

It should be clear by that legal responses are mostly based on events that mobilise the media and the demands formulated around them. However, the concrete configuration of the response given is a choice made by the political

[17] It is essential to remember that the public–private dichotomy, criticised by Western feminists as a fundamental binomial in the production of gender inequality, is questioned by feminists who do not align themselves with Western perspectives, such as Stony Brook University professor Oyèronké Oyěwùmí (2000), who argues that family arrangements in various territories on the African continent do not correspond to the idea of family that this dichotomy expresses.

system, which is yet another filter that leaves other possibilities out. Later in this book, I will discuss other possible approaches to the problem that have yet to be prioritised in Brazil.

But first, let us move into another territory: misogyny expressed in words and other communicative acts in the public sphere.

References

Abramovay, P., & Lotta, G. (2022). *A democracia equilibrista: Políticos e burocratas no Brasil*. Companhia das Letras.

Aronovich, L. (2022). A trajetória e resistência do Escreva Lola Escreva. *Estudos Feministas, 30*. Retrieved March 18, 2025, from http://www.scielo.br/j/ref/a/MZ3PGMd3bZmNFncPfBypMPv/abstract/?lang=pt

Arrais, A. (2014). *Justiça de Minas Gerais culpa jovem que teve imagens íntimas divulgadas na internet por se expor*. Marie Claire. Retrieved March 18, 2025, from https://revistamarieclaire.globo.com/Mulheres-do-Mundo/noticia/2014/07/justica-de-minas-gerais-culpa-jovem-que-teve-imagens-intimas-divulgadas-na-internet-por-se-expor.html

Bouchardet, C. (2020). Disseminação não consentida de imagens íntimas: Uma análise jurisprudencial das compensações por danos morais. *Dignidade Re-Vista, 5*(9) Retrieved March 18, 2025, from https://www.maxwell.vrac.puc-rio.br/46618/46618.PDF

Coding Rights. (2021, March 25). *Safer nudes!* Medium. Retrieved March 18, 2025, from https://medium.com/codingrights/safer-nudes-

Corrêa, S., Sívori, H., & Zilli, B. (2012). Internet regulation and sexual politics in Brazil. *Development, 55*(2), 213–218.

da Silva Santarém, P. R. (2022). *O direito achado na rede: A concepção do Marco Civil da Internet no Brasil*. Dialética.

de Cruz, F. C. B. (2015). *Direito, democracia e cultura digital: A experiência de elaboração legislativa do Marco Civil da Internet* (Master's thesis). University of São Paulo. http://www.teses.usp.br/teses/disponiveis/2/2139/tde-08042016-154010

G1/Fantástico. (2013, November). *'Não tenho mais vida', diz Fran sobre vídeo íntimo compartilhado na web*. G1. http://g1.globo.com/fantastico/noticia/2013/11/nao-tenho-mais-vida-diz-fran-sobre-video-intimo-compartilhado-na-web.html

Ganzarolli, M. Z. (2016). *Produção legislativa e gênero no Brasil* [Master's thesis, Universidade de São Paulo]. Repositório da USP. Retrieved March 18, 2025, from https://repositorio.usp.br/item/002778506

Gregori, M. F. (2008). Limites da sexualidade: Violência, gênero e erotismo. *Revista de Antropologia, 51*(2), 575–606.

Iglesias Keller, C. (2020). Policy by judicialisation: The institutional framework for intermediary liability in Brazil. *International Review of Law, Computers & Technology, 35*(3), 1–19.

Jereissati, T., & Macaya, J. F. M. (2021). Vazamento de nudes: Entre tensões e contradições. In B. Barbosa, L. Tresca, & T. Lauschner (Eds.), *TIC, governança da internet e gênero* (pp. 150–170). CGI.br.

Lins, B. A. (2021). *Caiu na net: Nudes e exposição de mulheres na internet*. Telha.

Lisbino, J. K. T., & Caridade, S. M. M. (2022). Exposição não consentida de conteúdos íntimos na perspectiva do Poder Judiciário brasileiro. *Suprema: Revista de Estudos Constitucionais, 2*(1). Retrieved March 18, 2025, from https://www.researchgate.net/publication/361624124_Exposicao_nao_consentida_de_conteudos_intimos_na_perspectiva_do_Poder_Judiciario_brasileiro

Mendonça, R. (2017, August 31). *O que o caso do homem que ejaculou em mulher no ônibus diz sobre a lei brasileira?* BBC News Brasil. Retrieved March 18, 2025, from https://www.bbc.com/portuguese/brasil-41115869

Neris, N., Ruiz, J. P., & Valente, M. (2017). Análise comparada de estratégias de enfrentamento a 'revenge porn' pelo mundo. *Revista Brasileira de Políticas Públicas, 7*(3), 333–347. https://repositorio.fgv.br/server/api/core/bitstreams/4ccd9399-f0b0-4981-9cac-d831b7b38083/content

Neris, N., Ruiz, J. P., & Valente, M. (2018). *Fighting the dissemination of non-consensual intimate images: A comparative analysis*. InternetLab. http://www.internetlab.org.br/wp-content/uploads/2018/11/Fighting_the_Dissemination_of_Non.pdf

O Globo. (2016). *Entenda o caso do estupro coletivo de adolescente*. Infográficos. Retrieved March 18, 2025, from https://infograficos.oglobo.globo.com/rio/entenda-o-caso-do-estupro-coletivo-de-uma-menor.html

Oyěwùmí, O. (2000). Family bonds/conceptual binds: African notes on feminist epistemologies. *Signs, 25*(4), 1093–1098.

Papp, A. C. (2014). *Em nome da internet: Os bastidores da construção coletiva do Marco Civil* (Final dissertation). University of São Paulo. https://issuu.com/annacarolinapapp/docs/em_nome_da_internet.

Perez, F. (2013, November 22). *Vingança mortal*. IstoÉ. https://istoe.com.br/336016_VINGANCA+MORTAL

Petição Pública. (2014). *Petição contra a violência de gênero*. https://peticaopublica.com.br/pview.aspx?pi=BR75370

Pimentel, S., Pandjiarjian, V., & Belloque, J. (2006). 'Legítima defesa da honra': Ilegítima impunidade dos assassinos — Um estudo crítico da legislação e jurisprudência da América Latina. *Cadernos Pagu Coleção Encontros*, 65–134.

Plaha, M., et al. (2022, August 22). *Por dentro do mundo secreto do comércio de nudes*. BBC News Brasil.

Retrieved March 18, 2025, from https://www.bbc.com/portuguese/geral-62630785
Singhal, A. (2015, June 19). *'Revenge porn' and search.* Google Public Policy Blog. https://publicpolicy.googleblog.com/2015/06/revenge-porn-and-search.html
Tambelli, C. (2016, December 13). *InternetLab e NDIS-USP levam nota técnica sobre violência de gênero na internet a Brasília.* https://internetlab.org.br/pt/noticias/internetlab-e-ndis-usp-levam-nota-tecnica-sobre-violencia-de-genero-na-internet-a-brasilia
Valente, M., & Neris, N. (2019). Para falar de violência de gênero na internet: Uma proposta teórica e metodológica. In G. Natansohn & F. Rovetto (Eds.), *Internet e feminismos* (pp. 105–125). Edufba.
Valente, M., Neris, N., & Bulgarelli, L. (2015). *Not revenge, not porn: Analysing the exposure of teenage girls online in Brazil.* GISWatch. https://genderit.org/sites/default/files/giswatch2015-brazil_0.pdf.
Valente, M., et al. (2016). *O corpo é o código.* InternetLab. [lista de autores incompleta—completar com todos os autores até 20, se possível].
Warken, J., & Helena, L. (2015, October 2). *Por que Stênio Garcia não se envergonha com o vazamento das fotos íntimas, e Marilene Saade sim?* Geledés. Retrieved March 18, 2025, from https://www.geledes.org.br/por-que-stenio-garcia-nao-se-envergonha-com-o-vazamento-das-fotos-intimas-e-marilene-saade-sim/

4 Hatred and Women's Freedom of Expression

Abstract

In this chapter, the focus shifts to speech: how organised masculinist ecosystems (the machosfera/manosphere) target women's expression and how law responds. Anchored in the long-running attacks against feminist writer and professor Lola Aronovich, this chapter examines the Lola Law (2018), which assigns the Federal Police competence to investigate online crimes involving misogyny, and situates it within broader debates on Brazilian hate speech law. It interrogates whether "women" qualify as a protected minority in hate speech frameworks and analyses the frictions with freedom of expression, including retaliatory suits and SLAPP-like tactics used to silence women critics. This chapter also brings stalking into view—often the connective tissue between online and offline intimidation—through the Anti-Stalking Law (2021) and its application. Finally, it links the monetised incentive structures of platforms to far-right politics and misogynistic attention economies, arguing for platform accountability alongside safeguards for legitimate criticism and women's participation in public debate.

Keywords

Hate Speech Law in Brazil · Freedom of Expression · Manosphere · Biologisation of gender difference · Stalking

In January 2008, when I started my blog, Write Lola Write, I didn't expect it to be a necessarily feminist blog, but a personal one. After all, it even has my name in the title. However, since I've been a feminist since I was eight years old, practically everything I write has a feminist, inclusive slant in defense of human rights. Fourteen years later, my blog is still active, and it's always gratifying to hear a reader say that she or he has started to fight and overcome their own prejudices by reading my blog. However, it's not all flowers. For more than eleven years, I have been threatened and attacked by organised groups of misogynists and neo-Nazis, which I have nicknamed Mascus (short for masculinists). My resistance and the difficulty in making reports inspired the creation of the Lola Law, which assigns the Federal Police to investigate misogynistic crimes on the internet. This is my account of the experience. We continue to resist (Aronovich, 2022*).*

M. Valente, *Online Misogyny in Brazil*, Sustainable Development Goals Series,
https://doi.org/10.1007/978-3-032-07727-1_4

Lola Aronovich is a journalist and university professor born in 1967 in Argentina and naturalised as a Brazilian citizen, who has been running a feminist blog called Write Lola Write since 2008. The blogosphere was born in the 1990s as a kind of virtual journal and was subsequently appropriated by journalists as a more dialogical means of communication (Christofoletti & Laux, 2008). Lola writes specifically about feminist issues and has resisted the transition to social networks. Her blog received 400,000 views a month at its peak in 2013 (Aronovich, 2022).

Since 2011, Lola has received online and offline attacks from organised misogynist groups—who, she discovered, had been talking about her in their communities and forums long before they took action. Together with other InternetLab researchers, I interviewed Lola and, separately, her lawyer, Paula Bernardelli, in 2021. The story of the attacks on Lola is intertwined with many major events of misogyny in Brazil.

From an early age, the blogger denounced misogynistic forums and groups that were breeding grounds for barbarity. In 2008, she reported on the creation of the Orkut community "Eloá became ham—good riddance"[1] right after the murder of fifteen-year-old Eloá Cristina Pimentel (Aronovich, 2008). Eloá was murdered by her ex-boyfriend after forced confinement followed by a disastrous police intervention, at which point he shot her. Comments in the community commemorated her death and invented lies about her. More than fifteen years later, her killer, Lindemberg Alves, is regarded as a hero among masculinists, as reported by political scientist Bruna Camilo, who wrote a PhD on the subject (Serafini, 2023; Silva, 2023). But who are they?

Masculinism is a construction that sees women as enemies of their interests and propagates notions of women's inferiority. Historically and from an international perspective, it can be traced the text *The Legal Subjection of Men*, written in 1908 by Ernest Belfort Bax, apparently motivated by John Stuart Mill's *The Legal Subjection of Women*. Another important reference is the Argentinian sociologist Esther Vilar's book *El Varón Domado*, from 1971, which argued that women control men across history, and not otherwise, with seduction techniques. But many of its contemporary contours find their origins in anti-feminist properly organised reactions from the 1980s, as described by Melissa Blais and Francis Dupuis-Déri (2012), predominantly in Canada, the U.S. and the UK; the foundation of groups such as the Men's Rights Activists (MRA's) and the Father's Association did legislative advocacy to counter what they saw as losses due to victories of the feminist movement, such as divorce laws (Vilaça, 2024). As a movement, it is growing worldwide, particularly in the U.S., Europe, and Latin America (Silva, 2023). The international literature differentiates several groups, such as the PUAS ("pick-up artists", who teach practices for conquering women based on this idea of inferiority), the MGTOW (men going their own way, who advocate practices to reassure male dominance), the Red Pills (men who think they have freed themselves from female dominance), and the incels (involuntary celibates, who claim to be rejected by women because they do not meet the desired standard, organising around this resentment). Their multiplatform organisation online has become known as the *manosphere* (Ging, 2019).

According to Camilo, whose research observed webpages and Telegram groups, although references to the Red Pill and other references of the *manosphere* such as the divisions between alpha, beta, and gamma men are influential, groups are not so strictly differentiated in Brazil as elsewhere (and are much less studied).[2] Masculinists rarely identify with one group only and rarely self-identify as masculinist. The communication studies researcher Gracila Vilaça argues that the phenomenon is *glocal*, showing tensions between processes of globalisation and local contexts that transform both, and proposes the term "*machosfera*" to refer to the Brazilian *manosphere*. The *machosfera* finds its origins in

[1] To "become ham" is a satirical expression for dying—ham meaning the corpse. The name in Portuguese was "Eloá virou presunto—já vai tarde".

[2] *Incels* are the most disseminated group in Brazil. Across masculinist pages and groups, a common vocabulary is shared. "Diabolheres" (devil women), "merdalheres" (shit women), "conservadias" (conservative whores), and "escravoceta" ("slaves of pussy") are some of the terms used across the board (Silva, 2023).

communities in Orkut from around 2005. In these groups, one of the topics was the discussion of the work of Nessahan Alita (apparently a pseudonym), who in the early 2000s theorised about the supposed manipulative nature of women in books in Portuguese such as "The Magnetism of Social Relations and the Feminine Profane". Olavo de Carvalho, who I mentioned before in the context of referring to the far right, emerges as another essential local reference, bridging both publics. According to Lola Aronovich, in an interview to Bruna Camilo, these are the most distinctive references of the Brazilian version of the *manosphere* (Ging, 2019).

Camilo's research also identified how the *bolsonarismo*—politics associated with Jair Bolsonaro—was both fuelled and fuelled masculinist discourses and practices around gender and sexuality on the internet. As stated, fearmongering around the concept of "gender ideology" has been central to Brazilian politics after the impeachment in 2016, and Bolsonaro has been praised as possessing masculine virility qualities (Ging, 2019). This follows similar lines to how, in the United States, the subreddit r/The_Donald (T_D) was founded as a site for Donald Trump supporters in 2015, developed a sophisticated meme iconography to dissimulate misogyny and racism, and became one of the homes of the U.S. manosphere. Donald Trump himself reposted T_D publications, fuelling the movement (Vilaça, 2024).

In a study focused on YouTube, The Federal University of Rio de Janeiro's NetLab found over 76 thousand videos in 7.8 thousand channels that can be characterised as misogynistic (Santini et al., 2024). Juxtaposed, these different studies show how masculinism can express differently in different platforms: on YouTube, they could clearly find distinctions between Red Pill, MGTOW, and PUA subcultures, and incel to a lesser extent. In common, these subcultures were using specific misogynistic grammars in Portuguese and promoting the idea that there is a social conspiracy for female domination, claiming for their control or isolation. The researchers could prove both an expressive growth in numbers of videos from 2022, and that 80% were being monetised—primarily through native YouTube tools, some with internal promotion of products, courses, and crowdfunding. That is, misogyny is giving them revenues.

In other spaces, the Brazilian *machosfera* can present itself in even more extreme versions. In her PhD research at the Federal University of Minas Gerais, Gracila Vilaça engaged in a digital ethnography of the subreddit /BrasilLivre ("Free Brazil") during 2021 and 2022, with a particular focus on memes. Due to its origins, architecture and content moderation practices, Reddit can be understood as a platform that is in the transition between the mainstream and the *deep web*. Although she found a general preference for voting for Bolsonaro, she describes that many of the members see themselves as more extremist to the right, frequently associating him with mainstream politics. In this subreddit, she found close ties between masculinism and libertarianism, vernacles from the *manosphere*, marked antifeminism and transphobia, and a strong affinity with neo-Nazism, as the ideal of man is intertwined with racial purity and neo-Nazi symbolism is mobilised. That means,

> The atmosphere that emerges from this is even more diffuse and chaotic than its transnational counterpart, and more openly affinised with the far right, in line with empathic populism and polarised leadership, and less overtly masculinist. Maybe the studied *machosfera* can also be understood as a 'gateway drug,' as Copland (2023) thinks of the manosphere. Maybe this homosociotechnical environment is even more addictive than its transnational version since its radicalisation depends less on vernacular literacy. (Vilaça, 2024, pp. 331–332)

Studying the *deep web* can be complicated, but a few examples help visualise the kind of content that circulates—and that eventually victimised Lola Aronovich. In 2018, the Federal Prosecutor's Office published screenshots of the blog *Rio de Nojeira* ("River of Filth", playing around Rio de Janeiro), created falsely under the name of Ricardo Wagner, a technology consultant. The creators of the blog were linked to *Dogolachan*, at the time Brazil's version of *4chan*, and considered to be the biggest channel for spreading misogynistic content in the country; they were supposedly trying to incriminate Wagner because of a disagreement in an online game. The blog is no longer online. A few examples of headlines from the Prosecutor's Office document give an idea of the level of violence:

> Suicide guide for black women: why black women need to die
> UniCarioca Carnival: a great place to rape drugged and drunk sluts
> Women with dark pussies and tits are disgusting
> Why [sic] should we rape lesbians these days?
> How to apply the gay cure to lesbians
> Marielle Franco, a ham* with a pedigree
> Long live the incel revolution, we support the massacre of Alek Minassian, he is a hero and we will not stop
> We support the massacre of Dimitrios Pagourtzis
> How to prepare acid to throw at feminist bitches

There is a contradiction at play here: the blog was simultaneously spreading extreme misogyny and racism and doing so under the name of someone it wanted to incriminate. But the content is not far off than what was posted on *Dogolachan*. There, women were treated as "fucking dumps", "the most hypocritical and deplorable creatures in the universe", sluts who "only know how to hook up with the worst kind of rubbish". Perpetrators of femicides were treated as heroes, five-year-old Russian children were praised for being free of "miscegenation and all this degeneration", and techniques for kidnapping and raping teenagers were discussed (Salvadori, 2018). Racism and LGBTphobia were also common, especially in direct posts against black women and lesbian women.

Such violence is not restricted to online environments. There are records of Brazilian masculinist spaces being used to organise mass shootings in the country, as has also happened elsewhere (Instituto Avon & Decode, 2021). And although the prevalence is much lower than in the U.S., where the Gun Violence Archive accounted for 488 episodes in 2024 only, such attacks are on the rise. In 2011, Wellington Menezes de Oliveira, 23, killed ten girls and two boys aged between thirteen and fifteen in a public school in Realengo, a Rio de Janeiro neighbourhood—the *Realengo Massacre*. He committed suicide after being shot in the leg by a police officer. Witnesses said that he shot the girls to kill, and the boys in the arms and legs. Wellington was a regular participant in masculinist blogs and forums, and in his videos, he referred to women as "impure beings." After the attack, some of these blogs shut down to avoid problems with the police. However, Wellington was deemed a hero in other masculinist spaces, such as *Dogolachan* (which, since 2018, has migrated to the *deep web*) (Coelho, 2021). In 2019, a *Dogolachan* moderator, known as Kyo, announced that he would shoot a woman in the back in the city of Penápolis, São Paulo state, where he lived, and then commit suicide. He was encouraged by other regulars and carried out the plan against an unknown woman.

Two weeks later, Guilherme Taucci Monteiro, seventeen, and Luiz Henrique de Castro, 25, killed seven people in a public school in Suzano, a neighbourhood of São Paulo—the *Suzano Massacre*. The press reported that the two killers were regulars at *55chan* and *Dogolachan*, where they had asked for advice and guidance during the planning of the attack. Posts on these forums celebrated the attack and satirised the victims (Declercq, 2019). There are more cases of femicide linked to these spaces (Coelho, 2021).

In 2023, a teenager stabbed four teachers and two students at a public school in Vila Sônia, a neighbourhood in São Paulo city. On Twitter, he used the nickname "Taucci", apparently in deference to the Suzano shooter (Dias & Kruse, 2023). 2023 witnessed a steep rise of attacks in schools in Brazil—at least 21. The public and academic discussion pointed out that behaviours and discourses familiar to these *chans* had begun to "rise to the surface" on social networks in previous years—that it, they did not belong to the *deep web* only anymore (Pires, 2023). The cases also made it clear that these online spaces, contrary to what some claim, are far from harmless.

Lola Aronovich reports that she always received insults and accusations on her blog, but that when she started writing about masculinists, she began to receive threats. She tells this story in a 2022 text called "The trajectory and resistance of Write Lola Write" in painful detail. She brings up emails with death threats, phone calls, chats planning attacks, and videos accusing her of crimes. In the interview she gave us, she told us how she has received a phone call every Christmas since then, saying that this will be her last Christmas. Criminal websites have been set up in her name and that of her husband. Complaints against her have been made at the Federal University of Ceará, where she works, and she has already faced eight lawsuits from men who wanted to hold her responsible for slander and defamation, which have caused her headaches and various costs. In one case, the plaintiff promised to kill her when she arrived in the city where the hearing was to take place. She had difficulty convincing the judge that holding the hearing in person was risky. A pair of female lawyers and a male lawyer subsequently resigned from her defence because of the threats they also began to receive.[3]

Lola also filed a police report and wanted to see her aggressors held accountable. And that is the story of a law.

4.1 The Lola Law

After the Realengo Massacre in 2011, *Silvio Koerich*, then one of the most popular blogs among masculinists, was briefly taken off the air, only to return more extremist: if before it still attempted at humour, it now showed what is known as *gore*: images of tortured, raped, and dead women, as well as texts defending the legalisation of rape, especially "corrective rape" for lesbians, the legalisation of paedophilia, the murder of women, blacks, and gays. In between, one could find many threats to Lola Aronovich and the then MP Jean Wyllys (Socialism and Liberty Party) and promises of massacres in the Social Sciences building at the University of Brasília, to kill "sluts and leftists".

Lola Aronovich reports that, between August 2011 and April 2012, different people made more than 70,000 complaints about the website to Safernet, an NGO I mentioned before, that partners with law enforcement to channel complaints about online crime and violence, but the Federal Police never got back to her about the investigations. It was the group Anonymous[4] (Baptista, 2020) that discovered the identity of the two main perpetrators: Emerson Eduardo Rodrigues and Marcelo Valle Silveira Mello. Both were briefly imprisoned in 2012 as a result of the Federal Police's "Operation Intolerance". When they were released in 2013, they again threatened Lola on the blog and in emails with prosecution and death. Emerson Rodrigues, in fact, sued her but dropped the suit. Marcelo Valle started a new blog: the famous *Dogolachan*. Aronovich found out about it because he left links on her blog, and from then on, she began to follow the daily threats to her, her husband, and her mother. There, Valle also sought to recruit young people for massacres and tested their loyalty by giving them tasks—several of which involved threatening Lola and recording videos with lies about her. They left traces; particularly when members quarrelled, they would expose each other, and she went on to put together a dossier and file police reports, but

> the Civilian Police were always too busy, and didn't seem to have much knowledge about the internet in general; at the Police Department for Violence Against Women, the first question was "What is your aggressor?", and I had to explain that I didn't know my aggressors personally and never communicated with them, in other words, they weren't mine at all; at the time (and to this day), Ceará didn't have a Police Department for Cybercrime; a Federal Police superintendent told me by email that the Federal Police only investigated crimes to which Brazil was an international signatory, such as racism and child pornography. (Aronovich, 2022)

Aronovich's account resonates with what I mentioned in the previous chapter, which comes from many other reports I have obtained in the over ten years I have researched the subject. Law enforcement can be a maze. It is not only hard for the citizen to navigate between the different units—their internal divisions are not always clear, which seems to be aggravated in cases like

[3]Interview given to InternetLab in 2021.

[4]A decentralised international collective and movement, with no explicit leadership, of hacktivists and activists, which has become known for its various cyberattacks against governments, companies, and the Church of Scientology.

online misogyny, where cultural resistance plays a role. Law enforcement is divided into federal and state authorities for investigating crimes, and the latter (the Civilian Police) is generally in charge of "common crimes". It also encompasses specialised units, like the Police Department for Violence Against Women and Police Department for Cybercrime.

The Police Departments for Violence Against Women are much better equipped to deal with physical violence, especially domestic violence, and they often lack the technical preparation to conduct investigations into acts committed online. The Police Departments for Cybercrime, where they exist (in the capitals of the states, and not all of them),[5] often claim that they only deal with crimes against property, such as scams involving bank accounts (Valente et al., 2016). In her book *Caiu na net* ("Leaked Online"), Beatriz Lins recounts a situation in which, on accompanying a victim to the São Paulo Police Department for Cybercrime in 2015, she heard from police officers that they only dealt with consumer offences, "like when you buy something [in a retailer shop] and it is not delivered". "I can't take any more of this nude stuff… Go to the Department for Violence Against Women, ask for the Carolina Dieckmann Law, not here!" (Lins, 2021, p. 114). In a case I followed from start to finish between 2015 and 2016, the victim of a mass attack took the case to a normal Civilian Police Department, filed a police report, tried to contact them to find out about the progress of the case, was never contacted and ended up giving up. It was still quite common for police officers not to be internet users or to use it marginally, and not to realise the extent of the violence in victims' lives. The situation can become Kafkaesque. For example, the 2016 account of a police chief from a São Paulo Police Department of Violence Against Women who sought help from the Civilian Police in a case of child sexual exploitation, in an interview to my research team about investigating NCII:

> We had a case of paedophilia. We seized the computer, we seized everything. But then the judge asked for confidentiality to be broken to find out which website the paedophile was using. We don't have the means, so we sent it to the Department of Homicide and Personal for paedophile crimes, and that Department said it didn't have the means to do this kind of thing either.
> They said it didn't fall within their remit. Then we sent it to the people responsible for Cybercrime; it didn't fall within their remit either. Then we sent it to… I was lost, almost putting the investigation in my purse and saying, "Look, Dr Fernando, I don't know where I'm going. I don't have the means, I don't even know where to start". So, I sent it to the Federal Police, and they didn't send it back to us, so I think they embraced it. (Valente et al., 2015)

The Brazilian Federal Constitution defines the powers of the Federal Police, including that additional cases can be determined by law if their commission has "interstate or international repercussions and requires uniform repression".[6] All residuals are within the competence of the Civilian Police Departments, which are governed by each of the 26 federative states. A law defining these other cases for the Federal Police was enacted in 2002, including, among crimes with interstate repercussions, investigations into human rights violations described in international treaties that Brazil signs. This is the reason why the Federal Police investigates crimes of racism and child sexual exploitation, the prosecution of which is provided for in international treaties, and claimed not to investigate misogyny.

There remains, however, a question of interpretation—or conviction. After all, Brazil is a signatory to the 1979 Convention on the Elimination of All Forms of Discrimination against Women, Article 2 of which defines that States undertake to "adopt appropriate legislative and other measures, with appropriate sanctions, prohibiting all discrimination against women". In addition, the Inter-American Convention on the Prevention, Punishment, and Eradication of Violence Against Women, known as the Convention of Belém do Pará, of 1994, which Brazil has also signed and promulgated, defines:

[5] SaferNet maintains a list, available at: https://new.safernet.org.br/content/delegacias-cibercrimes#mobile. Accessed on: April 8, 2025.

[6] Brazilian Federal Constitution, art. 144, § 1°, I.

> Art. 7—States Parties condemn all forms of violence against women and agree to adopt, by all appropriate means and without delay, policies to prevent, punish and eradicate such violence and to endeavour to:
> act with due diligence to prevent, investigate and punish violence against women;
> to incorporate into its domestic legislation such criminal, civil, administrative and other rules as may be necessary to prevent, punish and eradicate violence against women, and to adopt such appropriate administrative measures as may be applicable.

In any case, perhaps because of the open-ended nature of these provisions, or even because of a lack of prioritisation, the response given by the Federal Police to cases like Aronovich's was often that these misogyny cases fell outside their scope. As mentioned, women who brought online violence to the Civilian Police were not having better luck. Especially before the issue began to gain more public traction in 2016, women commonly reported coming to the police station with problems of online violence and being mocked and blamed, or being told: "girl, just close your computer".[7]

In 2016, after reading Aronovich's interviews about how difficult it was to get her attackers identified and held accountable, the former mayor of Fortaleza (where Lola is based) and then MP Luizianne Lins (Workers Party, PT) drafted Bill No. 4614/2016, which was sanctioned in 2018 as Law No. 13,642—the Lola Law. The Lola Law adds an assignment to the Federal Police's list of tasks: to investigate crimes "committed through the World Wide Web that disseminate misogynistic content, defined as those that propagate hatred or aversion to women". The aim was to solve Kafka's labyrinth and ensure that a more nationally articulated body, transcending the boundaries of the states of the federation, and at least supposedly with more material resources, would take a closer look at misogyny. This does not mean that other police units would be excluded from such investigations—the law that defines the powers of the Federal Police, Law No. 10,446/2002, states that their role is not exclusive—in all cases, the Military and Civilian Police of the states can investigate concurrently.[8]

When the bill was being debated, there were some opposing voices. For example, in the House of Representatives, when it was debated in the Committee on Public Security and the Fight against Organised Crime in 2017, MP Waldir (then a member of Republican Party) and the then MP Major Olímpio (Solidarity Party) voted in the opposite direction, arguing that there were already many initiatives to expand the Federal Police's remit, and they were not accompanied by an increase in personnel, structure, and resources to do justice to the expansion: in short, the Federal Police would not be able to cope (Câmara dos Deputados, 2017).

In any case, the law passed. As Lola rightly observes, it was the first time that the term "misogyny"was used in Brazilian legislation. However, this is also a limitation. In an interview with InternetLab in 2021, prosecutor Silvia Chakian[9] mentioned that, despite the Lola Law's brief definition of misogyny as content that "propagates hatred or aversion to women", its effectiveness is limited by the fact that there is no clarity as to which crimes could be covered by the investigations (Chakian, 2021). The idea here is that existing crimes—threats, extortion, slander, defamation—fall under the remit of the Federal Police when they involve misogyny. But how do we define whether they involve misog-

[7]Beatriz Accioly Lins (2021) recounts a similar case that occurred at a women's police station: the police chief, after stating that it was not possible to register a case of nCII in the system, suggested that the victim deactivate her social media profiles.

[8]Under Law No. 10.446/2002, Article 1: In accordance with item I of paragraph 1 of Article 144 of the Constitution, "when there is interstate or international repercussion that requires uniform repression, the Federal Police Department of the Ministry of Justice may, without prejudice to the responsibility of the public security bodies listed in Article 144 of the Federal Constitution, especially the Military and Civil Police of the States, conduct investigations of, among others, the following criminal offenses: [...]".

[9]Silvia Chakian coordinates a group to face domestic violence against women at the São Paulo Prosecutor's Office and is also a researcher who has written extensively on violence against women, including online.

yny? One lens of interpretation, in Chakian's view, would be the hypothesis set out in the Feminicide Law (Law No. 13,104/15), which provides for the crime of feminicide when the murder involves domestic and family violence, or "contempt for or discrimination against the condition of women". According to the prosecutor, this last hypothesis could serve as a guideline. However, she resents the absence of legal and social frameworks to address misogyny in Brazil.

This is precisely what researchers Luanna Souza et al. (2022) from the Federal University of Pará observed in a study from 2022, indicating a surge in the use of the term "misogyny"across social networks, media, and academic papers, during and after the impeachment of the former president Dilma Rousseff, in 2016—a turning point in Brazil's recent history, and an event intensely marked by misogynistic insults. They note that the concept lacks a precise definition and illustrate how numerous academic papers define misogyny in terms of its meaning (Souza et al., 2022). The most common definition is "hatred/aversion to women". Others have proposed associations with "male dominance", "essentialist discourse on women" (positively or negatively linking them to a stable and immutable genetic nature), "refusal of the feminine", as well as others that are less frequent. Their conclusion is that this lack of outlines may contribute to the ineffectiveness of the Lola Law.

There was a separate heated debate among feminists in 2023 about creating a specific crime for misogyny, including discrimination based on gender within the crimes of discrimination or prejudice outlined in the Antiracism Law (law No 7716/89), which covers "race, colour, ethnicity, religion or national origin". We will address this later in Chap. 6.

Despite these problems, the Lola Law was considered a victory: perhaps more symbolic than practical. The attacks have not stopped, but the visibility of the granaries of misogyny has increased. In December 2018, Marcelo Valle was arrested by the Federal Police in "Operation Bravata", which was investigating child sexual exploitation, racism, criminal association and terrorism, and sentenced, after back and forth, to eleven years in prison (Vianna & Kaniak, 2018). Other members then took over the leadership of *Dogolachan*. One of them was Kyo, who I mentioned for killing a woman in Penápolis and then committing suicide. That woman was called Luciana de Jesus do Nascimento, and he did not know her. *Dogolachan*'s members were showing force beyond the screens.

Another *Dogolachan* moderator continued to send messages to Lola, saying that they got stronger on the *deep web*, and the death threats would go on. During the pandemic, the *chans* began to organise episodes of zoombombing, although they did not plan to end the idealisation of physical attacks. The Civilian Police claims to have prevented ten school massacres in 2021, apparently by monitoring the *chans* (Leal, 2021). Meanwhile, Lola lives a routine in which she has to get used to the attacks she suffers and recognises that her case is just one of many that lack visibility.

Mentioning a former MP, Roberto Jefferson (Brazilian Labour Party), who, unhappy with a decision by four Supreme Electoral Court ministers on disinformation in 2022, chose to call the only female Justice, Carmen Lúcia, a "whore", "a crook", "rotten on the inside and hideous on the outside", and a "witch", Lola says:

> You don't have to do anything to be called a "whore" or a "witch"—it's enough to be a woman. But it's still shocking that the ex-MP should publicly hurl these words at a female Justice. Because if he says that about a Justice, a woman in a high position of power, you can imagine what he says about everyday women, anonymous, poor, black women who don't hold important positions. (Valenga & Guimarães, 2022)

4.2 Words Against Women and Hate Speech Law in Brazil

When dealing with verbal violence against women, it is displeasing, but necessary to introduce the blog *Tio Astolfo*. It was a website created in 2014 with the self-declared aim of "exposing the reality of a society corrupted and degenerated by leftism". In a text called "Women like to be beaten", the author—under a pseudonym—said:

> It's time for Western men to start assuming their role. Eliminating faggots and leftists and putting women back in the kitchen. Everyone would be happy, women's emotional problems would be over and men would have a world full of pussy, no longer needing to spend their time going to parties and listening to sluts' emotional mimicry. [...]
> This blog is to open the minds of these retarded teenagers, to humiliate these feminist sluts and make their vaginas honey.
> It's not a question of being handsome or elegant, it's a question of words. A woman is an object, and you have to impose control on her. It's like training dogs.

Other posts were guides with detailed recommendations for rape: "How to rape a woman at school: A step-by-step guide for minors", as well as extremely misogynistic texts such as

> Single mothers are genetic scum and should be eliminated
> Women are shallow and ignorant, I just want to f*, I can't empathise with them
> How to rape women at parties and discos: a step-by-step guide.[10]

The site began to be investigated by the Federal Police and the São Paulo State Prosecutor's Office for containing misogynistic and racist content; investigations (with the help of the Anonymous group) revealed that the same people who attacked Lola were behind the blog. As mentioned, one of them was arrested by Operation Bravado in 2018. The question that remains is: What to call these events and how to investigate them?

A large body of recent literature on hate speech recognises some of the challenges in defining the concept in Brazil. In 2020, we conducted an action-research project at InternetLab in partnership with IBEAC (Brazilian Institute for Community Studies and Support) and the Social Knowledge Network with a group of fourteen young women and men between the ages of 16 and 26 from different outlying neighbourhoods in the city of São Paulo. We held nine workshops, beginning with a common conceptual construction on hate speech against women, and then went on to develop 22 interviews with people with different socioeconomic backgrounds.[11] One of the insights we gained from the interviews was that the notion of hate speech was not well defined: many people referred to aggressive, unempathetic discourse or a lack of consideration for other people's opinions. A work of critical discourse analysis by Jhussyenna de Oliveira (2021), from the Federal University of Piauí, showed something similar in a survey of 250 participants: people tend to understand hate speech as something that has an effect on someone, but they are not clear on the definition of that someone, which brings the risk of "trivialising the problem in the belief that any dispute can be hate speech", or even minimising the victim's pain. Her conclusion: "society needs to learn to include the identity of victims in its representations, in other words, society needs to start recognising the rights of minorities, their place of speech and their historically situated pain".

Socially and even politically, hate speech is a loose term. For example, in July 2022, after the murder of the Worker Party's member Marcelo Arruda, Supreme Court Justice Alexandre de Moraes, reacting to a representation made by seven opposition parties, asked Jair Bolsonaro to comment on the "incitement to violence and hate speech" he had uttered against opponents. Some examples of such speech brought up by the parties in the representation were:

[10] Although the pages have been taken down, they can be found in services of internet archive. I will not publish the links, given the degree of violence and the disturbance they cause. Some media outlets reproduced part of the contents: *Fórum* (2015), *G1* (2015).

[11] And they ended up in public actions developed entirely by them—a collage of lambes, the #todescontraoódio (#allagainsthate) campaign and the *Pilotas* podcast. This project was part of the wider Recognise, Resist and Remedy project, which we conducted in partnership with the Indian organisation it for Change and which was funded by Canada's International Development Research Centre (IDRC). As mentioned elsewhere, this book is one of the results of that project. About the action-research component with young people, and the results of the activities that were carried out, see Martins and Oliveira (2021).

> Let's shoot the *petralhada*[12] here in Acre. We're going to put these pricks out of Acre.
> Like when Paulo Guedes, in 2018, put together that pile of candidates, and I said: "It's good that one single shot or just one grenade kills everyone at once".

In this representation, as well as in Moraes' request, there is a clear recognition that speeches produce real-world effects. But does it make sense to say that hate speech also applies to political opponents, or does that dilute the definition too much? After all, how is hate speech understood or applied?

One of the reasons why we have been tossing around this concept so much is that, as such, it does not have a long tradition of debate in Brazilian law. The first time it appeared in these terms in a relevant way was in the judgement of the notorious Ellwanger Case, in 2003, by the Supreme Court. I will address that in a moment. The conceptual debate is contested, but we can start with a widely accepted definition of hate speech, that of Jeremy Waldron, professor of law at New York University: the converging core of hate speech is the use of deliberately abusive, insulting, threatening, or inferior words directed at members of vulnerable minorities, with the aim of instigating hatred against these people (Waldron, 2012). The words may even be directed at a particular person, but they are considered hate speech when the target is a subalternised group to which that person belongs.[13] There are authors who, in their definition, determine which these groups are according to certain criteria, such as race and ethnicity, religion, gender, physical or mental disability, origin or sexual orientation; there are others who leave it open.[14]

Despite internal or transnational definitional challenges, there are international obligations to combat hate speech, and countries apply different extensions to the ban. The most significant is the International Covenant on Civil and Political Rights (ICCPR), approved by the UN General Assembly in 1966 and which came into force in Brazil in 1992. Article 20, paragraph 2 of this Convention states that "any advocacy of national, racial or religious hatred which constitutes incitement to discrimination, hostility or violence shall be prohibited by law". This is considered to be the only content-related speech prohibition in international law.

It contains many difficult concepts; because of this, in 2012, the Office of the United Nations High Commissioner for Human Rights (OHCHR) approved the Rabat Action Plan, which defines certain concepts and establishes what it calls a "threshold test". The concepts are: hatred and hostility (defined as intense and irrational emotions of opprobrium, enmity, and detestation towards the target group), advocacy (defined as the intention to publicly promote hatred towards the target group), and incitement (statements about national, racial, or religious groups that generate an imminent risk of discrimination, hostility, or violence towards these groups). This threshold test involves considering context (whether discrimination, hostility, and violence against the target audience are likely and causal), the speaker's position in society, intention (negligence and recklessness are not sufficient, and the speaker must "advocate" and "incite"), content and form (being direct, and considering style), the extent of the speech acts (for example, whether the means of dissemination have a wide reach), and the reasonable likelihood that the speech will incite real action against the target audience. This interpretation significantly limits the application of the concept of incitement to hatred, since, although serious cases are often not

[12] "Petralhada" is a pejorative term to refer to supporters of the Workers Party, the largest leftist party in the country (Lula's party).

[13] For a more detailed discussion of this see Valente (2020). See also, da Silva et al. (2011), Meyer-Plug (2009).

[14] There are many competing definitions or those with slight variations. In 2020, a Brazilian research centre called CEPI-FGV published a Guidebook for Hate Speech Analysis, hate speech as "manifestations that negatively evaluate a vulnerable group or an individual as a member of a vulnerable group, to establish that they are less worthy of rights, opportunities or resources than other groups or individuals who are members of other groups, and consequently legitimise the practice of discrimination or violence". Here, the deservingness of rights, opportunities, or resources and the legitimisation of violence, rather than incitement, gain prominence. See Luccas et al. (2020).

prosecuted, vague legislation also risks persecuting minorities in many countries. The Rabat Plan emphasises another important point: establishing that politicians and religious leaders have a duty to actively combat hatred.

As a member of the OAS (Organisation of American States), Brazil has been a signatory since 1992 to the 1969 Inter-American Convention on Human Rights (Pact of San José da Costa Rica), which has a strong focus on guaranteeing freedom of expression, but provides in its article 13(5) that "the law shall prohibit all propaganda in favour of war, as well as all advocacy of national, racial or religious hatred that constitutes incitement to discrimination, hostility, crime or violence". The language is similar to that of the Covenant, and the Inter-American Commission on Human Rights has spoken out on a number of occasions to the effect that advocacy of hatred should be curbed only when it comes with a clear intention and the real and effective possibility of committing crimes, to avoid leading to sanctions for opinions. As is evident, gender (and sexuality) is not part of these conventions. One explanation is that they were devised and created in the context of post-World War II, post-Holocaust Europe, and the decolonisation process (Barker & Jurasz, 2018).

Despite these absences, a change of winds is underway. In 2022, Brazil enacted two other OAS conventions (from 2013): the Inter-American Convention against Racism, Racial Discrimination and Related Forms of Intolerance and the Inter-American Convention against All Forms of Discrimination and Intolerance. They are an important milestone and guide from at least two points of view. Firstly, because they advance the state's obligations to legislate not only against incitement to hatred but also against the circulation of content that does so. Secondly, because of the broad category of protected groups which they provide for—the first applies to racial discrimination ("race, colour, descent or national or ethnic origin"), and the second to

> gender, age, sexual orientation, language, religion, political or other opinion, social origin, economic position, migrant, refugee or displaced person status, birth, stigmatised infectious or contagious condition, genetic characteristic, disability, incapacitating mental suffering or any other social condition. (OAS, 2013)

They contain similar provisions: in addition to affirmative action and public policies, they oblige signatory countries to prevent, eliminate, prohibit, and punish, "in accordance with their constitutional norms and the provisions of this Convention", acts such as support for discriminatory activities (including their financing) and the publication, circulation, and dissemination, including via the Internet, of hateful and intolerant materials.

As mentioned, countries give different contours to these obligations. Given its great influence on the internet debate, the most important case to differentiate is the United States, a signatory to the ICPPR, but not the last two I mentioned. In the United States, the dominant jurisprudence sees freedom of expression as a right that takes priority over all others. Hate speech is thus understood as protected speech, i.e., speech that cannot be banned, even if it is hurtful and reprehensible. Only speech that leads to an imminent—clear and present—danger of an illegal act is restricted, what are known as fighting words or provocative words. Behind this doctrine is the value of guaranteeing public order and peace, not the protection of victims' rights (Sarmento, 2006).

In a 1969 case, the Supreme Court overturned the conviction of Clarence Brandenburg, who, at a Ku Klux Klan meeting, lamented alleged "anti-white Caucasian" policies, made racist remarks against Blacks and Jews, and spoke of revenge. The argument of the decision—which did not mention racism—was that illegal advocacy or campaigning is permitted by the First Amendment of the American Constitution (Brugger, 2007). Later decisions expressed a rather radical position of the Supreme Court along these lines in cases involving the burning of crosses to intimidate Black people.[15] There is a belief involved in this model that the free debate of ideas will lead

[15] "R.A.V. vs. City of Saint Paul", from 1992, and "Virginia vs. Black et al.", from 2003. See: Sarmento (2006), Stone et al. (2016).

to the best conclusions, and that hate speech is fought with more speech. At the root of this thinking lies a distrust of the state as a mediator of acceptable discourse and a rather formalistic conception of the right to freedom of expression, which believes that this right will flourish with the mere absence of state coercion and not with factual conditions, such as the security to express oneself free from oppression.

The approach differs significantly from that adopted by international treaties on the subject and by the law of many countries, especially European ones, where values such as dignity, honour, and equality are given greater weight when assessing the lawfulness of hate speech. For example, in German law, there is no requirement that the incitement of hate speech is concrete for there to be a specific criminal act (for this, there is a specific crime, that of incitement); it needs to raise the general risk of disruption of public peace, the occurrence of hate crimes, other violations against minority groups: the "danger of a danger" (Brugger, 2007, p. 118). Such a vision is also called militant democracy, that is, a regime that sees the prohibition of hate speech as necessary for the society's exercise of effective and plural points of view, particularly from traditionally excluded groups, with reciprocal recognition of equality. The liberation of hate speech produces less speech than its prohibition because of who it silences (Sarmento, 2006). Although there is no history in Brazil of dealing with hate speech through the lens of militant democracy, there is a long tradition, driven by social movements, of pleading for the regulation of speech, understanding that it produces effects in the world. However, this has always been done in other terms: racism, LGBTphobia, misogyny or even discrimination. For example, in his book *What is Discrimination?*,[16] the Brazilian law professor Adilson José Moreira (2017) argues that discourses are discriminatory practices—conducts not expressions—fuelling stigmas that affirm the essential inferiority of minorities and corroborating the perception that all members of minority groups are inferior, which can ultimately lead to violence. Discourse, Moreira claims, produces effects in the world on a cultural and material level; the focus on effects takes into account the concrete experiences of the people affected by it (Matsuda, 1989; Delgado, 1982).

In an interview with InternetLab in 2021, Fabiana Benedito, a journalist and member of the World March of Women's Communicators Collective in Brazil, expressed an interesting concern about the everyday uses of the word "hate", which does not distinguish between discriminations that are very much part of Brazil's history:

> We have resorted to a feeling, to hatred, but it's not hatred of just anyone, it's not hatred like any other feeling. It's a hatred directed mainly at women, Black people and LGBT people, and hatred of women has a name, hatred of Black people and LGBT people also has names. Naming is an exercise: to say it's sexist, it's racist, it's an important movement. (Martins & Becari, 2021)

And what does Brazilian law say about hate speech? One of the reasons why we have been running around so much with this concept is that, as such, it does not exist in legislation. However, some provisions would fit some versions of the concept. The most important of these is Law No. 7716/1989, known as the Antiracism Law or the Caó Law, which, in its twentieth article, defines it as a crime to "practice, induce or incite discrimination or prejudice based on race, colour, ethnicity, religion or national origin", and which also forbids acts that promote Nazism. We can see that there is no reference to sex, gender, or sexuality nor to age or other social markers. And what about speech that could be classed as hate speech but is against women, trans people, non-binary people, or homosexuals?

The Supreme Court handed down two important decisions that outlined and expanded the scope of this legislation. The first was in the Ellwanger case in 2003. Sigfried Ellwanger had published a book under the pseudonym S. E. Castan, entitled *Holocaust, German or Jewish? Behind the scenes of the lie of the century*. Because of this, he was indicted for racism by the Rio Grande do Sul State Prosecutor's Office, and when the case reached the Supreme Court,

[16] *O que é Discriminação?*, in Portuguese.

Ellwanger's defence claimed that the crime was statute-barred since the book had been published in 1988. Although racism is an imprescriptible crime according to the Federal Constitution, the defence said that what Ellwanger had done could not be considered racism because, it claimed, Jews were a people, not a race. Justice Maurício Corrêa, the case rapporteur, ruled that race is a concept with no biological substrate and rather a historical, political, and social one—and that, in this concept, Jews constitute a race. The Court also debated the different legal goods at stake—freedom of expression and human dignity—and concluded that the abusive exercise of freedom of expression can be restricted. Even so, the concept of hate speech has not been widely adopted in the decisions of the Brazilian judiciary.[17]

The Supreme Court's second important decision was in the case of the criminalisation of homophobia and transphobia and equated them to crimes of racism in 2015. A small diversion is necessary: two years earlier, in 2013, the Federal Prosecutor's Office filed a complaint with the Supreme Court against MP Marcos Antônio Feliciano, an evangelical pastor that has been in five different parties in the last 15 years, who, in 2011, had posted on Twitter: "The rottenness of homo-affective feelings leads to hatred, crime and rejection". The Federal Prosecutor's Office sought to classify the case under the Antiracism Law, in the terms of the decision we have just commented on in the Ellwanger case—a "cultural and sociological" definition; the decision in 2014 favoured the MP (not upholding the complaint), and different Justices argued that, although it was likely to exceed the limits of freedom of expression, the MP's speech did not constitute a criminal offence, for lack of an explicit provision.

A year later, in 2016, the Supreme Court judged a lawsuit challenging the Brazilian state for constitutional omission (a "Direct Action of Unconstitutionality in Omission" or ADO), a mechanism provided for in the Brazilian Constitution to provoke the judiciary in cases where the Parliament recognisably delays in issuing a norm that regulates a right. The Popular Socialist Party (PPS) was the one who initiated ADO 26. The rapporteur, Justice Celso de Mello, recognised various forms of violence against LGBTQIAP+ people and the segregationist nature of the "gender ideology" narrative and stated that homophobia and transphobia can be framed as racism in the terms of the Ellwanger case: a "cultural and sociological" definition.

The court agreed on some theses, determining two important things: that the crimes of the Antiracism Law can be used to frame homophobia and transphobia and that homotransphobic practices qualify the crime of homicide, that is, when a homicide involves homotransphobia, the penalty will be higher. The second thesis was that religious temples can demonstrate against homosexuality, as long as these demonstrations do not constitute hate speech—and here, hate speech was defined as "externalisations that incite discrimination, hostility or violence against people because of their sexual orientation or gender identity".

During this process, the Brazilian public sphere largely quarrelled around whether it was appropriate for the Supreme Court to broaden the interpretation of racism offences, or whether this was the legislature's prerogative. There was also an important, albeit timid, debate about how appropriate the criminalisation strategy was for dealing with LGBTphobia (as well as racism).

Years after the decision, in 2022, the National Council of Justice published a survey showing that there were still few prosecutions characterising the criminal act as LGBTphobic nationwide. In addition to mapping the decisions in the judiciary, the authors of the research identified in interviews that it is rare for cases of LGBTphobia to be reported and turned into criminal proceed-

---

[17]Research published by Professor Rosane Leal da Silva in 2011 systematised all the decisions involving Orkut in the higher courts up to that point. As I have already mentioned, Orkut was Brazil's most popular social network in the 2010s. Only 1% of the cases (six of them) referred to the definition of hate speech I mentioned above. Most of these cases were initiated by the Prosecutor's Office, "an institution that has as one of its foundations the defence of social interests, representing on behalf of causes that transcend the individual, as is the case with this type of discriminatory discourse" (da Silva et al., 2011).

ings, i.e. few reach the judiciary. One of the reasons is the victims' fear of re-victimisation at police stations. There has also been difficulty in mapping, producing data and preparing police officers to deal with these cases. Some states have included fields on sexual orientation and gender identity in their police investigation forms, but police officers often refrain from filling them in. This, coupled with the fact that judicial decisions themselves often do not mention LGBTphobia, generates an "erasure of elements of LGBTphobia and LGBTQIA+ plaintiffs along the institutional chain" from the investigation to the lawsuit. The conclusion is: "in addition to thinking about the effectiveness of the prohibition of discrimination, we need to think about access to justice as a longer path" (CNJ, 2022). And, of course, the law as just one of the ways to combat LGBTphobia.

What about misogyny or gender-based hate? In Brazilian law, the only provision for the concept of "misogyny"is in the Lola Law, which, as has already been discussed, assigned the Federal Police to investigate internet crimes that "disseminate misogynistic content", defined as those that "propagate hatred or aversion to women". We also saw that the Feminicide Law of 2015 includes "contempt for or discrimination against women" as one of the two hypotheses that qualify a homicide as feminicide. But this applies to murder cases, i.e. when misogyny has reached its peak. There is no provision in the law for misogynistic discourse as such: when faced with it, the avenues offered by the law are the "common" ones, which do not qualify misogyny as something specific. For example, the cases in which misogynistic speech can be qualified as defamation or a threat, without specifying whether they are misogynistic or not, and within an individualised lawsuit.

Between 2020 and 2021, we at InternetLab carried out a study to understand what the Brazilian judiciary did when facing cases involving online misogyny.[18] Studying freedom of expression in the Brazilian judiciary is not a simple task because there is not really what you would call a jurisprudence of freedom of expression. The criteria for restriction or balance with other rights are often applied in very different ways. As there is no provision for misogyny in Brazilian law and the rulings do not mention the term, we face an even more difficult task, both methodologically and in gauging conclusions. We needed to search the databases using a large set of keywords to try to find cases that could be subsumed to the definition of misogyny since it was impossible to search by the mention of a law or a specific criminal offence.[19] We also aimed to separate only those cases in which the aggressor used a misogynistic term in "public" environments or shared by more people than just the aggressor and the victim—in order to fulfil the criterion of incitement that is at the heart of the concept of hate speech. In other words, we consider posts in feeds, groups, pages, tweets, stories, and the like. We found many cases of private aggression containing strong misogyny, but we did not analyse them to try to isolate the episodes that occurred in the public sphere. As I mentioned in the previous chapter, defining what is public and what is private, on the internet, is not always simple, because content travels quite dynamically—from messaging apps to social networks and vice versa, blurring the boundaries. But these

[18]We scraped data from six Courts of Justice (Bahia, Federal District and Territories, Pará, Minas Gerais, Santa Catarina, and São Paulo) using the R programming language. I would like to thank programmer Alessandra Gomes, who carried out this work with great competence, as well as the researchers Blenda Santos, Catharina Pereira, Clarice Tavares, Ester Borges, Fernanda K. Martins, Jade Becari, Juliana Fonteles, Natália Neris, and Thiago Oliva, who worked on this project at various stages, read judicial decisions, and led other initiatives that emerged as developments from the initial project. Regarding the jurisprudence research mentioned here, one of the materials produced, presenting preliminary results, was: Fernanda Martins et al. (2020).

[19]We used "misogyny", "misogynist", "misogynist and discourse", "feminism", "feminist", "violence and women", "sexism", "sexist", "machismo", and "machista", combined separately with "internet", "social network", "Facebook", "WhatsApp", "Twitter", and "YouTube". As these words generated many false positives, we ran another algorithm separating the decisions most likely to be relevant based on the repetition of keywords.

boundaries are also blurred by the legal system: many cases that occur in public are read as cases of domestic violence, as long as they involve current or former partners of the victims. As a result, the public dimension of violence and the understanding of the social imaginary of how women are read and treated are erased.[20]

Our conclusions, therefore, gave many more clues as to which cases reach the judiciary and the ways in which they are dealt with, than firm conclusions can be replicated. Therefore, the examples I bring here are somewhat anecdotal. One of the things we discovered was that many cases involved a reading of women's lives and morals and fell within a typology that finds close resemblance with other studies, both from us and from other researchers. We classified eight types of cases: hypersexualisation, association of women with prostitution (understood as a disvalue), questioning of women's performance in terms of motherhood, interlinking between gender prejudices and other social markers of difference (i.e. race, ethnicity, sexuality, etc.), questioning of women's professional capacity (such as associating professional success with sexual favours), threats, NCII, and, finally, pointing out "moral defects", such as suggestions of betrayal, scamming, and bad character.

Sexuality was very manifest, whether in the form of criticism or exposure of sexual practices in public. This confirms the conclusions of other studies carried out in Brazil. For example, in a questionnaire administered to teenagers in Brasilia, University of Brasilia professor Valeska Zanello identified sexual behaviour as the type of name-calling considered the worst by both women and men—in the case of men, name-calling with a passive sexual character, such as "faggot", "pussy", and "cuckold" (Zanello, 2008).[21] The second "worst" category is what she calls "relational character traits": "values attributed to women as being 'naturally' their own", such as the "feminine essence" linked to caring for others, the expectation of delicacy, of giving. The insults of selfish, arrogant, cold and bad mum are of this nature—and are also a form of social control.

In our research, we found that, in fact, in the criminal sphere, the cases were classified under other categories, such as threats, crimes against honour (slander, libel, and defamation), and "disturbance of tranquillity". The vast majority of aggressors were male[22]; most of them were former partners,[23] some of them current. And most of the cases went to the courts as domestic violence, even though we restricted the search to "public" cases.[24] In civil cases—where financial reparation is generally sought (but it can be an injunction, such as a request for content removal), rather than a criminal offence—the types of cases were much more diverse, and less than a third involved partners or ex-partners. These results may indicate the difficulty of understanding hate speech in the public sphere when the case does not involve domestic violence.

In some cases, it was particularly apparent that misogyny is not recognised. For example, there was a case judged by the Minas Gerais Court of Justice involving the Brazilian Funk group UDR. Brazilian Funk is a genre that takes influence from Afro-Brazilian religions, Miami bass, freestyle, popularised in Rio de Janeiro favelas in the 1980s. It is both very popular and very stigmatised—even criminalised (Cymrot, 2022). UDR musicians were convicted for songs they posted on the internet, which they claimed were satirical. And despite the deplorable content of the songs, there seems to have been a lot of selec-

[20] In an interview, public prosecutor Silvia Chakian mentioned the possibility that this framing is being used strategically by both defence attorneys and the Public Prosecutor's Office, due to the lack of more suitable legal provisions for cases that occur in public. See Silvia Chakian (2021).

[21] "Boiola", "viadinho", e "corno", respectively, in Portuguese.

[22] Seventy-seven of the 81 cases, judging by the names—an approach that certainly leads to mistakes, though likely not major ones.

[23] Sixty-one cases, six of which involved current partners.

[24] Domestic violence is not a crime in itself; the Maria da Penha Law establishes certain special circumstances when a crime occurs in connection with an intimate, domestic, or family relationship, but it does not create new offenses (except for one, added later, regarding the violation of protective measures).

tivity in the result. The content included racism, religious intolerance, transphobia, and misogyny—some verses were odes to rape (as in the song "Bonde da Mutilação" or "Mutilation Gang"). The complaint, however, was for the offences of racism and religious intolerance (as well as incitement to crime), and misogyny and transphobia are not even mentioned in the decision. This does not even seem to stem from the fact that they do not find legal expression; the issue seems to be a lack of vocabulary and recognition in the sociocultural sphere.[25] In any case, the selectivity that I have recognised here is essential if we are to critically debate the way out of criminalisation.

A body of research on applying antiracism legislation in the Brazilian judiciary has reached important conclusions that dialogue with this diagnosis. The Antiracism Law (Law No. 7716/89) underwent a meaningful change in 1997 as the current description of the crime of racism was introduced. This same reform created the offence of *racial insult* in the Criminal Code, a qualified form of the common insult, i.e. with a higher penalty. In 2023, the law was reformed to equate the offences of racism and racial insult: racial insult was expressly made one of the forms of the offence of racism, while before, it was only a crime under the Criminal Code, with more lenient penalties. It was also made explicit that the so-called recreational racism—offences uttered as "jokes" or "pranks"—is racism.

Before this change, which has not yet been translated into much research, a study by researchers Marta Machado, Márcia Lima, and Natália Neris from the Brazilian Center for Analysis and Planning (Cebrap) identified that the vast majority of cases that reached the courts were verbal offences, i.e. racist slurs. Among the significant number of acquittals, they identified that the most common reason was a lack of evidence, either of the event or of the "intention to discriminate"—without adequate justification and without uniform criteria. In some cases, judges stated that the case did not involve racism—for example, with the argument that "Black piece of shit" was the equivalent of "short piece of shit". In many cases, the acquittal was on the grounds that the offence occurred "in the heat of the discussion". One of the researchers' findings is that the decisions show a failure to recognise racism in Brazilian society or how insults are in maintaining social dynamics (Machado et al., 2016). More recent research by the Getúlio Vargas Foundation in Brazil, in partnership with Afro-Cebrap and InternetLab, looking at court decisions involving racism on the internet, shows that the race and gender of the victims and perpetrators are rarely mentioned in the decisions (Machado et al., 2022).

What will happen after the 2023 change (which only applies to cases that occur after it) is still to be understood. Even so, an episode that became known on social media shows the face of the problem: the same year, the famous Brazilian singer Ludmilla sued the TV host Marcão do Povo, who called her "poor and a monkey". She lost the case at first instance because the judge ruled that there was no intention to offend (O Globo, 2023).

The parallel with the study on misogyny in the Judiciary is obvious: although legal provisions play a role, judges' failure to recognise the terms of the conflict is fundamental to the lack of concrete effectiveness of these laws. The absence of a legal vocabulary in the case of misogyny certainly contributes to this since there is not even a provision on which to base the analysis.

It is worth remembering that if the cases are not homogeneous, neither is the judiciary. Despite the trend, there are some surprising cases. For example, among those we analysed, the São Paulo Court of Appeals ruled in favour of a Public Civil Action, a form of class action that can be presented by state actors and some civil society associations, brought by the São Paulo State Public Defender's Office for the removal of videos on Facebook, Twitter, and YouTube which incited violence against women and LGBTQIAP+ people.[26] On 11 March 2016, the same court con-

[25]The reference for the decision is *Criminal Appeal No. 1.0024.12.266703-3/001*.

[26]Court of Justice of São Paulo, Interlocutory Appeal No. 2130844-48.2016.8.26.0000, December 14, 2016.

firmed the conviction of the Brazilian brewing company Ambev at first instance in a case brought by Procon, Brazil's consumer protection agency, to pay a fine for abusive advertising because it was discriminatory. It was an advert for a beer brand, Skol, where a "summer muse" was cloned and delivered to men in various places; some refused because the "muse" had come "defective". The "moral of the story" was that if Skol's creator had invented the muse of summer, she would always come defectless to all men (in correlation with the brand's beer). The decision explicitly addresses gender issues:

> In this context of the commodification of women, you cannot ignore gender issues and say, as the author does, that the advert only invokes symbols of summer, such as the sun, the sea, a scene in which men and women appear celebrating in beachwear. In fact, what you see in the film are "cloned women", loaded into trolleys, the kind you see in supermarkets, being delivered by men to men. In the author's own words, the idea is to convey the message that, in that fantastic world, women with the muse phenotype would be available to any man, just like Skol beers. The advert's argument is more than unfortunate, as it "objectifies" women, serving them up for the consumer's enjoyment. In other words, the female gender is transformed into a consumer object. [...] Finally, Brazilian advertising, recognised worldwide for its creative capacity, has shown that the public's intelligence cannot be subjugated: [...] Procon's action is the result of the conscience that inhabits the collective, in the sense that unlikely associations between women's bodies and consumer objects cannot be encouraged.[27]

4.3 Women: A Minority?

The low level of recognition of misogyny that seems to be possible to identify in the judiciary and in society, and the absence of a legal conceptualisation of misogyny or its equation with other forms of discrimination, raises an important question about women. One way to begin to address this issue is: What is a minority, and who can be a victim? In a 2005 paper, the Brazilian sociologist Muniz Sodré discusses the quantitative and qualitative notions of minorities, which are so important for representative democracy.

> In democracy, they say, the will of the majority prevails. That's true, but it's a quantitative argument. Qualitatively, democracy is a regime of minorities, because only in the democratic process can the minority make itself heard. A minority here is a qualitative voice.

Being a minority, thus, refers to the possibility of having an active voice and intervening in decision-making bodies—a location that is not topographical, but topological. The minority place is where flows of transformation of an identity or a power relationship take place, and it is impossible to separate the notion of minority from legal-social vulnerability (a political party is not a minority) and from the counter-hegemonic struggle, especially through discursive strategies. Thus, says Sodré, Black people, homosexuals, women, indigenous peoples, environmentalists, etc., are minorities.

With this, Muniz Sodré (2005) implicitly questions the importance of the European concept of minority—the recognition of quantitative minority groups within a Nation-state, as formulated in international law—restricted to ethnicity and national belonging, and to the concept of legal subjects. While these concepts were being developed between the 1960s and the 1970s, social groups in colonised countries were still fighting for their recognition as legal subjects. Because of this European origin, post- and decolonial theorists criticise the use of the concept of minorities, which seems to refer to something crystallised, an individual and collective quality of subjects, concealing power relations—it is these, in fact, that "minoritise" people. Referring to "minorities" as something universal, in an uprooted way, glosses over complex local realities and equates different collectivities under the same category. (This can also be emphasised about "hate speech", which, we have seen, contains differences between the groups that are victimised and even varying recognition.)

[27] An unavailing vote by judge Coimbra Schmidt considered the advert a good piece of humour, stating that "on the beaches, women's outfits are increasingly skimpy. It is a fact that the ideal of the muse has been part of the male imagination since ancient times". Tribunal de Justiça de São Paulo, Apelação n. 0005431-07.2010.8.26.0053, 7a Câmara de Direito Privado, 11 mar. 2016.

In an article from 2022, Raquel Freitas and Luciana Nóbrega, from the Federal University of Ceará, show how none of the most current constitutions in Latin America use the concept of minorities but rather the concepts of self-determination, recognition of difference, and diversity of social groups—particularly in the Andean countries, where the struggles of social groups have led to the recognition of the autonomy of ethnic and racial groups (Freitas & Nóbrega, 2022). For this reason, there are many activists and theorists who, from a decolonial perspective, prefer to talk about socially and politically minoritised or subalternised groups.

And what about women? As the University of Basel professor Andrea Maihofer says, theory currently accepts widely that gender and sex are not anthropological constants, essential to human beings as nature (although there are differences of opinion about how the process of social construction of gender takes place). Even so, in the social sphere, biological differences are sufficient to explain gender inequalities (Maihofer, 2016). The University of Brasilia professor Maria Helena Fávero argues that this "naturalisation" or "biologisation"of gendered practices, of what is "typically feminine or masculine", and crucially of the dichotomy of "emotion versus reason", is one of the most important justifications for men's exercise of power over women.[28]

The biologisation of differences makes the dispute over them complex, which is evident in the popular conservative discourse on "gender ideology" in Brazil. It must be remembered that, despite this biologisation, different groups of women suffer discrimination and violence in very variable ways, depending on their position and identity in relation to the markers of race, ethnicity, social class, territory, and others. In any case, the specific erasure of the "gender" variable has a lot to do with biologisation. Even the figure of the victim is a way of giving recognition and intelligibility to situations of suffering. This process also invisibilises victims who do not correspond to constructed ideals, as Unesp professor Cynthia Sarti (2011) says.

The conquer of celebrated women's rights milestones in the field of domestic violence, such as the Maria da Penha Law, obviously has to do with the high incidence and seriousness of this type of violence. In turn, the fact that other types of violence, particularly those that concern women's participation in the public sphere, receive less attention also seems to be related to this biologisation—women are not even seen as subjects who are present in the public sphere or who should be there.[29]

Despite this diagnosis that misogyny is socially and legally under-recognised, there are some notable cases in which the justice system has dealt with this specific problem from a collective perspective. For example, in 2021, the Federal Prosecutor's Office won a case in the first instance against the Federal Government for discriminatory speeches and acts by Jair Bolsonaro government's speeches and acts against women. The argument, replete with data on violence against women, was developed to prove that these statements caused collective moral damage. The Office referred to statements such as:

> Jair Bolsonaro: "Brazil cannot be a paradise for gay tourism. Anyone who wants to come here and have sex with a woman is free to do so. Now, it can't become known as a paradise for the gay world here".
> "She wanted a scoop. She wanted to lick a scoop! At any price against me."[30]
> "Then I invited them [...] to fly here and in Europe. If there's one hectare of (devastated) forest, you're

[28]Fávero shows how boys and girls feel emotions in very similar ways, but girls are socialized to express emotions more often; furthermore, the types of emotions deemed acceptable differ for each gender (Fávero, 2011). However, "the fact that Western gender categories are presented as inherent to nature (of bodies), and operate within a dichotomous duality—male/female, man/woman—where the male is presumed superior and, therefore, the defining category, is particularly alien to many African cultures. When African realities are interpreted through these Western assumptions, what we find are distortions, linguistic mystifications, and often a total lack of understanding due to the incommensurability of categories and social institutions" (translated by Juliana Araújo Lopes).

[29]I have discussed this in more detail in Valente (2022).

[30]Referring to journalist Patrícia Campos Mello, who investigated his campaign practices, a story that will be explored further in this book.

right. That's the big reality. Brazil is a virgin that every pervert from abroad wants. Excuse the women here, OK?"
"There's a fluffy MP from São Paulo and another half-Japanese MP who are criticising him on social media. If they were doing good things, the first would be thinner and the second would be less of a shameless prick … I think lying makes you fat, lying makes you fat."
Paulo Guedes, Minister of Economy: "I'm seeing progress on several fronts, but the concern is: they cursed Bachelet, they cursed Macron's wife, they called his wife ugly. 'Oh, Macron said they're setting fire to the Brazilian forest, the president gave it back. He said his wife was ugly'. All right, it's fun. There's no problem, it's all true, the president did say it. And it's really true, his wife is really ugly."
Damares Alves, Minister of Human Rights: "Women should be submissive. Within Christian doctrine, yes. Within Christian doctrine, within the Church, we understand that in a marriage between a man and a woman, the man is the leader of the marriage. So this is a perception within my church, within my faith. [...] What a pretty [female] MP. Just the fact that you're in parliament. You didn't even have to open your mouth. Just the fact that you're here tells young people out there that they can get here, too."
"Why do parents exploit [their children sexually]? Is it because of hunger? We're going to take businesses to the island of Marajó, we're going to meet the needs of those people. Some experts even told us here in the cabinet that the girls there are exploited because they don't have knickers. They don't wear knickers, they're very poor."
Ernesto Araújo, Minister of External Relations: "Today, a man looking at a woman is already attempted rape."

The Federal Government was ordered to pay a fine of five million reais and to carry out awareness campaigns on women's rights worth ten million reais (about 1.7 million USD). The judge who decided the case affirmed that the speeches of public agents and servants, particularly in the exercise of their public functions, have special weight on people, and stated that these speeches offend the dignity of women and are not covered by freedom of expression.[31]

[31]Ação Civil Pública Cível (65) n. 5014547-70.2020.4.03.6100/6a Vara Cível Federal de São Paulo.

4.4 Freedom of Expression? Lawsuits Against Women

In Brazil and many countries in the world, any argument favouring content removal strategies or prevention against misogynistic speech will be quickly objected to on the grounds of freedom of expression. This is not a minor issue: vaguely formulated legal concepts can lead to the censorship of legitimate speech on account of other powerful interests. The public debate and expression of ideas on issues, including gender, is a democratic requisite. But two major points are rendered invisible by the simplistic objection. The first is that, as I have been pointing out referring to research in Brazil, misogyny is not even widely recognised, whether socially, culturally, or legally. Few court rulings ever set misogyny against freedom of expression, because misogyny itself rarely even appears in legal arguments—just like racism. The second is that this argument considers the freedom of expression of those who issue misogynistic speeches but not of the victims of the speeches. And there is a very close link between misogyny and the expression of women and other subjects affected by it.

In 2021, Irene Khan, the UN Special Rapporteur on Freedom of Expression, published a report on gender and freedom of expression, which identified that harassment, censorship, and discrimination affect women's ability to express themselves online worldwide. It was not the first time international organisations have looked at this issue.[32] She argues that while online plat-

[32]Already in 2013, the UN Human Rights Council adopted a resolution affirming the role of women's freedom of opinion and expression in their interaction with society, especially in economic and political participation, and a "deep concern" that violence such as discrimination, intimidation and harassment and violence, *including* in public spaces, prevent women from exercising their human rights (A/HRC/RES/23/2, available at: https://www.refworld.org/docid/53bd1c254.htm. Accessed on: March 18, 2025). These intersections were the subject of the independent expert report on protection against violence and discrimination based on sexual orientation and gender identity in 2019: https://undocs.org/A/74/181. Accessed on: March 18, 2025) and the Special Rapporteur for Minorities at the UN General Assembly in 2021 (A/HRC/46/57, https://undocs.org/en/A/HRC/46/57.

forms have become increasingly important for women's expression, they have also been used to silence women's voices through harassment and abuse. I discussed the use of the internet (and platforms) for self-discovery, collective solidarity, and the formation of feminist counter-publics in the second chapter. But the evolution I portray in this book also shows an escalade, over time, of misogynistic strategies of silencing and their normalisation. The 2022 CIGI survey, mentioned a few times, showed higher numbers of women and LGBTQIAP+ people who had their internet use affected after episodes of violence. And Brazil leads the way in these figures: 56% of the Brazilian population (compared to 38% of people in the global figures) and 60% of women said their freedom of political expression had been affected (Valente, 2023).

The debate on freedom of expression and misogyny is so distorted that it does not usually take into account or adequately value a fundamental point: the lawsuits against women who publicly denounce violence, which are on the rise and have been called lawfare. Some cases have gone public.

After filing a police report for rape that was not pursued (according to her lawyers, the investigation was superficial and the enquiry was closed, but the accused was not acquitted), Brazilian journalist Amanda Audi spoke out on social media about the case and named the accused, university professor Alexandre Andrada. He won an injunction against her in 2021, banning her from talking about the case. However, her lawyer and activist Isabela Del Monde reported that he continued to post and give interviews on the subject (Del Monde et al., 2022). In 2022, Audi won both the civil and criminal lawsuits against her, arguing that it was legitimate for her to speak about the case and the way the complaint was handled, and that the plaintiff had not proven that the facts were false.

At around the same time, two other famous people sued women who reported having suffered sexual violence from them: Neymar, the football star, and the Brazilian funk artist Nego do Borel. Only the latter—a Black, Brazilian funk musician—did not have his injunction granted, which points to the contradictions of justice in Brazil—who does it shield?[33] In 2023, TV host Titi Müller revealed that she was prevented from talking about the seven lawsuits between her and her ex-husband Tomás Bertoni by an injunction after she spoke on social media about having suffered physical and psychological violence since her pregnancy. According to her, the extent of the ban involved not speaking about him or his family on social media (CNN Brasil, 2023). The restriction was revoked two months later (G1, 2023). Our research in the Brazilian judiciary also identified some cases, most of them with favourable outcomes for the women.[34] But, as already discussed referring to Lola Aronovich's case, being prosecuted is by itself already costly and intimidating.

Accessed on: March 18, 2025).

[33]Although both of them are Black, Nego do Borel is connected to a sitgmatised cultural expression, while football players are highly valued. About these cases, see also Góis (2021).

[34]In the five state-level courts of second instance that we analysed, we found five cases that fit this category. In four of them, the women won; in one, she did not. The four cases where the women prevailed were as follows: a man requested that Twitter and Facebook remove content and accounts, and implement filters to prevent future posts about him from those accounts (Interlocutory Appeal No. 2143875-96.2020.8.26.0000, Court of Justice of São Paulo—TJ-SP); a man requested protective measures under the Maria da Penha Law against his ex-wife to prevent her from speaking about him on social media (Civil Appeal No. 1004126-87.2017.8.26.0323, TJ-SP); a woman who posted online about federal congressman Alberto Fraga (PL-DF), accusing him of inciting femicide after he reportedly said that "a woman who talks tough needs to be beaten", was sued for moral damages but won the case (Civil Appeal No. 0030262-36.2015.8.07.0001, Court of Justice of the Federal District—TJ-DF, May 10, 2017); a student in Blumenau who had posted online about sexism among male students succeeded in having her removed post reinstated (Civil Appeal No. 2014.002980-7, Court of Justice of Santa Catarina—TJ-SC, May 26, 2014). In one case, however, a female student who posted about abuse following a relationship with a professor was sued by him and lost both in the first and second instances (though the compensation amount was reduced). The court ruled against her on the grounds that she had not proven the events (Civil Appeal No. 0500792-59.2013.8.24.0045, TJ-SC, February 7, 2018).

It goes without saying that people who have had their reputations damaged on the web can seek redress. But in a country where, as the lawyer and researcher Tainã Góis (2021) points out, 39% of women have suffered sexual violence and only 10% of these cases are reported, it has to be recognised that the problem does not lie in empty reports but in the immense lack of reports. If the internet has begun to be used as a space for aggregating demands and as a way of making cases against powerful people visible, lawsuits of this nature and the threat of them, when designed to silence, silence not only the women involved but all those who could report cases of potential violence.

The terms of the public debate on the conflict between freedom of expression and equality are often formalistic and do not consider people's concrete capacity to express themselves. Moving further, the most simplistic objections tend to defend the speech of White men, especially when referring to the fight against "political correctness". If the debate is about free thought and expression, we need to talk about what concerns women, in all their diversity, and the conditions in which they can exercise it. We need to talk about the link between passing laws to combat TFGBV and freedom of expression.

4.5 The Anti-Stalking Law

In the last chapter, I spoke about the passing of the Rose Leonel Law and the Sexual Importunacy Law, which came in the wake of a debate about gender-based violence that had gained body and expression in the Brazilian public sphere. Years later, in 2021, the Stalking Law (Law No. 14,132/2021) was passed, which created the offence of stalking in the Criminal Code, with the following text:

> Art. 147-A. Stalking someone, repeatedly and by any means, threatening their physical or psychological integrity, restricting their ability to move or, in any way, invading or disturbing their sphere of freedom or privacy.
> Penalty—imprisonment from 6 (six) months to 2 (two) years and a fine.
> § Paragraph 1 The penalty is increased by half if the offence is committed:
> i—against a child, adolescent or elderly person;
> ii—against a woman because of her sex, under the terms of §2-A of Article 121 of this Code;
> iii—by means of a conspiracy of two (2) or more persons or with the use of a weapon.
> § Paragraph 2 The penalties in this article shall apply without prejudice to the penalties for the underlying violence.
> § Paragraph 3: The criminal proceedings depend on the victim's representation [a formal authorization].

At least since the 1930s, there have been many examples of the criminalisation of stalking around the world. In Brazil, the origin of this law was a bill by MP Leila Barros (Brazilian Socialist Party, PSB). As she herself mentioned in the bill's justification, these situations previously fell under the "criminal contravention" of "disturbing the tranquillity of others". A criminal contravention is less serious than a criminal offence from a legal point of view, like a misdemeanour or a violation. MP Barros argued that stalking had become more serious because of social media, and it needed a new legal standing. In fact, obsessive and compulsive stalking behaviour can take on very serious contours: a 1999 survey in the United States stated that 76% of femicides in the country were preceded by stalking (McFarlane et al., 1999). The internet provides extra opportunities for such behaviour. Over the ten years, I have been working in the field of online violence, I have been contacted by victims of various types of cases, and have conducted initial talks to help conduct them to protection services. There have been many cases of stalking.

I followed Natalia's case for years.[35] Her ex-boyfriend would not accept the end of the relationship and kept contacting her obsessively. After she blocked him on all the social networks and messaging apps, he created fake profiles and added several of her acquaintances and work colleagues, created different emails to send her messages that were at times passionate, at times aggressive and with threatening sub-text, contacted people to ask about her, asked mutual friends and family members to ask her to talk to

[35] Fictitious name.

him. Sometimes, he would cool off; months later, he would return. Natália moved country and started a new work, and was very afraid that he would write to her new bosses, as she would feel very exposed. Among the emails she did not reply to, one day came one describing her new address, with the message that he would soon be on a plane to meet her. She began to fear leaving the house alone and went through various materials, psychological and emotional upheavals.

From the point of view of the tools available to protect the victim, it is quite difficult to prevent such behaviour: blocking or reporting the profiles is ineffective because the person creates multiple profiles, and the communications come from unexpected places. Individual actions may not be illegal. Creating a fake profile and sending messages are not prohibited acts. And, of course, stalking often results in other violence—the fear of it adds another layer of suffering. In Natália's case, fortunately, this did not happen, and the aggressor at one time stopped. At least until now. Because he was an ex-boyfriend, the shortest route would have been to apply for a protective order under the Maria da Penha Law, but she gave up after talking to a lawyer and realising the hardships involved in doing that from another country. If the stalker, however, was a stranger or someone with no previous romantic relationship, protective measures would not be an option, but she could go down the route of suing for the "criminal contravention" of disturbing tranquillity (which was finally abolished by the Stalking Law).

In MP Leila Barros' initial bill, there was a provision that the police authority would immediately inform a judge at the beginning of the investigation, to facilitate granting protective precautionary measures to the victim—in other words, in addition to the penalty, protection. This provision was dropped when the bill was voted on in the Senate's Constitution, Justice and Citizenship Committee (CCJ), because of an understanding that the Code of Criminal Procedure already provided for the submission of the investigations to a judge in the case of catching someone in the action (which is undoubtedly stricter than what Barros was proposing). The initial version also did not mention children, the elderly, or women. It was in the House of Representatives after no less than eleven other bills with similar content had already been proposed, that the final wording was given. The gendered nature of this violence, which expresses notions of ownership over the other, was partially recognised. Partially, because it was not an increase in the penalty based on gender that was envisaged, but "against a woman because of her condition as a female"—a wording that echoes the moral panic surrounding the word gender in the Brazilian Parliament and in politics in the context of the presidency of Jair Bolsonaro, who would sanction the law in 2021.

Article 147-A has been included in the Criminal Code's chapter on offences against personal liberty, so it concerns the right to come, go, and act. There is no requirement for an actual deprivation of individual freedom in order for it to be classed as persecution; the article seeks to protect against the very threat to physical and psychological integrity, and for this, there must have been insistence and concrete elements threatening liberty (Gennarini, 2021).

From the beginning of the discussion of the bill, some criticised the open and imprecise nature of the crime of persecution (Pacheco, 2021). It is quite common that when a crime or any legal concept is created, people and groups concerned with individual freedoms argue that, no matter how good the intentions, that concept can be used for unwanted purposes. This was also the case, for example, when the Anti-Terrorism Bill (passed as Law No. 13,260/2016) was debated: the imprecise definition of terrorism would allow interpretation according to convenience and the framing of various standard practices of social movements as terrorism.

The Stalking Law has, in fact, been used for cases of stalking, such as those described. A news piece from 2021 reported that, in Ceará alone, twenty people had gone to a police station with cases that were framed as such, nineteen of them women and one man (Brisa, 2021). However, the way in which the offence of stalking was actually used for deviant purposes was quite unpredictable.

In 2020, a trio of young people from Minas Gerais and Paraná created the Sleeping Giants Brazil profile on Twitter. Like the Sleeping Giants in the United States, they began to promote actions for advertising companies to position themselves in the face of hateful or disinformation content sponsored by them in the context of the pandemic and the Jair Bolsonaro government. The strategy was simple: advertising money provides the conditions for those who make this type of content grow and thrive, and sponsors are either not fully aware or turn a blind eye, and then public embarrassment turns off the tap. Sleeping Giants Brazil took action against *Jornal da Cidade Online*, an extreme right-wing outlet known for fabricating news, and began calling on Twitter for brands such as McDonald's, Facebook, and Domino's Pizza to take a public stance. The brands began to withdraw. In response, *Jornal da Cidade Online* filed a lawsuit demanding that Twitter identify who was behind the account. Twitter claims to have resisted, but lost, and handed over the IPs. As a result, two of the members of Sleeping Giants Brasil went public, identifying themselves, to prevent the lawsuit from exposing their families as well (Biller, 2020).

But the Sleeping Giants Brazil faced yet another lawsuit. After running a campaign, they were sued by radio station Jovem Pan, which alleged defamation and asked for their profiles to be blocked and their bank and phone records to be breached (Coalizão Direitos na Rede, 2023), and by the TV host Sikêra Jr., also a target of the campaign because of his LGBTphobic remarks.[36] In 2021, Sikêra Jr. obtained an injunction to stop the campaign and sued Sleeping Giants Brasil for financial losses; the group sued back, claiming bad faith litigation.[37] But the part that interests us explicitly here is that, in June 2021, the Manaus Police Department for Cybercrime started an investigation following a police report by Sikêra Jr. to investigate three crimes: libel, defamation, and the crime of stalking (MZ Notícia, 2021).

Sikêra Jr.'s lawyers detailed the way the Sleeping Giants Brazil developed the campaign to demonetise his show—tagging advertisers and asking other people to demand them as well—claiming that it consisted of stalking, without going into more detail about what characterises this crime. Based on these grounds, the police chief requested an extensive breach of the telematics secrecy of the group's accounts with various internet companies, which was granted. It was then that the third member of the group came to light. As this book was being written, the group was still waiting for the investigation to move forward.

This case illustrates the need to remain alert to open-ended legal formulations, particularly in criminal law, because they can be used for very different purposes than initially thought. In this case, the instrumentalisation of the Stalking Law against the Sleeping Giants Brazil goes against the interest of combating violent and misogynistic practices since the group seeks to cut off funding for those who propagate hate speech propagators—and does so in an intelligent and non-violent way, by exposing the contradictions between the values brands profess and the causes they actually fund. Legal action against them attempts to silence and intimidate and, at the very least, generates difficulties and costs. So the concern is not unfounded.

As a side note, in the same year, the Criminal Code was amended to include a crime of psychological violence against women:

> Art. 147-B. Causing emotional harm to a woman that harms her and disturbs her full development or that aims to degrade or control her actions, behaviour, beliefs and decisions, through threats, embarrassment, humiliation, manipulation, isolation, blackmail, ridicule, limitation of the right to come and go or any other means that causes harm to her psychological health and self-determination:
> Penalty—imprisonment, from 6 (six) months to 2 (two) years, and a fine, if the conduct does not constitute a more serious crime. (Included by Law No. 14.188, of 2021)

[36]At that specific time, for calling LGBTQIAP+ people a "wretched race", but he is known for lines like "can you imagine having a faggot child and not being able to kill it?", "You disgust me", etc.

[37]And the Federal Public Prosecutors Office, two years later, sued Sikêra Jr. on the basis of Law No. 7716/89 (Intervozes, 2023). He was also convicted in January 2025 in a civil lawsuit brought by the Federal Public Defender's Office; there are other pending lawsuits.

While the very general text may imply it can be used against different practices, the amendment was in the context of strengthening measures around the Maria da Penha Law, that is, relating to domestic violence, and to include a provision on psychological violence in the Criminal Code, reflecting its recognition as a form of violence under that law. The general character of this provision raises concerns similar to those pointed regarding the stalking provision. This Article would become more critical for TFGBV in the future, as it was the basis for an initiative to criminalise *deepfakes*. But that is a topic for Chap. 6.

References

Aronovich, L. (2008, October 21). *A ordem dos homens de bem quer que as mulheres morram*. Escreva Lola Escreva. Retrieved March 18, 2025, from https://escrevalolaescreva.blogspot.com/2008/10/ordem-dos-homens-de-bem-quer-que-as.html

Aronovich, L. (2022). A trajetória e resistência do Escreva Lola Escreva. *Estudos Feministas, 30*. http://www.scielo.br/j/ref/a/MZ3PGMd3bZmNFncPfBypMPv/abstract/?lang=pt

Baptista, R. (2020, November 24). *"Senti que existe justiça", diz Lola sobre vitória em ação contra misógino*. UOL Tilt. Retrieved March 18, 2025, from https://www.uol.com.br/tilt/noticias/redacao/2020/11/24/lola-aronovich-celebra-vitoria-judicial-em-caso-contra-mascu.htm

Barker, K., & Jurasz, O. (2018). *Online misogyny as hate crime: A challenge for legal regulation?* Routledge.

Biller, D. (2020, December 13). *Swift backlash for Brazil students targeting misinformation*. Associated Press. Retrieved March 18, 2025, from https://apnews.com/article/brazil-rio-de-janeiro-misinformation-coronavirus-pandemic-latin-america-ba4a7dbd4b57a53a6c4748aeb94b9bde

Blais, M., & Dupuis-Déri, F. (2012). Masculinism and the antifeminist countermovement. *Social Movement Studies: Journal of Social, Cultural and Political Protest, 11*(1), 21–39.

Brisa, M. (2021, July 31). *Ceará registra 20 casos de stalking desde sanção de lei; entenda o crime*. O Povo.

Brugger, W. (2007). Proibição ou proteção do discurso do ódio? Algumas observações sobre o direito alemão e o americano. *Direito Publico, 4*(15) Retrieved March 18, 2025, from https://www.portaldeperiodicos.idp.edu.br/direitopublico/article/view/1418

Câmara dos Deputados. (2017, November 10). *Diário da Câmara dos Deputados* (p. 553). https://imagem.camara.gov.br/Imagem/d/pdf/DCD0020171110001980000.PDF#page=553

Chakian, S. (2021). *Existem outras formas de contenção social que não apenas a legal-penal [Interview]*. InternetLab. Retrieved March 18, 2025, from https://internetlab.org.br/pt/especial/existem-outras-formas-de-contencao-social-que-nao-apenas-a-legal-penal

Christofoletti, R., & Laux, A. P. F. (2008). Confiabilidade, credibilidade e reputação: No jornalismo e na blogosfera. *Intercom: Revista Brasileira de Ciências da Comunicação*. Retrieved March 18, 2025, from https://revistas.intercom.org.br/index.php/revistaintercom/article/view/194

CNN Brasil. (2023, February 23). *Titi Müller é proibida de falar do ex-marido, Tomás Bertoni, nas redes sociais*. CNN Brasil. Retrieved March 18, 2025, from https://www.cnnbrasil.com.br/entretenimento/titi-muller-e-proibida-de-falar-do-ex-marido-tomas-bertoni-nas-redes-sociais/

Coalizão Direitos na Rede. (2023, March 22). *Manifestação de apoio ao Sleeping Giants Brasil (SGBR)*. Coalizão Direitos na Rede. Retrieved March 18, 2025, from https://direitosnarede.org.br/2023/03/22/manifestacao-de-apoio-ao-sleeping-giants-brasil-sgbr

Coelho, L. (2021, March 9). Sol, Luciana, Elidia, massacres de Suzano e Realengo: As 23 vítimas do terrorismo misógino. *Ponte Jornalismo*. Retrieved March 18, 2025, from https://ponte.org/sol-luciana-elidia-massacres-de-suzano-e-realengo-as-23-vitimas-do-terrorismo-misogino

Conselho Nacional de Justiça (CNJ). (2022). *Discriminação e violência contra a população LGBTQIA+: Relatório da pesquisa*. CNJ/PNUD. Retrieved March 18, 2025, from https://www.cnj.jus.br/wp-content/uploads/2022/08/relatorio-pesquisa-discriminacao-e-violencia-contra-lgbtqia.pdf

Cymrot, D. (2022). *O funk na batida: Baile, rua e parlamento*. Edições Sesc SP.

da Silva, R. L., Nichel, A., Martins, A. C. L., et al. (2011). Discursos de ódio em redes sociais: jurisprudência brasileira. *Revista Direito GV, 7*, 445–468.

de Oliveira, J. R. (2021). Uma reflexão crítica sobre a representação social do discurso de ódio. *Investigações, 34*(2) Retrieved March 18, 2025, from https://periodicos.ufpe.br/revistas/INV/article/view/248457

de Souza, L. T., Petroli, D. P., & Magalhães, L. V. N. (2022). A Lei Lola e os usos acadêmicos da misoginia no Brasil. *Paradigma, 31*(2), 231–257.

Declercq, M. (2019, March 13). *Nos chans, se celebra o massacre na escola de Suzano*. Vice. Retrieved March 18, 2025, from https://www.vice.com/pt/article/qvya87/nos-chans-ja-se-celebra-o-massacre-na-escola-de-suzano

Del Monde, I., et al. (2022, June 2). *Isabela Del Monde: Jornalista processada por expor abuso ganha ação: Judiciário fez justiça*. UOL Universa. Retrieved March 18, 2025, from https://www.uol.com.br/universa/colunas/isabela-del-monde/2022/06/02/jornalista-processada-por-expor-estupro-ganha-acao-judiciario-fez-justica.htm

Delgado, R. (1982). Words that wound: A tort action for racial insults, epithets, and name-calling. *Harvard Civil Rights-Civil Liberties Law Review, 17*, 133–182.

Dias, P. E., & Kruse, T. (2023). *Em carta, autor do ataque em escola de SP cita bullying, tristeza e ódio*. Folha de S. Paulo. Retrieved March 18, 2025, from https://www1.folha.uol.com.br/cotidiano/2023/03/em-carta-autor-do-ataque-em-escola-de-sp-cita-bullying-tristeza-e-odio.shtml

Fávero, M. H. (2011). *Psicologia do gênero: Psicobiografia, sociocultura e transformações*. UFPR.

Fórum. (2015, July 27). *Site dá passo a passo de 'como estuprar uma mulher'*. Fórum. Retrieved March 18, 2025, from https://revistaforum.com.br/mulher/2015/7/27/site-da-passo-a-passo-de-como-estuprar-uma-mulher-13406.html

Freitas, R. C., & Nóbrega, L. N. (2022). *Indignação epistêmica e decolonização do conceito de minorias/Epistemic indignation and decolonization of the concept of minorities*. Direito e Práxis. Retrieved March 18, 2025, from https://www.epublicacoes.uerj.br/index.php/revistaceaju/article/view/62119

G1. (2015, July 28). MPE apura blog com guia do estupro 'testado' na Unesp de Araraquara. *G1*. Retrieved March 18, 2025, from http://g1.globo.com/sp/sao-carlos-regiao/noticia/2015/07/mpe-apura-blog-que-prega-estupro-e-afirma-que-crime-foi-testado-na-unesp.html

G1. (2023, April 21). *Justiça derruba liminar que proibia Titi Müller de falar sobre ex-marido*. G1. Retrieved March 18, 2025, from https://g1.globo.com/pop-arte/noticia/2023/04/21/justica-derruba-liminar-que-proibia-titi-muller-de-falar-sobre-ex-marido.ghtml

Gennarini, J. C. (2021). A criminalização do stalking. *Direito Penal e Processo Penal, 3*(1), 67–79.

Ging, D. (2019). Alphas, betas, and incels: Theorizing the masculinities of the manosphere. *Men and Masculinities, 22*(4), 638–657.

Góis, T. (2021, January 30). *Pode a sobrevivente falar? O assédio judicial em casos de violência sexual*. Carta Capital. Retrieved March 18, 2025, from https://www.cartacapital.com.br/opiniao/pode-a-sobrevivente-falar-o-assedio-judicial-em-casos-de-violencia-sexual

Instituto Avon, & Decode. (2021). *Muito além do cyberbullying: A violência real do mundo virtual*. Instituto Avon. Retrieved March 18, 2025, from https://institutoavon.org.br/wp-content/themes/avon-wp/images/estudo-21/E-BOOK%20-%20Avon_Ebook_Ciberbullyng_2021.pdf

Intervozes. (2023, February 2). *MPF pede prisão de Sikêra Jr. e multa por crime de racismo*. Carta Capital. https://www.cartacapital.com.br/blogs/intervozes/mpf-pede-prisao-de-sikera-jr-e-multa-por-crime-de-racismo/

Leal, A. (2021, August 17). *Dez massacres em escolas foram evitados em 2021 no Brasil com apoio de agência americana, diz governo federal após caso no RN*. O Globo. Retrieved March 18, 2025, from https://oglobo.globo.com/brasil/seguranca-publica/dez-massacres-em-escolas-foram-evitados-em-2021-no-brasil-com-apoio-de-agencia-americana-diz-governo-federal-apos-caso-no-rn-25158621

Lins, B. A. (2021). Caiu na net: Nudes e exposição de mulheres na internet. Telha.

Luccas, V. N., Gomes, F. V., & Salvador, J. P. F. (2020). *Guia de análise de discurso de ódio*. Centro de Pesquisa em Ensino e Inovação (CEPI), FGV. Retrieved March 18, 2025, from http://bibliotecadigital.fgv.br:80/dspace/handle/10438/28626

Machado, M. R. A., Lima, M., & Neris, N. (2016). Racismo e insulto racial na sociedade brasileira: Dinâmicas de reconhecimento e invisibilização a partir do direito. *Novos Estudos Cebrap, 35*, 11–28.

Machado, M. R. A., dos Santos, A. L. P., Silva, A. V., et al. (2022). *Segurança da população negra brasileira: Como o sistema de justiça responde a episódios individuais e institucionais de violência racial: Sumário executivo*. Núcleo de Justiça Racial e Direito (FGV-SP). Retrieved March 18, 2025, from http://bibliotecadigital.fgv.br:80/dspace/handle/10438/32916

Maihofer, A. (2016). O gênero como construção social: Uma consideração intermediária. *Direito e Práxis, 7*(3), 874–888.

Martins, F. K., & Becari, J. (2021). *Entrevista com Fabiana Benedito | Especial discurso de ódio*. InternetLab. Retrieved March 18, 2025, from https://internetlab.org.br/pt/noticias/entrevista-com-fabiana-benedito-especial-discurso-de-odio/

Martins, F. K., & Oliveira, K. (2021, February 8). *Jovens protagonizam ações de combate ao discurso de ódio contra mulheres*. InternetLab. Retrieved March 18, 2025, from https://internetlab.org.br/pt/noticias/jovens-protagonizam-acoes-de-combate-ao-discurso-de-odio-contra-mulheres

Martins, F. K., Valente, M., Borges, E., Tavares, C., & Gomes, A. (2020, November 12). *Violence against women online and the courts: Preliminary observations*. InternetLab. Retrieved March 18, 2025, from https://internetlab.org.br/en/news/violence-against-women-online-and-the-courts-preliminary-observations/

Matsuda, M. (1989). Public response to racist speech: Considering the victim's story. *Michigan Law Review, 87*(8), 2320–2281.

McFarlane, J. M., Campbell, J. C., Wilt, S., et al. (1999). Stalking and intimate partner femicide. *Homicide Studies, 3*(4), 300–316.

Meyer-Plug, S. R. (2009). *Liberdade de expressão e discurso do ódio*. Revista dos Tribunais.

Moreira, A. J. (2017). *O que é discriminação?* Casa do Direito.

MZ Notícia. (2021, September 28). *Estudantes de direito são suspeitos de crime contra apresentador Sikeira Junior em PG*. MZ Notícia. Retrieved March 18, 2025, from https://mznoticia.com.br/estudantes-de-direito-sao-suspeitos-de-crime-contra-apresentador-sikeira-junior-em-pg

O Globo. (2023, March 28). *Ludmilla perde processo judicial contra apresentador após ser chamada de 'macaca'; cantora irá recorrer.* O Globo. Retrieved March 18, 2025, from https://oglobo.globo.com/cultura/musica/noticia/2023/03/ludmilla-perde-processo-judicial-contra-apresentador-apos-ser-chamada-de-macaca-cantora-ira-recorrer.ghtml

Organization of American States (OAS). (2013). *Convenção Interamericana contra o racismo, a discriminação racial e formas correlatas de intolerância.* Retrieved March 18, 2025, from https://www.oas.org/en/sla/dil/docs/inter_american_treaties_A-69_Convencao_Interamericana_disciminacao_intolerancia_POR.pdf

Pacheco, V. P. (2021, April 5). *O crime de perseguição: Breves críticas sobre o stalking no direito brasileiro.* Migalhas. Retrieved March 18, 2025, from https://www.migalhas.com.br/depeso/342950/o-crime-de-perseguicao

Pires, T. (2023). *Ataque à escola não é decisão individual e reflete contato com extremistas, diz pesquisadora.* Brasil de Fato. Retrieved March 18, 2025, from https://www.brasildefato.com.br/2023/03/29/ataque-a-escola-nao-e-decisao-individual-e-reflete-contato-com-extremistas-diz-pesquisadora

Salvadori, F. (2018). Site racista do Rio é novo ataque de trolls de extrema direita. *Ponte Jornalismo.* Retrieved March 18, 2025, from https://ponte.org/site-racista-do-rio-e-novo-ataque-de-trolls-de-extrema-direita

Santini, R. M., Salles, D., Belin, L. L., Belisário, A., Mattos, B., Medeiros, S. G., Mello, D., Grael, F., Seade, R., Borges, A., Murakami, L., Cardoso, R., Dau, E., Loureiro, F., Yoneshigue, B., do Carmo, V., & Maia, F. (2024). *"Aprenda a evitar 'esse tipo' de mulher": Estratégias discursivas e monetização da misoginia no YouTube.* NetLab—Laboratório de Estudos de Internet e Redes Sociais, Universidade Federal do Rio de Janeiro (UFRJ).

Sarmento, D. (2006). A liberdade de expressão e o problema do "hate speech". In D. Sarmento (Ed.), *Livres e iguais: Estudos de direito constitucional.* Lumen Juris.

Sarti, C. (2011). A vítima como figura contemporânea. *Caderno CRH, 24*, 51–61.

Serafini, M. (2023, March 16). *Como os red pills espalham ódio contra as mulheres nas redes sociais.* Carta Capital. Retrieved March 18, 2025, from https://www.cartacapital.com.br/sociedade/coaches-de-misoginia/

Silva, B. C. S. L. (2023). *Masculinismo: Misoginia e redes de ódio no contexto da radicalização política no Brasil* (PhD thesis). PUC Minas.

Sodré, M. (2005). Por um conceito de minoria. In R. Paiva & A. Barbalho (Eds.), *Comunicação e cultura das minorias.* Paulus.

Stone, G. R., Seidman, L. M., Sunstein, C. R., et al. (2016). *The first amendment* (5th ed.). Wolters Kluwer.

Valenga, D., & Guimarães, P. (2022, October 25). *Lola Aronovich: Misoginia de Bolsonaro incentiva seus aliados a fazerem o mesmo.* Catarinas. https://catarinas.info/lola-aronovich-misoginia-de-bolsonaro-incentiva-seus-aliados-a-fazerem-o-mesmo

Valente, Mariana; Neris, Natalia; Bulgarelli, Lucas. "Not Revenge, Not Porn: Analysing the Exposure of Teenage Girls Online in Brazil". Giswatch, 2015. Disponível em: https://genderit.org/sites/default/files/giswatch2015-brazil_0.pdf. Acesso em: 15 out. 2022.

Valente, Mariana; Neris, Natalia; Ruiz, Juliana; Bulgarelli, Lucas. O corpo é o código: estratégias jurídicas de enfrentamento ao revenge porn no Brasil. São Paulo: InternetLab, 2016.

Valente, M. (2020). Liberdade de expressão e discurso de ódio na internet. In J. E. Faria (Ed.), *A liberdade de expressão e as novas mídias* (p. 79). Perspectiva.

Valente, M. (2022). No place for women: Gaps and challenges in promoting equality on social media. In E. Celeste, A. Heldt, & C. I. Keller (Eds.), *Constitutionalising social media* (pp. 101–118). Bloomsbury Publishing. Retrieved March 18, 2025, from https://www.alexandria.unisg.ch/handle/20.500.14171/109576

Valente, M. (2023). *Online gender-based violence in Brazil: New data insights.* CIGI. (Supporting a Safer Internet Paper).

Vianna, J., & Kaniak, T. (2018, May 10). *PF prende uma pessoa em operação contra racismo, ameaça, incitação e terrorismo praticados na internet.* G1. Retrieved March 18, 2025, from https://g1.globo.com/pr/parana/noticia/pf-faz-operacao-contra-crimes-de-racismo-ameaca-e-incitacao-e-terrorismo-praticados-na-internet.ghtml

Vilaça, G. F. (2024). *Ambiências homossociotécnicas: Uma investigação sobre a machosfera, memes de internet e o r/brasilivre com o Reddit* (PhD thesis). Universidade Federal de Minas Gerais.

Waldron, J. (2012). *The harm in hate speech.* Harvard University Press.

Zanello, V. (2008). Xingamentos: Entre a ofensa e a erótica. In *8° Seminário Internacional Fazendo Gênero, Florianópolis.* Retrieved March 18, 2025, from https://www.researchgate.net/publication/221706218_Xingamentos_entre_a_ofensa_e_a_erotica

5 Writing, Reporting, Campaigning

Abstract

This chapter follows the gendered costs of visibility for women journalists, academics, activists, and especially women in politics. Using the assassination of Rio councillor Marielle Franco (2018) as a hinge event, it shows how violence—amplified and orchestrated online—deters civic participation, disproportionately harming Black, Indigenous, and LGBTQIAP+ women. It synthesises evidence on mental health and professional impacts; examines platform content-moderation logics and their gaps; and tracks the mobilisation that yielded the Political Violence Against Women Law (2021) in Brazil, which typifies and penalises acts that hinder women's political rights across online/offline spaces and creates preventive and protective mechanisms. After unpacking data about TFGBV against visible women and platform actions, it addresses content moderation, its working, limits, and recent global backlashes, from a gendered perspective. The chapter reads political violence as both a democratic problem and a gender/race problem, urging institutional capacity-building (investigation, protective orders, party duties), networked support for targets, and platform activity against coordinated abuse—so women can exercise speech and representation on equal terms.

Keywords

Gender-based political violence · Elections · Participation and representation · Content moderation · Platform regulation · Public and private divide

On 14 March 2018, Rio de Janeiro city councillor Marielle Franco and her driver Anderson Gomes were shot dead in the central region of Rio de Janeiro, returning from a debate promoted by her party, the Socialism and Liberty Party, with young Black women at Casa das Pretas ("Black Women's House"). Marielle had been a councillor in Rio de Janeiro since 2017—she was the fifth most-voted councillor in the city in 2016. Born and raised in the Favela da Maré, she was a she was a Black, bisexual woman, who had written about public security in Rio in her master's degree in public administration at the Fluminense Federal University. Marielle was no neophyte in politics: she had worked with councillor Marcelo Freixo, who was known for supporting investigating the militia in Rio de Janeiro and having a strong platform on public security. She was a vocal defender of women's and LGBTQIAP+ rights and a critic of police abuses, and considered one of the great political figures, as well as a promise of her generation. In 2024, three men—two politicians, one policeman—were arrested

M. Valente, *Online Misogyny in Brazil*, Sustainable Development Goals Series,
https://doi.org/10.1007/978-3-032-07727-1_5

for being the masterminds of the crime, apparently because of Marielle's opposition to bills that legalised land grabbing by the militia in certain Rio de Janeiro territories (O Globo, 2024).

Marielle Franco is a brutal milestone in confronting the multiple forms of violence suffered by women, especially Black, Indigenous, lesbian, bisexual, and transgender women, in Brazilian politics. These are forms of violence that go beyond institutional politics and affect other women engaged in public issues. In this chapter, I will deal with violence that takes place on the Internet against women, Black, and indigenous people and LGBTQIAP+ people who take a stand in public spaces, as well as the content-moderation activities of digital platforms—leading up to the debate on political violence and the law that was passed in 2021 to try to deal with this phenomenon of growing visibility.

In a world where the dominant ideology assumes that the public space belongs to the masculine, rational archetype, and the private space to the feminine, emotional and intimate, women who occupy the public space encounter a challenge that is expressed in numbers—such as the very low representation of women in institutional political spaces—and in violence related to misogyny. For Black, Indigenous, and LGBTQIAP+ women, these difficulties are compounded by discrimination arising from these other identities.

Although this dichotomy between public and private, which structures gender divisions, is still dominant in social representations, it has been questioned by feminists for decades. As already mentioned, Black feminists in Brazil and the United States question the representation of women as confined to private space because Black women were enslaved in the past and later had to work outside their homes to survive—they never experienced such confinement. "Under slavery, US Black women worked without pay in the allegedly public sphere of Southern agriculture and had their family privacy routinely violated", says Patricia Hill Collins (2019), in a statement that also applies to Brazil. According to Collins and Angela Davis, this division, which remained the dominant ideology, meant other oppressions for Black women—but also other resistances from these unique standpoints. In Brazil, domesticity, private space, and gender were strongly configured in the post-Abolition period, when the power of wealthy White housewives was reconfigured, and motherhood and keepers at home were ennobled. These wealthy White women began to supervise the now-paid domestic work carried out by mainly Black and former enslaved women in relationships permeated by servile assumptions (Monticelli, 2017). In this process, as Lélia Gonzalez (2020, p. 58) reminds us, the double journey is a more intense reality for Black women.

These considerations are essential for understanding the complexity of the division between private-female and public-male. Even so, this dominant ideology produces and reproduces gender inequalities. A significant part of violence against women takes place in the private sphere, and it is in this space that patterns of exploitation and domination limit their autonomy in other spaces. It is also where the foundations are laid for public life, which presupposes unpaid domestic care work. The idea that politics takes place in the public sphere, particularly in the state's domain, devalues work in the private family sphere and, as Brazilian political scientist Flávia Biroli (2020) points out, prevents criteria that are valid in the public sphere from being valid in the home. Thus, feminists fight for the recognition of femicide and the public and community confrontation of domestic violence by affirming that the private is political.

Biroli further argues that the depoliticisation of the private sphere aligns with the idea that relations in the public sphere are abstract, based on universal and impartial values. This justification supports hierarchies and the reproduction of privileges,[1] rooted in the notion of the "universal

[1]The strict separation between the public and private spheres was fundamental to the establishment of bourgeois values, according to Habermas, and to gender relations, patriarchy, and colonial relations, according to feminist and postcolonial critiques. Moreover, the debate that began in the second half of the twentieth century regarding the underrepresentation of women in politics, in Latin America and other parts of the world, also began to

subject", as claimed by Brazilian researcher Joanna Burigo (2022). These notions of impartiality are challenged by Nirmal Puwar, a sociology professor at Goldsmiths University, in her book *Space Invaders: Race, Gender and Bodies Out of Place* (2004) Puwar asserts that bodies perceived as conforming to the norm, namely White men, are regarded as the "normal" inhabitants of these spaces. This normalisation is reinforced through repetition. Consequently, the presence of female and non-white bodies becomes unsettling, regardless of what these so-called "space invaders" are attempting to propose.

Having a strong presence in the public sphere says something, albeit incomplete, about the suffering of violence by women all over the world—and particularly online violence. CIGI's 2022 research, which I've mentioned several times throughout this book, had a whole section on "high-profile individuals", meaning "high visibility": human rights defenders, journalists, politicians, influencers, or women who have a significant following. The incidence of online violence in all these categories is strikingly higher than that of the average person: while, in the eighteen countries studied, 59% of users report having suffered harm on the internet, in these specific categories the proportion is between 73% and 77%. Of the "high-profile" LGBTQIAP+ people, 82 per cent say they have been affected by violence specifically arrested for being the masterminds of the crime, apparently because of Marielle's identity, expression, and sexual orientation, and 42 per cent of high-profile women say they have been targeted because of their gender identity (compared to 26 per cent of high-profile men, or 25 per cent of general users). High-visibility women also report more serious effects of violence on their daily lives; for example, 48 per cent of those who have suffered violence report difficulties in their ability to concentrate and mental health, compared to 41 per cent of men and 37 per cent of general users; 51 per cent of high-visibility LGBTQIAP+ people report suicidal feelings, compared to 39 per cent overall (which also includes the LGBTQIAP+ section) (Valente, 2023).

From 2018 onwards, the debate around violence against politically active women intensified, along with increased reports and visibility of the issue. It is evident that the rise of the extreme right, conflicts over race and gender issues, and the legitimisation of such violence by political leaders have significantly contributed to this growth. Therefore, it is crucial to examine how this impacts journalists, academics, and women in politics, to understand the nature and specifics of this form of violence, its online dimension, and the role of internet platforms. In this context, we explore the history, achievements, and contradictions of a law that has confronted gender-based political violence.

5.1 Women Journalists and Academics

In 2015, TV Globo's newscast Jornal Nacional posted a picture of their host, Maju Coutinho, on their Facebook page. The post was flooded with racist and misogynistic offences posted at very close times, which raised suspicions of a coordinated action. The investigation led to four men who, with pseudonyms, organised an online community to carry out the attacks on a set day and time. Two of them were convicted of racism and racial insult in 2020 (G1, 2020), and the conviction was upheld in the São Paulo Court of Appeals (G1, 2020). The episode led other TV Globo journalists to launch the hashtag #SomosTodosMaju (#WeAreAllMaju), which began to be replicated broadly on social media.

That same year, the Brazilian journalist Aline[2] wrote an article for an independent media outlet about her experience as a nerd woman in nerd communities and the exclusions and discrimination she suffered. It was not long before users of

focus on a political economy of privilege to destabilize the category of "women," which conceals internal differences within this group.

[2]Fictitious name. I followed the case closely at the time. The journalist allowed her story to be recounted but prefers not to be identified.

a Brazilian *chan* opened a campaign of attacks that would not stop for weeks. They started with mockery and moved on to debate how to abuse her until one user posted his address, apparently obtained from a database of a credit scoring company he claimed to work for. What they started doing is known as *trolling*. According to researchers Clarice Tavares and Ester Borges, trolling is a specific violent behaviour that targets an individual, group, idea or cause, with the intention of hitting the target and destabilising the conversation. These attacks are often misogynistic, racist, ableist, and LGBTphobic in nature and differ from other attacks in their performative action to transform the debate into something else (Tavares & Borges, 2021). The word may make it seem harmless, and *trolls* also present themselves as representatives of the culture of irreverence. But far from it: as researcher Whitney Phillips (2015) argues in the excellent *This is Why We Can't Have Nice Things*, trolling culture is intimately connected with conventional, gendered notions of domination, and there are countless examples of serious consequences.

Aline started receiving all kinds of packages in the post, from sex shop items to live animals and even absurd things that took up her time and energy, like when she had a cement lamp post delivered to her house. Her neighbours all received a parcel with a T-shirt with her picture on it and fat-phobic slurs. They knew her address, and she didn't know where it would end up. In the *chans*, they said they wouldn't stop until she committed suicide. She left her house.

She took the case to a Civilian Police station, handed over evidence and waited for a contact that never came. She lost work opportunities as a freelance journalist, because some editors were afraid to publish her and become targets as a result. She also self-censored: she reports thinking twice before writing anything about gender.

In a 2021 report, UNESCO published a survey involving 714 female journalists from 113 countries: 73% of them had suffered work-related violence (Posetti et al., 2021). One of the stories in the survey is that of award-winning Filipino journalist Maria Ressa, whose story of persecution by the Philippine government and its supporters is well known. Ressa said that, at peak times, she received 90 hate messages an hour on Facebook alone and around 2000 insults a day. She is attacked not only for being a journalist but also for the colour and texture of her skin and for her sexuality.

Lebanese Al Jazeera presenter Ghada Oueiss reported receiving at least one death threat every day she goes live. Research shows that attacks on female journalists are not only very frequent, but they are also usually misogynistic and intimate, and extend to family, sources and colleagues. British researcher and professor Becky Gardiner (2018) surveyed 70 million comments posted between 2006 and 2016 on the website of the British newspaper The Guardian and showed that, of the ten most frequent targets of attacks, eight were women. In addition, Black women, Asian women, and women from other socially minoritised ethnic groups were disproportionately affected. Another survey carried out by the Indian organisation IT for Change in the states of Karnataka and Tamil Nadu revealed that women journalists are often attacked continuously and together, by several attackers at the same time, and some are forced to leave online spaces because of violence against family members (Gurumurthy et al., 2019).

There is no shortage of cases in Brazil, and some recent episodes are very paradigmatic. Patrícia Campos Mello was insulted by a source, Hans River, who had given her information about a mass WhatsApp messaging scheme by Jair Bolsonaro's campaign in 2018. In a statement to the Fake News Commission in 2020, River said that he had made the statements because the journalist had offered sex in exchange. The case led to an avalanche of insults and threats against Mello, which were reproduced (and encouraged) by MP Eduardo Bolsonaro, the former president's son. The then president, in an interview in front of the Alvorada palace, endorsed: "She wanted a scoop. She wanted to lick the scoop!", and laughed with the others present.[3]

[3] Free translation to «Ela queria dar o furo», a sexual reference to a journalistic scoop. "Furo", in Portuguese, is a work both for a "journalistic scoop" and for "hole".

Three different rulings forced River, Eduardo Bolsonaro, and former president Jair Bolsonaro to compensate the journalist (Brandino, 2021). Journalist Bianca Santana also won a lawsuit against Bolsonaro in 2021, because a year earlier he had claimed in one of his lives that she was spreading fake news, attributing to her a story that she didn't even write. This led Bianca Santana to receive death threats (Lemos, 2021).

In March 2021, journalist Juliana dal Piva received a message from Frederick Wassef, the Bolsonaro family's lawyer, after she published a podcast about corruption investigations on Jair Bolsonaro and family: "do there what you do here in your work, to see what the marvellous political system that you love so much would do to you. There in China you would disappear, and they wouldn't even find your body". She filed a civil lawsuit and published the message on social media, denouncing what had happened; in 2022, at first instance, she won damages, but was also ordered to pay the same amount she would have received, for having "injured the defendant's privacy" by publicising the intimidating message (Brebatti & Barbosa, 2023). Fortunately, her part of the conviction was overturned by the São Paulo Court of Justice the following year. It was a clear distortion of the right to privacy, which does not prevail in a case like this.

This is evidently not always the case, but the three cases narrated have connections with people linked to the then Bolsonaro government, which points to a dynamic that has been repeated in violence against women journalists in Brazil. In the 2022 mapping by the Brazilian Association of Investigative Journalism (Abraji) of gender attacks against journalists, of the 145 identified, more than 50% of the cases were what became known as "stigmatising speeches"; in the following category (33.8%) were threats and intimidation, both online and offline. It is striking that no less than 67.6% of stigmatising speeches were made by authorities and prominent figures, and 45.9% were systematic campaigns involving the internet (Abraji, 2023).

Many other surveys provide data on the prevalence of female journalists or gender-based attacks in episodes of violence against journalists in Brazil. Another example: A study by Reporters Without Borders and the Institute of Technology and Society in 2021 indicated that women journalists were critically referenced thirteen times more than their male colleagues (Repórteres Sem Fronteiras & Instituto de Technologia e Sociedade, 2021); another survey by a consortium of organisations, in which InternetLab participated, showed that also in 2021, four out of five journalists most cited in attacks were women; it was evident that, on Twitter, attacks against Black women journalists were more aggressive (InternetLab et al., 2022). An important point that this study revealed was that the discrediting of journalism is a strategy for destabilising democratic pillars; the gendered nature of the attacks comes either as an easy shortcut for doing so because misogyny is socially widespread or as a misogynistic expression that rides the wave of this discrediting.

The dynamic of attacks on journalists has become extremely visible and has had great repercussions, particularly during the 2022 elections. With slightly less visibility, given the shorter reach of their work, academics and activists have also suffered similar attacks. In 2018, University of Brasília professor Debora Diniz left Brazil after suffering virtual lynchings and death threats against herself, her family, students, and the rector. The professor became better known after she spoke at a public hearing before the Supreme Court in 2016 when she defended the right to abortion up to the 12th week of pregnancy. Diniz said she took the decision to leave because of the contagion effect: people around her became targets too. Investigations were slow due to difficulties in identifying cybercrimes (Rossi, 2019). Larissa Bombardi, a geography professor at University of Campinas and researcher into the impacts of pesticide use in the country, began receiving threats from agents linked to agribusiness and also went into exile in 2019 (Venturini et al., 2022). Márcia Tiburi, a philosophy professor, also left Brazil the same year due to threats.

Robert Quinn, from the organisation Scholars at Risk, has argued that the increase in Brazilian academics seeking help since 2017 was linked to rhetoric from political leaders stigmatising the university environment (Lisboa, 2020). For example, in 2019, Education Minister Abraham Weintraub said that higher education institutions in Brazil were full of "shambles" (Agostini, 2019). A 2022 study by the Centre for the Analysis of Freedom and Authoritarianism (LAUT) identified many reports of recommendations made by university administration suggesting avoiding or vetoing the use of expressions—and gender and sexuality were among the areas most closely monitored. Even so, there is little study or debate on the relationship between gender, race, and sexuality, and the persecution of academics in Brazil.

5.2 Gender-Based Political Violence

In 2024, Brazil elected the highest number of women to local mandates in its history: almost 18 per cent of mayors and city councillors (Barreira, 2024). Two women were elected as mayors of the 26 state capitals in the countries—an extreme subrepresentation, but an increase in relation to 2020, when no woman was elected to a capital (Paulo, 2024; Martins & Silva, 2020). Funding for women's and Black people's candidacies is proportionally lower than for other candidacies (Ramos et al., 2020; Mardegan et al., 2022). In 2022, 17.7 per cent of women were elected to the House of Representatives and 16 per cent to the Senate—below the regional and world average (Inter-Parliamentary Union, 2023). This means that women's voices are neglected in politics and, consequently, in society, as they are under-represented by spokespeople for their needs and interests (Biroli, 2016). After progressive governments instituted gender and race equality policies, as well as the presence of activism and the entry into the state of important cadres from the feminist movement, a woman was elected president for the first time in the country's history, but deposed before the end of her second term, and replaced by her vice-president, who made up a 100 per cent male and white ministerial cabinet (Bevins, 2016).

During Dilma Rousseff's impeachment, the extreme misogyny of the speeches that circulated led the debate to gain more body and space in activism; many academic papers began to be written (de Oliveira, 2021). Although gender-based political violence and its expression in laws had been discussed for a longer time in other Latin American countries,[4] and there existed already a diagnosis that it was a way of pushing subjects out of public political life, in that episode misogyny in Brazil became very explicit: from magazine and newspaper covers calling the president crazy and out of control to the sticker of Rousseff with her legs open that opponents began to stick on the entrance to the petrol tank of their cars—to be "penetrated by a bomb". There is, therefore, no denying that misogyny is a challenge to women's expression. Here, with two extra layers, the consequences are felt in political representation, with straightforward effects on the lives of Brazilian women and men, and with the dangers very present—a fact that Marielle Franco's murder in 2018 was a testimony to.

In 2016 and 2018, InternetLab's #OtherVoices project recorded several initiatives aimed at giving visibility to the candidacies of women, Black, Indigenous, and LGBTQIAP+ people (Neris & Valente, 2017). We knew that social networks had undeniably been playing a role for activist candidates who (also) build an online audience. When we mapped the initiatives in 2018, the debate on misogyny and gender-based political violence was so intense that in 2020, we decided to take a turn and focus on this type of violence against female candidates, monitoring it more systematically. This is how MonitorA was born, a project in partnership with AzMina magazine and Volt Data Lab. This project materialised the problem in numbers and made it possible to identify trends and narratives in the type of gender-based

[4] "Other Latin American countries have typified this kind of violence—Bolivia, Mexico and Peru—or assumed a broader concept of violence in national laws—Argentina and Venezuela". [Outros países latino-americanos tipificaram esse tipo de violência—Bolívia, México e Peru—ou assumiram um conceito mais amplo de violência nas leis nacionais—Argentina e Venezuela.] (Biroli, 2016; Krook et al., 2016).

political violence in the 2020, 2022, and 2024 elections across the country.

In 2020, we monitored 175 profiles of candidates from all regions, following various diversity criteria: ethnicity and gender. The candidates received an average of forty offensive comments on Twitter, Instagram, and YouTube every day during the first round. The cis and trans women candidates got an average of forty offensive comments on Twitter every day during the first round. Although this figure is shocking, the main issue we observed was not numerical but related to the nature of the offences. Some male candidates even received more offence on social media, which depended on many factors. For example, Guilherme Boulos, who was running for mayor of São Paulo, received a massive number of insults, given the size and visibility of his candidacy. However, we noticed that men, particularly white cis men, were offended by their political or professional performance, while women were offended by who they were, by their bodies and intellectual capacity, by their behaviour from a moral and sexual perspective, by factors linked to their family (such as motherhood). Black women suffered extreme dehumanisation, as was the case with Marina Silva (Rede Party) and Benedita da Silva (Workers Party, PT), both of whom were compared to animals ("tartaruga", "milk cow", "pig") and were called names for their supposed lack of beauty. GBT+ and Black men also received attacks based on their personal characteristics (Revista Azmina; InternetLab, 2021). Parenthetically, a study by the organisation VoteLGBT on the same electoral process showed that 49% of LGBTQIAP+ candidates who ran for office in 2020 reported having received attacks because of their sexual orientation, 32% because they were women, and 29% because of their gender identity; 54% sought assistance from their party, but in 56% of cases the party did not take action (VoteLGBT, 2022). And, between one election and the other, the Brazilian organisations MariaLab and Casa1 also observed, using the MonitorA framework, violence on Twitter against LGBTQIAP+ elected politicians, identifying intersections of misogyny, lesbophobia, and transphobia. It is common to be called "crazy", to be confronted with domesticity ("mistress", "lady") and references to not belonging to the political world (Araújo et al., 2022).

By 2022, the existence of gender-based political violence was well established, and the debate had reached the institutional spheres. The continuation of the observatory sought to refine the conclusions in order to offer better answers regarding misogyny on social networks in the political context: what differentiates heated, or even hostile, political debate from language that inferiorises historically marginalised groups, and what needs to be done in each case? (Martins, 2022). To answer this question, we observed that some misogynistic and discriminatory narratives were being constructed during the elections. For example: Michelle Bolsonaro and Janja Lula da Silva, the wives of the candidates who faced each other in the second round, were protagonists, even though they were not running, and both were the target of hostility related to religion and morality. The attacks on Michelle Bolsonaro sought to prove a dissonance between her religion and her behaviour and slipped into misogyny; more aggressively, the attacks on Janja were laced with intolerance against African religions combined with misogyny: for example, "pomba gira" was used as a reference to her alleged previous sex life (InternetLab & Revista AzMina, 2023).[5] In the ethnography we carried out at TikTok in partnership with Lux Ferreira, we also captured the immense mobilisation of Michelle Bolsonaro's femininity: in videos of Bolsonaro and his supporters, she was referred to as a "princess", "real first lady", and images of female Lula supporters such as the politicians Benedita da Silva and Gleisi Hoffmann as supposed examples of women on the opposite spectrum, with opposing characteristics (InternetLab & Revista AzMina, 2023). And in 2024—an edition that was impacted by platforms' actions to limit researcher access to data, which made us focus

[5] Pomba gira, a guardian and protector in Candomblé and Umbanda, appears in these curses as a representation of evil, immorality and vulgarity, according to the interpretations of some Christian communities. See Simas and Rufino (2018), InternetLab & Revista AzMina (2023).

on YouTube and Telegram—we found, for example, that, although women made up only 15% of the candidates in the second round, they received more than 68% of the offences during the television debates.

In all editions, it also became evident how lexicon can be used subtly to convey misogyny. Manuela D'Ávila, in 2020, was often called a "communist", which is an essentially political adjective. In the context, however, it was clear that communist was used as a proxy for a person without desirable moral, religious, or sexual values. Two years later, candidate Jair Bolsonaro said to journalist Vera Magalhães during a presidential debate on the Bandeirantes TV network: "Vera, I couldn't have expected anything else from you. I think you sleep thinking about me. You must have a crush on me. You can't take sides in a debate. A disgrace to Brazilian journalism". "You're a disgrace" began to be reproduced on the networks, particularly against women, subtly translating notions of gendered moralities. These examples also show the power of discourses emanating from powerful political figures. In 2024, Tábata Amaral (Brazilian Social Party, PSB), who was running for mayor in São Paulo, received 48% of all attacks in the candidates' debates transmitted on YouTube she participated in, and one of the most common tropes was infantilisation.

In 2022, we identified that men were also attacked for their characteristics when they belong to subalternised groups. MP Kim Kataguiri (Union Brazil Party) was attacked because of his Japanese ancestry: he was called "ugly Jap" and "Kim Kata Koquinho" ("Kim Coconut Catcher", in an attempt to mimic the Japanese language), and his identity was used in a pejorative way. To cite another example, Fernando Holiday (then running for Novo Party) was reproached for perceived inconsistencies between his speech and his ethnic-racial belonging, but with racist and violent vocabulary: "You are a disgrace to Black Brazilians! I'm disgusted by a guy like you". Despite the attempt to raise the issue of race, a statement like this is not related to what Holiday thinks, but to being a Black man who thinks what he thinks. Both these candidates belong to the conservative spectrum.

In addition to the content, the architecture of the space matters. In 2020, we had already identified that Twitter was the network with the most attacks—a diagnosis that corroborated other research, such as Amnesty International's in 2018 (Amnesty International, 2018)—and we set out to think about why, beyond content moderation policies. In this research, it became clear that the way a platform is built, what it allows and what it doesn't allow (which I identified above as architecture) plays a significant role. For example, Twitter has an architecture that favours exchanges between people who do not follow each other, showing posts shared by their contacts and giving great reach to posts gaining traction. This is very different from Instagram, where people interact primarily with their added network, or even TikTok, where, even when watching videos by people they don't follow, people end up receiving much more content they like due to the way the recommendation criteria are constructed (TikTok is known for offering a lot of what you would want, based on your behaviour on the platform itself, something that Instagram has incorporated more recently).

Thus, in 2022, MonitorA identified that, on Instagram, the most common words addressed to candidates Erika Hilton (Socialism and Liberty Party, PSOL) and Duda Salabert (Democratic Labour Party, PDT), both elected to the House of Representatives and much attacked online for being trans women, were "hang in there", "take care of yourself", "courage" and, specifically for Duda, "resistance" (since she had received death threats in August 2022), and "community", "unite", "congress", "association", "popular" and "let's go" for Erika. They were supporters and admirers who used the candidates' networks to show solidarity. On Twitter, in 2020, Erika Hilton was the most targeted candidate among those we monitored: 8.5% of all the comments directed at her contained insults, many of them transphobic.

After learning this data, Erika Hilton decided to sue fifty of the people who assaulted her.[6]

[6] "After being targeted by transphobic and racist attacks,

MonitorA and similar initiatives, such as those looking at journalists that I mentioned earlier, give concreteness and materiality to a problem that can be very abstract for those who don't experience it—and difficult to recognise and prove for those who do.

MonitorA has allowed us to take a closer look at another phenomenon that is difficult to solve: dogpiling. These are additive practices that may not in themselves be illegal or involve violating terms of use but cause damage and suffering because they create an atmosphere of threat (in this, they are reminiscent of stalking, although they are committed by multiple people). For example, dozens or hundreds of people go to a profile of a Black candidate and say: "Give up running, you don't deserve to be there". This phrase wouldn't be classed as illegal, and it probably doesn't violate the platforms' policies to be removed by them. But the aggregate character creates emotional chaos and can lead victims to a "breaking point", as Sydney University professor Emma Jane (2016) said after interviewing many victims of online hate. The problem, then, is not just the content of the messages but the way in which this is perpetrated, generating work and energy in reading, reporting, blocking, and acting against. And even this may not be enough: Filipino journalist Maria Ressa, who, as I mentioned earlier, sometimes receives an unimaginable amount of insults per hour, says that "you never know when it's going to jump out of the virtual and into the physical world" (Posetti et al., 2021).

In view of this, it is possible to say that the platforms' architectures and business models favour, more or less, hatred and, in particular, misogyny? In 2020, in an episode of The New York Times podcast The Daily, Jack Dorsey, founder and then-CEO of Twitter (before it was sold to Elon Musk), bemoaned what he called mistakes in fundamental choices involving the platform. He said that small choices—what gives a post more visibility to other users, a like or a share? A like and a share, or a like and a comment?—made users and media companies favour sensationalism over division. He wanted to open up more of the algorithm's Black box and push for changes (Jackson & Ibekwe, 2020). The path Twitter took next was quite different. The important takeaway, however, is that every architectural choice influences how people converse on these platforms, massive spaces organised by algorithms. These choices are also based on what type of content and interaction generates the most visibility for advertisers. And, of course, people also take ownership in creative ways, i.e. they have agency and bring their values to these spaces.[7] This is why, as complex as it may seem, discussing misogyny needs to cross the discussion about business models in the digital environment, platform governance and, more broadly, the internet as well.

Lastly, it is still worth insisting, because of how central it is: even when our focus is on the internet, recognising the continuum between online and offline is imperative. What is the ultimate gravity of what we are talking about? Andréia de Jesus, a state MP in Minas Gerais (Workers Party, PT), asked for a police escort in 2022 because she had received more than 3500 threats on the internet after demanding an investigation into a police operation in the south of the Minas Gerais state. In one of the threats, they said that her fate would be "the same as Marielle Franco's" (Gomes, 2022). Both are Black women. Áurea Carolina, who was also a state MP (Socialism and Liberty Party, PSOL), also Black, gave up running for a second term in 2022; according to her, the main reason was her belief in the need for alternation of power, the wear and tear of political violence weighed her down. In addition to situations of harassment while in

Erika Hilton plans to sue 50 people," (Brasil 247, 2021). Unfortunately, Hilton wasn't the only Black and transgender candidate to be attacked during the elections; Carol Dartora from Curitiba, Ana Lúcia Martins from Joinville, Benny Briolly from Niterói, and Duda Salabert from Belo Horizonte also received death threats by email. The threats have several similarities: they were directed at Black and/or transgender women who were elected for the first time by popular vote and with large margins of victory, for the most part (Rupp, 2021).

[7] See the discussion in the second chapter, in dialogue with Letícia Cesarino's work.

office, "in a very explicit and direct way, I even received threats in anonymous letters, messages, aggressive, discriminatory, and offensive comments on social media. But in a hidden way, there have been many situations since I was a councillor", she told the Lupa News Agency (Macário et al., 2023).

In 2021, MP Mônica Seixas (Socialism and Liberty Party, PSOL) heard from deputy Wellington Moura (Republicans) in the State Assembly of São Paulo that he would put a halter in her mouth, in a clearly racist speech. When she left the plenary crying, she was surrounded by fifteen men shouting "crazy" and "go take your Gardenal" (González, 2022). At one point, Mônica had a major crisis and went on medical leave. Duda Salabert, the first trans councillor in Belo Horizonte and the most-voted parliamentarian in 2020, has received transphobic emails and letters with death threats (Carmo, 2022). Erika Hilton, mentioned earlier for being a big target on social media, periodically receives death threats by email. "We're going to kill you with a bomb, we're going to blow up your houses and tear your bodies apart" was an example of a threat she received in 2022 after she filed a lawsuit against Jair Bolsonaro. Also in 2022, Isa Penna, a state MP for São Paulo, then from the Socialism and Liberty party, received a death threat by email linked to her actions in favour of the impeachment of state MP Douglas Garcia (Republicans), a Bolsonaro supporter, for his attack to journalist Vera Magalhães, and filed a police report. It was the third time that year (Rodrigues, 2022). Manuela D'Ávila (Communist Party of Brazil), who has held several public offices and was then federal MP, decided not to run for re-election in 2022, referring to political violence. She has a long history of being the target of gendered disinformation and receiving rape and death threats, including to her infant daughter (D'Ávila, 2022). These are stories that demonstrate the daily life of being a woman politician in the country, especially being a woman who represents certain agendas, especially in the case of Black women. In turn, the recent historical increase in the presence of these women in these spaces shows their resistance, and their combative mandates also show that they confront silencing.

5.3 Online Content Moderation

Elisa Riemer is a visual artist, feminist, and lesbian. In 2023, she was punished by Instagram, apparently for posting nude content while publicising a work she has been dedicating to since 2019, with collages that use old images of naked women—in photographs or photographs of sculptures. Some of the posts in the series were deleted and she was informed that her content would only be distributed to 10 per cent of her followers for two months. She recorded a video asking for the case to be publicised (and for her profile to be integrated so that she wouldn't lose so much reach).[8]

On January 7, 2025, Mark Zuckerberg, Meta's CEO, posted a video on Instagram and Facebook and a text on Threads, announcing significant changes to the company's approach to content moderation (Hendrix, 2025). Beyond discontinuing the fact-checking programme at least in the United States—the issue that garnered the most media attention—he proclaimed that Meta would begin permitting various offensive references to LGBTQIAP+ people, would relax policies on insults against women, such as comparing them to objects and property and claiming they are incapable of holding professions, and would remove automated controls or filters for most policies (except those related to the most serious issues like terrorism, child sexual exploitation, and drugs). He justified this last point by citing false positives, such as Elisa Riemer's case. However, the proposed solution seems to go against the refinement of policies and their enforcement—and women's safety online.

Instagram's policies at the time of Riemer's case allowed nudes in protest and "in images of paintings and sculptures" (as well as in some other cases, such as breastfeeding and health conscientisation), but Riemer's collages did not pass

[8] Video available at: https://www.instagram.com/p/Cps8yFkvTkh/?hl=en. Accessed on: April 8, 2025.

the sieve. Many years before, images of nudity used politically, for example, in the Slut Walk and other movements of the period, began to be blocked by social networks. Between 2012 and 2013, there was a national and international debate against censoring nudity. This was the case with a Facebook page that reproduced a newspaper cover with a small image of nudity, a well-known image of Simone de Beauvoir, or images of a protest against the World Cup in Rio de Janeiro in 2014, with a naked activist (Folha de S. Paulo, 2014; Hungria, 2013; de Belém, 2012; Rebaixada, 2014). Some cases were even more frivolous, such as a "naked" porcelain doll and a mermaid cake, whose images were blocked (Terra, 2014). Others had great political expression, as was the case with an image posted by the Ministry of Culture in 2015, with a photograph from 1909 showing an Indigenous Botocudo woman with her breasts exposed—blocked by Facebook and restored after the controversy (de Souza, 2015). Faced with many controversies, the most widely used platforms began to adopt more nuanced policies, allowing nudity in some cases.

The role and meaning of nudity are far from univocal in feminisms. In any case, here we are not talking about decisions made by feminists but by the platforms, which set the standards for communication within their walled spaces. When internet services, on their own initiative, move posts, suspend accounts, limit their reach (to fewer people), or put a "label" on a post as a filter indicating sensitive content, they do what in internet policy jargon is known as content moderation.[9] Content moderation involves the platforms' own rules, set out in their terms of use (and, in the more user-friendly version, the "community guides" or "platform policies"), but it also involves the procedures and systems that are used to enforce these rules.

Control over the application of these terms of use can be automatised (for more on this, see Gorwa et al., 2020). For example, it is known that Facebook and Instagram do not allow nudity and have a different policy for female and male nipples—which has even created problems for trans and non-binary people, whose specific demands are often not recognised (Martins, 2022). Many women and other people who don't identify as women have had the experience of posting a nude photo and having it removed; this usually happens automatically through an algorithmic filter that identifies what is in the image without a person having to check. However, internet platforms also employ content moderators, professionals whose job is to analyse posts in accordance with the platform's terms of use. The degree of adoption of automated tools and the types of cases in which control is carried out by automatons or humans vary from platform to platform.

These companies provide very little public information about their content moderation activities, usually citing moderator safety and the desire to prevent manipulation or "gaming the system"—where rules are exploited by malicious agents to bypass them. Of course, although the companies do not admit this, the more information they release publicly, the greater the scrutiny and criticism they face. Recent years have seen repeated reports that have sparked scandals over content moderation decisions and the poor working conditions of moderators, who are often outsourced (Tobin et al., 2017). Less attention has been given to the fact that content moderation involves significantly more investment and dedication in some countries—generally the wealthiest—than in others. The most notable example was in Myanmar, where in 2018, a massacre occurred amid a wave of hatred and incitement to violence against the Rohingya minority on Facebook. At that time, there was only one content moderator in Dublin capable of understanding Burmese, the language spoken in Myanmar, responsible for 1.2 million users in that country (Milmo, 2021).

Content moderation can have a more immediate impact on people's lives than other legal mechanisms. Essentially, when an image of

[9] An excellent book that discusses the issues and dilemmas of content moderation is Tarleton Gillespie, *Custodians of the Internet: Platforms, Content Moderation, and the Hidden Decisions that Shape Social Media*. New Haven: Yale University Press, 2018.

nudity is shared, a platform can respond swiftly to a notification and remove it, so the harm can be addressed much faster than if the victim has to take the case to court. But the two are interconnected.

In Brazil, since the Marco Civil da Internet (Brazilian Civil Rights Framework for the Internet) established that platforms could be held responsible only after the victim's notification in cases of NCII, the decision has influenced content moderation (Valente et al., 2016): the more a platform removes such content after a user reports it, the less liable it will be. This has created incentives for automated removal policies. However, moderation exists not only to shield platforms from legal liability; different platforms may aim to cultivate specific environments targeted at particular audiences. For instance, the audiences and uses of Twitter and TikTok differ, even though they overlap. On X, nudity is permitted; on TikTok, it is not.[10]

In general, although we focus on content that platforms do not remove, the removal of lawful and legitimate content can have very damaging effects on people—as was the case with Elisa Riemer—and on public debate. Suppose a post by a visible feminist activist in the midst of a political conflict is wrongly removed. Even if she manages to go through the internal procedures that platforms have for challenging wrongful removals, it is possible that the post will be restored at a time when it is no longer relevant. In 1999, a well-known seminal author in platform regulation studies, Lawrence Lessig (1999), wrote that, on the internet, *code is law*. What the code (and, we would add, the terms of use and other moderation practices) determines becomes reality, and we need to look at that reality. At the same time, the case of nudity is very illustrative of the major challenges that platforms face when it comes to moderating content: many platforms adopt a stricter policy on nudity as a way of avoiding the sexual exploitation of children and adolescents, or the non-consensual dissemination of intimate images. For example, it may not be easy to determine, with the bit of information commonly available, whether a photo is of an adult or a teenager, or whether it was authorised by an adult.

The larger the platform, the more complex the system is likely to be. For example: in the case of misogynistic speech, it may be that the platform uses an automated tool, an artificial intelligence system that seeks to identify these cases by analysing the context, and the removal is automated; it may be that the tool identifies potential cases of misogynistic speech and this generates an alert for content moderators, so that they can check whether that post violates the terms of use; it may be that moderators analyse the post after a complaint is made on the platform itself by a user. Some organisations, such as Wikipedia, have a moderation system that is quite different from the commercial models: it is entirely carried out by volunteer users, who create and enforce the rules—for example, the notoriety rules, which mean that a bio of a person considered to be notorious is deleted by the community. This is also content moderation (Oliva et al., 2020).

And what is the relationship between the content moderation rules and the legislation on the lawfulness of content? They are not entirely congruent. There is content that is illegal in the legislation and not part of the rules established by the platforms themselves. This is the case with crimes against honour: it may be that an insult, i.e. offending someone's individual honour, is considered a crime by the judiciary or even generates compensation for the person who has suffered the offence, but a platform does not prohibit all offences of this kind. It is common, for example, for a company to seek redress because it believes it has been harmed by a user's unfair assessment, but this does not mean that the platform will remove all potentially harmful content (and it makes sense that it would not, not least because the balance between freedom of expression and damage or injury to honour is not simple). With the current shift towards less control in some of the largest social media platforms' policies and their enforcement, as Meta has followed

[10] X Adult Content Policies: https://help.x.com/en/rules-and-policies/adult-content. TikTok Community Guidelines: https://www.tiktok.com/community-guidelines/. Retrieved in August 2025.

suit from X, these situations of incongruence will be more frequent.

There is also the opposite situation where content that legislation does not ban is prohibited by platforms. I have already mentioned Facebook and Instagram's nudity policies; Brazilian law does not prohibit nudity to this extent. The rules are quite strict for children and teenagers, according to the Statute of the Child and Adolescent, but for adults, the offence is committing an obscene act in public (in article 233 of the Criminal Code), and obscenity is not defined by law. Naturally, this creates conflicts in interpretation—what constitutes nudity and obscenity? When should acts that could be seen as obscene be allowed?—remembering that these provisions of the Criminal Code date from 1940. The Ministry of Justice also influences the parameters for nudity by establishing an Advisory Rating for audiovisual content. However, nudity that is commonplace in newspapers and magazines is banned on these platforms because of their stricter policies. It is also noteworthy that nudity, a topic so representative of gender issues and highly controversial within feminist movements, is a central element in these conflicts.

In 2025, the most used social media services in Brazil have policies that provide for the removal of NCII, threats, incitement to violence and sexual exploitation. All the major social media sites used in Brazil—Facebook, Instagram, LinkedIn, Snapchat, X, TikTok, and YouTube—have policies to deal with "hate speech", "hate promotion", or "hateful conduct" against characteristics considered vulnerable. They all include either gender or gender identity——among race, class, religion, and others. In 2025, Meta's explicit change in policies watered down protections for women and LGBTQIAP+ people, and YouTube quietly changed its "hateful conduct policy" to exclude "gender identity and expression" and to keep "sex, gender, or sexual orientation", a day after Donald Trump's inauguration, but claimed that the change was in wording, not in the heart or workings of the policy (Wiggins, 2025). LinkedIn protects "gender identity", but removed a line prohibiting "misgendering and deadnaming of transgender individuals" (Bell, 2025). This comes in the midst of Trump's war against DEI—diversity, equity, and inclusion—in hiring (Mahdawi, 2025), arguments on censorship on social media (The White House, 2025a), "wokeness" in AI (The White House, 2025c), and tech regulation in general, framed as "overseas extortion" against US companies, threatening trade sanctions (The White House, 2025b). The pressure is clearly mounting against moderating speech.

Many of the provisions, however, at the time of writing, are still there. Although they do not strictly provide for *misogyny*, in a sense they go beyond the Brazilian legislation, banning speech that, if not framed as a threat, defamation, or some other type of offence, would perhaps not be considered illegal under the current law, which, as we have seen, does not directly provide for a ban on misogynistic speech: at the time of writing. Facebook's policy is quite specific, dividing hate speech into three categories and offering detailed examples for all of them[11]—although, since January 25, women can be compared to household objects or be called one's property. But even before these changes, one criticism of this and other policies is that they incorporate a notion of "protected category", which is typical of North American anti-discrimination law. Therefore, saying something about a woman and the same thing about a man are equal violations, even if one case is much more likely to lead to violence than the other.

As said, from a legal point of view, platforms are allowed to have stricter rules than the law. In this case, it is desirable that they do so. For example, in the case of political gender violence, it is important that platforms have policies to guarantee the safety and expression of potential victims of this violence, regardless of the legal provision. In the jargon of social media companies, these policies and actions are known as Trust and Safety and have begun to be structured as specialised areas within corporations.

[11] Available at: https://transparency.fb.com/pt-br/policies/community-standards/hate-speech/. Accessed on: April 8, 2025.

The fact that content is banned by the platforms' private policies does not mean that it will be removed or that all cases will be easy to decide. In some contexts, platforms remove more than what seems reasonable given the purpose of the policy, as was the case with Elisa Riemer. In others, they do not remove cases of blatant violence in violation of their policies. For example, in 2020, when there was a wave of murders of girls by criminal gangs "decreed" on social networks in the state of Ceará, Facebook stated that it had no knowledge of the posts and accounts and only removed them when inquired about it by the media—and that was way before the recent announcements (Folha de S. Paulo, 2020).

From 2021, that is, way before the recent crises, significant lay-offs have impacted and reduced Trust and Safety teams inside the industry (Moran et al., 2025). Meanwhile, there is a growing debate about how much freedom these platforms should have to determine these rules in such a unilateral way, and the recent alignment between platforms and Donald Trump's administration has made this problem even sounder.

As I discussed in the third chapter, the Marco Civil established a regime whereby, as a general rule, Internet applications could be held legally responsible for illegal content if a judicial decision to remove it has not been complied with. However, it did not address the (private) activity of content moderation on platforms, leaving, in the precise assessment of researcher Clara Iglesias Keller (2020), too much room for private content control.

In many places around the world, subsequent legislation has started to pay more attention to the issue of content moderation, recognising that there is no way to discuss social networks and certain other types of services without this private activity—and establishing parameters for them. One of the strategies considered is that of "co-regulation". For example, in 2016, after the terrorist attack in Brussels, the European Commission signed a code of conduct with Facebook, Twitter, YouTube, and Microsoft, in which the companies committed to making it clearer to users which content is not permitted, as well as being obliged to promote initiatives to counter hate speech and remove what was called "illegal hate speech"—which assumes that non-illegal hate speech exists—within 24 hours of receiving a report from a user requesting removal.

The definition of hate speech in the agreement was: "any conduct publicly inciting violence or hatred directed at a group of persons or a member of such a group, defined by reference to race, colour, religion, descent or national or ethnic origin", i.e. there is no reference to gender. The fact that it came after the Brussels attacks also shows how, in Europe, the problem is often associated with terrorism. A code of conduct is not law and does not establish sanctions for non-compliance, but it is a "softer" intervention to try to ensure that objectives are met, before implementing more interventional actions.

However, there are already widely known examples of more assertive actions. The most discussed framework is the European Union's Digital Services Act (DSA), approved in 2022, which leaves the liability framework in place, but also adds due diligence requirements for the development and functioning of such services, to govern the basic design of services, content moderation procedures, advertising, and transparency. Due diligence responsibilities are typically based on the size and social relevance of the services, with an emphasis on process and design rather than individual content (Buiten, 2021; Husovec & Laguna, 2022). For example, online platforms must provide more granular publication of the rules adopted, explanations in the case of removals and the right to appeal decisions. The European Union's 2018 Copyright Directive obliges some platforms to create automated filters to remove content that violates copyright, i.e. automated moderation in these cases, and also tools to prevent content that has already been taken down from returning to the platform. This is reminiscent of the case of the video with sex scenes of Daniella Cicarelli and Tato Malzoni, when YouTube took down the videos requested by the judge, but others with the same content were immediately posted.[12]

[12] YouTube was a novelty at the time. In January 2007, the judge in charge of the case, dissatisfied with YouTube's

In Brazil, new rules for content moderation have also been discussed, at least since the debate over Bill 2630/20, originally known as the "Fake News Bill". It was initially examined from a stricter perspective of controlling disinformation, and as it evolved, it included measures outlining the responsibilities of platforms in content moderation, especially during crises, as well as requiring greater transparency in these activities. After four years of debate, the Bill was killed by the opposition in the House due to a lack of consensus, notably following strong opposition from right-wing parties. In June 2025, a significant development occurred when the Supreme Court declared Marco Civil partially unconstitutional, with important implications for the moderation of misogynistic content. I will discuss that in Chap. 6.

In September 2025, Congress also passed a new law protecting children and adolescents online (Law no. 15,211—the Digital Statute of Children and Adolescents). Although a bill had been under discussion for longer, the approval was a quick response to the viral success of a video by an influencer named Felca, who denounced how social media was failing to moderate sexualized content of teenage girls and sexual grooming. The law established mechanisms for IT product and service providers to verify that this age group is not utilising services that are inadequate for their developmental needs. In addition, it employs a safety by design approach, in conjunction with a notice and takedown rule, to remove content that is deemed harmful to this group, including incitement to self-mutilation and suicide. In cases of sexual exploitation and abuse, a proactive role is assigned, encompassing the removal of content and the notification of the relevant authorities. Notwithstanding the absence of a gendered approach within the legal framework, the legislation addresses issues that, as previously discussed, affect girls to a disproportionate extent. In summary, the Marco Civil general liability framework is being dismantled in favour of a content-type-specific approach, and there will undoubtedly be consequences in how misogyny is moderated by platforms in the near future.

Up to this point, it should have become clear that, from a legal perspective, facing online misogyny involves direct regulation of conduct, the regulation of service providers hosting, curating, and promoting such content, and other forms of employing the law, such as policies for prevention and protection. Returning to the issue of political violence against women, the Brazilian Congress acted to pass a response to demands against this problem and other broader initiatives aimed at political parties.

5.4 Political Violence Against Women Law

In August 2021, the Political Violence against Women Law (Law No. 14,192/2021) was passed, concerning violence both in the electoral period and in the exercise of political rights and public functions, i.e. periods beyond the elections. The original bill was proposed by deputy Rosângela Gomes (Republicans) in 2015 and was shorter than the one that ended up being approved. In other words, the bill had already been proposed a long time before, but pressures began to mount, and with the proposal of new bills in 2018 and 2020, which were attached to this original one, the proposal moved forward and incorporated some of their proposals, with an almost final text approved in the Chamber in 2020. Rapporteur Ângela Amin (Popular Party), in her vote, spoke specifically of social networks as facilitators of political violence against women, even citing data from the 2020 MonitorA project. In the Senate, the bill received minimal changes and was approved at the end of 2020.

The law encompasses several elements. Firstly, it establishes a general rule prohibiting discrimination and unequal treatment based on sex or race in political representation and public functions. It then defines what constitutes political violence against women: "any action, conduct

failure to control another appearance of the video, requested that the platform be blocked nationwide. The case became known, far beyond the dissemination of the images, as the first occasion on which Brazil was faced with this peculiarity of YouTube.

or omission aimed at preventing, hindering or restricting the political rights of women" and elaborates further: "any distinction, exclusion or restriction in the recognition, enjoyment or exercise of their rights and fundamental political freedoms, on the grounds of sex". An initial observation is that what was protected here was sex, not gender, and the fact that this occurred despite many feminists advocating for the use of the term "gender" to encompass more than biological sex reflects the conservatism that characterised the Brazilian Congress at the time. It is worth remembering that Brazil was adopting, in foreign policy, a stance of vetoing any use of the word "gender" (Chade, 2019).

The remaining parts of the law can be divided into three sections. Firstly, there was an effort aimed at political propaganda: the Electoral Code already set out a series of bans on political propaganda, and the law added another propaganda that "depreciates the condition of women or encourages discrimination against them on the grounds of their sex, colour, race or ethnicity". Here, the phrase "depreciation for the condition of women" is similar, though not identical, to the language of the Feminicide Law, which I discussed in Chap. 4 when mentioning the Lola Law (and the lack of a comprehensive definition of misogyny in Brazilian law). In the Feminicide Law, the term used is "contempt for the condition of women". *Contempt*, rather than depreciation, is also the word employed throughout the rest of the law. From the choice of words, we can observe that the Brazilian legal understanding of misogyny is beginning to develop, albeit in a nascent manner.

The second part involves establishing new offences or modifying existing ones. In the Electoral Code, a new crime was created, namely violence based on sex or colour, race, or ethnicity, to prevent or hinder campaigning or the exercise of office:

> Art. 326-B. Harassing, embarrassing, humiliating, persecuting, or threatening, by any means, a female candidate for elective office or holder of elective office, using contempt or discrimination against her status as a woman or her colour, race, or ethnicity, with the aim of preventing or hindering her electoral campaign or the performance of her elective mandate.
>
> Penalty—imprisonment from 1 (one) to 4 (four) years and a fine.
>
> Sole Paragraph. The penalty is increased by 1/3 (one third) if the offence is committed against a woman who is i. pregnant, ii. over 60 years old, iii. disabled.

Along these lines, the law also amended four other offences that already existed in the Electoral Code. An increase in the penalty was added to the first, Article 323, called "dissemination of facts known to be untrue in the electoral campaign or during the campaign period", if this dissemination involves "contempt or discrimination against the condition of women or their colour, race or ethnicity", and also in the case of the production of videos with untrue content (the intention here was to criminalise deepfakes). Looking at untrue content whose basis, or confirmation bias, is gender discrimination has been called "gendered disinformation". The law then goes on to increase penalties in the same cases for the offences of libel, slander, and defamation in electoral propaganda.

The third part of the law includes rules for political parties and electoral processes: it amends the Law on Political Parties to specify that party statutes must establish procedures for "preventing, repressing and combating political violence against women"; and modifies the Elections Law to ensure that the gender quota for candidacies (at least 30 per cent, at most 70 per cent of "each sex") is also adhered to in electoral debates.

It is worth noting that a few weeks after the bill was passed, Law No. 14,197/21 was also enacted, establishing a new offence within the National Security Law: "Art. 359-P. Restricting, preventing or hindering, through the use of physical, sexual or psychological violence, the exercise of political rights by any individual based on their sex, race, colour, ethnicity, religion or national origin". The issue here is broader: the exercise of political rights. With these two laws, Brazil aligned itself with other Latin American countries that include provisions on political violence against women in their legislation. Additionally, beyond the vocabulary issues—which we have already discussed regarding the limitations of the very concept of woman and discrimination based on sex—their limited duration already reveals some constraints in their application, particularly in the first law, which pertains to female candidates and elected representatives.

A survey conducted by the Electoral Intelligence Centre, in partnership with InternetLab and coordinated by lawyer and researcher Samara Castro, examined how the Law on Political Violence against Women was applied during the first electoral process in which it was in force in 2022 (InternetLab & Revista AzMina, 2023). There was difficulty accessing data, which is one of the study's conclusions: there is a need for greater transparency in these cases. Using multiple methods, the research identified only twelve cases of complaints based on the law during the campaign, despite the Federal Public Prosecutor's Office reporting 62 ongoing investigations. Apparently, these cases did not develop into formal complaints to the courts during the electoral period. Of these twelve cases, five involved complaints related to offensive attacks on women candidates, with only one occurring online; they were referred to the Public Prosecutor's Office because they were initiated by the victims. However, this is not the proper procedure for offences under Article 326-B, which is a "public in- conditioned criminal action", as discussed in Chap. 3. In summary, no decisions based on this law were made during the first electoral period following its approval.

One possible reason could be a process of adaptation, which involves various electoral actions. For example, in 2022, the Superior Electoral Court and the Attorney General's Office signed a protocol to prioritise conduct and procedural rites for cases of political violence against women. Channels were opened to receive complaints online, and training was organised. Experiences of this kind need to mature if they are to be widely disseminated. Nevertheless, based on interviews with female candidates, the study questioned whether there are points where the law could already provide for improvements or even deeper conceptual issues. Victims don't always have the emotional or legal tools or even the knowledge of the law to realise that they have suffered political violence, or they don't yet have the motivation to report the offenders. One question that arose was: could it be that some female candidates, during the electoral period, avoid raising the banner of being victims of violence, for fear that this will be seen as weakness in the eyes of society and their opponents?[13] Another issue that became evident was that the Public Prosecutor's Office lacked the structure and institutional capacity to complete investigations in time. In 2024, by repeating this study, now under the coordination of lawyer and researcher Ana Claudia Santano, we confirmed that cases are not concluded within the timeframe of the election, and, through interviews with candidates, campaign coordinators, and lawyers, that they fear activating the Political Violence Against Women Law during elections might negatively impact their performance. However, they also argued that judicial authorities often share the view that women are victimised and fail to recognise political violence, leading them to consider whether pursuing this course is worthwhile (InternetLab et al., 2025).

Outside of the electoral period, there have been a few known cases of the law being used in complaints by the Public Prosecutor's Office or the candidates themselves. For example, the Electoral Public Prosecutor's Office filed a complaint against state MP Rodrigo de Amorim (Brazil Labour Party, PTB) for attacks on MP Benny Briolly (Socialism and Liberty Party, PSOL) during a session in the Legislative Assembly of that state and via email, and against state deputy Wellington Moura (Republicans), who told deputy Monica Seixas (Socialism and Liberty Party, PSOL) that he would "put a halter in her mouth" when he was chairing the session. Federal MP Sâmia Bomfim also filed a criminal complaint against posts on a website stating "Sâmia Bomfim, I won't rape you because you don't deserve it", and then councillor Erika Hilton filed a police report and criminal charges against a woman after being threatened with death. In other words, the law has broader objectives.

In any case, the above-mentioned studies on the enforcement of the law suggest that one of its

[13] See, for example: Letícia Paiva, "Campanha de Tebet rejeita questionar violência política de gênero na Justiça". Jota, 24 ago. 2022.

main objectives, ensuring parity and rights during the electoral period, has not been achieved. It hints at the limitations of the law and the capacity of institutions, but also raises a recurring question: what is the role and limit of criminalising conflicts, and what other tools could be more effective and desirable? They mention, for example, the need to consider protective measures, inspired by the Maria da Penha Law, which would be quicker and more effective in safeguarding rights during electoral campaigns, and emphasise the importance of diligent work within the parties, where many gender-related rights still require protection.

References

Abraji. (2023). *Monitoramento de ataques a jornalistas no Brasil: Edição 2022*. https://abraji-bucket-001.s3.sa-east-1.amazonaws.com/uploads/publication_info/details_file/4d6cb1b2-ca1a-4d7b-9c7b-1edcea1bb294/ABRAJI_Monitoramento_de_ataques_a_jornalistas_no_Brasil_2022__PT_.pdf

Agostini, R. (2019). *MEC cortará verba de universidade por 'balbúrdia' e já enquadra UnB, UFF e UFBA*. O Estado de S. Paulo. https://www.estadao.com.br/educacao/mec-cortara-verba-de-universidade-por-balburdia-e-ja-mira-unb-uff-e-ufba/

Amnesty International. (2018). Toxic Twitter: A Toxic Place for Women. Disponível em: https://www.amnesty.org/en/latest/research/2018/03/online-violence-against-women-chapter-1-1/.

Araújo, D., et al. (2022). Violência política, gênero e sexualidade: Contribuições para a análise do discurso de ódio contra grupos socialmente minorizados. In B. Barbosa, L. Tresca, & T. Lauschner (Eds.), *TIC, governança da internet e gênero 2*. CGI.br.

Barreira, P. (2024). *Resultado das eleições municipais mostra baixa representatividade de mulheres e negros*. Rádio Senado.

Bell, K. (2025). *LinkedIn quietly removed references to deadnaming and misgendering from its hateful content policy*. Engadget. https://www.engadget.com/social-media/linkedin-quietly-removed-references-to-deadnaming-and-misgendering-from-its-hateful-content-policy-190031953.html

Bevins, V. (2016, May 13). *In post-impeachment Brazil, the new conservative cabinet is 100% white men*. Los Angeles Times. https://www.latimes.com/world/mexico-americas/la-fg-brazil-impeach-diversity-20160513-snap-story.html

Biroli, F. (2016). Political violence against women in Brazil: Expressions and definitions. *Revista Direito e Práxis, 7*(15), 557–589. https://doi.org/10.12957/dep.2016.25164

Biroli, F. (2020). Ciência, política e gênero. In F. Biroli et al. (Eds.), *Mulheres, poder e ciência política: Debates e trajetórias* (pp. xx–xx). Editora da Unicamp.

Brandino, G. (2021). *Justiça condena Hans River a indenizar repórter da Folha em R$ 50 mil por danos morais*. Folha de S. Paulo. https://www1.folha.uol.com.br/poder/2021/04/justica-condena-hans-river-a-indenizar-reporter-da-folha-em-r-50-mil-por-danos-morais.shtml

Brasil 247. (2021, June 6). *Após ser alvo de ataques transfóbicos e racistas, Erika Hilton irá processar 50 pessoas*. Geledés. https://www.geledes.org.br/apos-ser-alvo-de-ataques-transfobicos-e-racistas-erika-hilton-ira-processar-50-pessoas

Brebatti, K., & Barbosa, B. (2023). *Opinião: Decisão da Justiça pode impactar trabalho de mulheres jornalistas*. Blog do Paulinho. https://blogdopaulinho.com.br/2023/03/20/decisao-da-justica-pode-impactar-trabalho-de-mulheres-jornalistas/

Buiten, M. C. (2021). The digital services act: From intermediary liability to platform regulation. *JIPITEC—Journal of Intellectual Property, Information Technology and E-Commerce Law, 12*(5), 5. https://nbn-resolving.de/urn:nbn:de:0009-29-54917

Burigo, J. (2022). *Patriarcado, gênero, feminismo*. Zouk.

Carmo, L. G. (2022, August 26). *Em ano de eleições no Brasil, mulheres na política denunciam ameaças recorrentes*. Global Voices. https://pt.globalvoices.org/2022/08/26/em-ano-de-eleicoes-no-brasil-mulheres-na-politica-denunciam-ameacas-recorrentes/

Chade, J. (2019, June 27). *Brasil veta termo 'gênero' em resoluções da ONU e cria mal-estar*. UOL.

Collins, P. H. (2019). *Pensamento feminista negro: Conhecimento, consciência e a política do empoderamento* (D. G. Silva, Trans.). Boitempo.

D'Ávila, M. (Ed.). (2022). *Sempre foi sobre nós: Relatos da violência política de gênero no Brasil* (3rd ed.). Rosa dos Tempos.

de Belém, E. F. (2012, March 18). *Nudez de Simone de Beauvoir e o moralismo do Facebook*. Jornal Opção. https://web.archive.org/web/20160712090424/http://jornalopcao.com.br/colunas/imprensa/nudez-de-simone-de-beauvoir-e-o-moralismo-do-facebook

de Oliveira, J. R. (2021). Uma reflexão crítica sobre a representação social do discurso de ódio. *Investigações, 34*(2) https://periodicos.ufpe.br/revistas/INV/article/view/248457

de Souza, A. (2015, April 17). *Ministério da Cultura vai entrar na Justiça contra Facebook por foto de índia bloqueada*. O Globo. https://oglobo.globo.com/brasil/midia/ministerio-da-cultura-vai-entrar-na-justica-contra-facebook-por-foto-de-india-bloqueada-1-15910229

G1. (2020, March 9). *Justiça condena dois homens por racismo e injúria racial contra a jornalista Maju Coutinho*. https://g1.globo.com/sp/sao-paulo/noticia/2020/03/09/tj-de-sp-condena-dois-homens-por-racismo-e-injuria-racial-contra-a-jornalista-maju-coutinho.ghtml

Gardiner, B. (2018). "It's a terrible way to go to work": What 70 million readers' comments on The Guardian revealed about hostility to women and minorities online. *Feminist Media Studies, 18*(4), 592–608.

Gillespie, T. (2018). *Custodians of the internet: Platforms, content moderation, and the hidden decisions that shape social media.* Yale University Press.

Gomes, A. (2022, April 11). *Deputada negra de MG que contabiliza 3,5 mil ameaças de morte perde escolta policial.* Brasil de Fato. https://www.brasildefato.com.br/2022/04/11/deputada-negra-de-mg-que-contabiliza-3-5-mil-ameacas-de-morte-perde-escolta-policial

Gonzalez, L. (2020). *Por um feminismo afro-latino-americano.* Zahar.

González, M. (2022, November 30). *Como a violência impacta saúde mental e afasta mulheres da política.* Mina. https://minabemestar.uol.com.br/mulheres-da-politica-saude-mental/

Gorwa, R., Binns, R., & Katzenbach, C. (2020). Algorithmic content moderation: Technical and political challenges in the automation of platform governance. *Big Data & Society, 7*(1), 1–15. https://doi.org/10.1177/2053951719897945

Gurumurthy, A., et al. (2019). *Getting it right online: Young women's negotiations in the face of cyberviolence in Karnataka.* IT for Change. https://itforchange.net/sites/default/files/1618/Karnataka_Report_Righting-Gender-Wrongs_1.pdf

Hendrix, J. (2025, January 7). *Transcript: Mark Zuckerberg announces major changes to Meta's content moderation policies and operations.* Tech Policy Press. https://techpolicy.press/transcript-mark-zuckerberg-announces-major-changes-to-metas-content-moderation-policies-and-operations

Hungria, J. (2013, May 31). *Facebook censura vaga referência a nudez na página do Blue Bus.* Blue Bus. https://web.archive.org/web/20130617133351/http://www.bluebus.com.br/facebook-censura-vaga-referencia-a-nudez-na-pagina-do-blue-bus/

Husovec, M., & Roche Laguna, I. (2022). *Digital services act: A short primer* (SSRN scholarly paper no. 4153796). Social Science Research Network. https://doi.org/10.2139/ssrn.4153796.

Iglesias Keller, C. (2020). Policy by judicialisation: The institutional framework for intermediary liability in Brazil. *International Review of Law, Computers & Technology, 35*(3), 1–19.

InternetLab, & Revista AzMina. (2023). *MonitorA 2022: Observatório de violência política de gênero.* InternetLab, AzMina e Núcleo Jornalismo. https://monitora.org.br/

InternetLab, INCT.DD, Instituto Vero, et al. (2022). *Como operações de influência entre plataformas são usadas para atacar jornalistas e enfraquecer democracias?* https://internetlab.org.br/pt/noticias/como-operacoes-de-influencia-entre-plataformas-sao-usadas-para-atacar-jornalistas-e-enfraquecer-democracias/

InternetLab, Revista Azmina, Núcleo Jornalismo, & LABHDUFBA. (2025). *MonitorA: Relatório sobre violência política contra candidatas(os) online.* Edição 2024. https://monitora.org.br/relatorios/

Inter-Parliamentary Union. (2023). *Women in Parliament 2022.* https://www.ipu.org/resources/publications/reports/2023-03/women-in-parliament-2022

Jackson, L., & Ibekwe, D. (2020, August 7). *Jack Dorsey on Twitter's mistakes.* The New York Times. https://www.nytimes.com/2020/08/07/podcasts/the-daily/Jack-dorsey-twitter-trump.html

Jane, E. A. (2016). *Misogyny online: A short (and brutish) history.* Sage.

Krook, M. L., Restrepo Sanín, J., et al. (2016). Género y violencia política en América Latina: Conceptos, debates y soluções. *Política Y Gobierno, 23*(1), 127–162.

Lawrence, L. (1999). Code: And Other Laws Of Cyberspace. New York: Basic Books.

Lemos, M. (2021). *Bianca Santana vê 'vitória coletiva' em condenação de Bolsonaro.* UOL. https://noticias.uol.com.br/politica/ultimas-noticias/2021/08/20/bianca-santana-ve-vitoria-coletiva-em-condenacao-de-bolsonaro.htm

Lisboa, A. P. (2020). *Acadêmicos brasileiros se exilam por ameaças de morte.* Correio Braziliense. https://www.correiobraziliense.com.br/app/noticia/eu-estudante/ensino_ensinosuperior/2020/03/13/interna-ensinosuperior-2019,834162/academicos-brasileiros-se-exilam-por-ameacas-de-morte.shtml

Macário, C., et al. (2023, March 8). *'Violência política contra as mulheres é agravada pela desinformação', diz ex-deputada Áurea Carolina.* Lupa. https://lupa.uol.com.br/jornalismo/2023/03/08/violencia-politica-mulheres-desinformacao-aurea-carolina

Mahdawi, A. (2025, March 13). *'Guess what? You don't matter': What Trump's war on DEI means for every American who's not a straight white man.* The Guardian. https://www.theguardian.com/us-news/2025/mar/13/trump-war-dei-american-straight-white-man-diversity-equity-inclusion

Mardegan, I., Fabbron, J., & Ramos, L. (2022, September 28). *Raça, gênero e representatividade nas cotas eleitorais.* Nexo Jornal. https://www.nexojornal.com.br/ensaio/2022/09/28/Ra%C3%A7a-g%C3%AAnero-e-representatividade-nas-cotas-eleitorais

Martins, F. K. (2022, September 6). *MonitorA 2022: A diferenciação necessária entre insultos e ataques no debate sobre moderação de conteúdo.* InternetLab. https://internetlab.org.br/pt/noticias/monitora-2022-a-diferenciacao-necessaria-entre-insultos-e-ataques-no-debate-sobre-moderacao-de-conteudo

Martins, F. B., & Silva, V. R. (2020). *Eleições 2020.* Gênero e Número. http://generonumero.media/eleicoes2020

Milmo, D. (2021, December 6). *Rohingya sue Facebook for £150bn over Myanmar genocide.* The Guardian. https://www.theguardian.com/technology/2021/dec/06/rohingya-sue-facebook-myanmar-genocide-us-uk-lega

Monticelli, T. (2017). A administração, as negociações e as desigualdades constituídas no lar: Reflexões sobre uma cultura da domesticidade no Brasil. *Revista Feminismos UFBA, 5*(2/3), 85–98. https://periodicos.ufba.br/index.php/feminismos/article/view/30316

Moran, R. E., Schafer, J., Bayar, M., & Starbird, K. (2025). The end of trust and safety?: Examining the future of content moderation and upheavals in professional online safety efforts. In *Proceedings of the 2025 CHI Conference on Human Factors in Computing Systems (CHI'25)* (Vol. 176, pp. 1–14). Association for Computing Machinery. https://doi.org/10.1145/3706598.3713662

Neris, N., & Valente, M. (2017). *#OutrasVozes: Gênero, raça, classe e sexualidade nas eleições de 2016*. InternetLab. http://www.internetlab.org.br/wp-content/uploads/2017/02/relatorio_outras_vozes.pdf

O Globo. (2024, October 30). *Assassinato de Marielle e Anderson: Os detalhes de um crime "quase perfeito"*. O Globo. https://oglobo.globo.com/rio/noticia/2024/10/30/assassinato-de-marielle-e-anderson-os-detalhes-de-um-crime-quase-perfeito.ghtml

Oliva, T., Pavarin Tavares, V., & Valente, M. (2020). *Uma solução única para toda a internet? Riscos do debate regulatório brasileiro para a operação de plataformas de conhecimento*. InternetLab. https://papers.ssrn.com/abstract=40961891-action-social-media-violence

Paiva, L. (2022, August 24). *Campanha de Tebet rejeita questionar violência política de gênero na Justiça*. Jota.

Paulo, F. D. S.. (2014, February 26). Facebook censura postagem da *Folha* com nudez. Folha de S. Paulo. http://www1.folha.uol.com.br/poder/2014/02/1418174-facebook-censura-postagem-da-folha-com-nudez.shtml

Paulo, F. D. S.. (2020, January 5). *COM decretações via rede social, assassinato de meninas dispara no CE*. https://www1.folha.uol.com.br/cotidiano/2020/01/com-decretacoes-via-rede-social-assassinato-de-meninas-dispara-no-ce.shtml

Paulo, P. P. (2024, October 28). *Apenas duas capitais elegem prefeitas mulheres em 2024*. G1. https://g1.globo.com/politica/eleicoes/2022/eleicao-em-numeros/noticia/2024/10/28/apenas-duas-capitais-elegem-prefeitas-mulheres-em-2024.ghtml.

Phillips, W. (2015). *This is why we can't have nice things: Mapping the relationship between online trolling and mainstream culture*. MIT Press.

Posetti, J., Shabbir, N., Maynard, D., et al. (2021). *The chilling: Global trends in online violence against women journalists*. UNESCO. https://unesdoc.unesco.org/ark:/48223/pf0000377223

Ramos, L. O., Barbieri, C. H. C., Herscovici, A., et al. (2020). *Candidatas em jogo: Um estudo sobre os impactos das regras eleitorais na inserção de mulheres na política*. FGV Direito. http://bibliotecadigital.fgv.br:80/dspace/handle/10438/29826

Rebaixada. (2014, February 23). *Como o Facebook censurou a postagem antiga, estamos republicando*. https://web.archive.org/web/20140921025008/http://rebaixada.org/como-o-facebook-censurou-a-postagem-antiga-estamos-republicando-nudez-em-pro/

Repórteres Sem Fronteiras, & Instituto de Tecnologia e Sociedade. (2021). *Relatório: Ataques ao jornalismo se alastraram nas redes*. https://rsf.org/sites/default/files/relatorio_ataquesaojornalismo_rsf_3.pdf

Revista AzMina, & InternetLab. (2021). *MonitorA: Relatório sobre violência política online em páginas e perfis de candidatas(os) nas eleições municipais de 2020*. AzMina, InternetLab e Volt Data Lab. https://www.internetlab.org.br/wp-content/uploads/2021/03/5P_Relatorio_MonitorA-PT.pdf

Rodrigues, H. (2022, September 19). *Isa Penna é ameaçada de morte; autor exige que Douglas Garcia não seja cassado*. Fórum. https://revistaforum.com.br/politica/2022/9/19/isa-penna-ameacada-de-morte-autor-exige-que-douglas-garcia-nao-seja-cassado-123506.html

Rossi, M. (2019). *Debora Diniz: 'Não sou desterrada. Não sou refugiada. Qual é a minha condição?'* El País. https://brasil.elpais.com/brasil/2019/02/22/politica/1550871025_250666.htm

Rupp, I. (2021, January 10). *Ameaças de neonazistas a vereadoras negras e trans alarmam e expõem avanço do extremismo no Brasil*. El País. https://brasil.elpais.com/brasil/2021-01-10/ameacas-de-neonazistas-a-vereadoras-negras-e-trans-alarmam-e-expoem-avanco-do-extremismo-no-brasil.html

Simas, L. A., & Rufino, L. (2018). *Fogo no mato: A ciência encantada das macumbas*. Mórula.

Tavares, C., & Borges, E. (2021). *Falando sobre ataques online e trolls: Um guia para jornalistas e criadores de conteúdo na internet*. InternetLab; Redes Cordiais. https://internetlab.org.br/wp-content/uploads/2021/06/guia_trolls_paginasimples_12062021_ok.pdf

Terra. (2014, March 20). *Confeiteira tem imagem de bolo retirada do Facebook por nudez*. Terra. https://www.terra.com.br/byte/confeiteira-tem-imagem-de-bolo-retirada-do-facebook-por-nudez,eab201ef86fd4410VgnVCM5000009ccceb0aRCRD.html

The White House. (2025a, January 20). *Restoring freedom of speech and ending federal censorship*. https://www.whitehouse.gov/presidential-actions/2025/01/restoring-freedom-of-speech-and-ending-federal-censorship/

The White House. (2025b, February 21). *Defending American companies and innovators from overseas extortion and unfair fines and penalties*. https://www.whitehouse.gov/presidential-actions/2025/02/defending-american-companies-and-innovators-from-overseas-extortion-and-unfair-fines-and-penalties/

The White House. (2025c, July 23). *Preventing woke AI in the federal government*. https://www.whitehouse.gov/presidential-actions/2025/07/preventing-woke-ai-in-the-federal-government/

Tobin, A., Varner, M., & Angwin, J. (2017, December 28). *Facebook's uneven enforcement of hate speech rules allows vile posts to stay up*. ProPublica. https://www.propublica.org/article/facebook-enforcement-hate-speech-rules-mistakes

Valente, M. (2023). *Online gender-based violence in Brazil: New data insights*. CIGI.

Valente, M., Neris, N., Ruiz, J., & Bulgarelli, L. (2016). *O corpo é o código*. InternetLab.

Venturini, A. C., Carvalho, D. R., Sales, F. R., et al. (2022). *Violações à liberdade acadêmica no Brasil: Caminhos para uma metodologia*. Centro de Análise da Liberdade e do Autoritarismo (Laut). https://laut.org.br/violacoes-a-liberdade-academica-no-brasil/

VoteLGBT. (2022). *A política LGBT+ brasileira: Entre potências e apagamentos*. https://www.votelgbt.org/s/2022-PT-A-POLITICA-LGBT-BRASILEIRA.pdf

Wiggins. (2025, April 3). *YouTube scraps gender identity harassment policies*. The Advocate. https://www.advocate.com/business/youtube-scraps-gender-identity-protection

6 AI Chips in, and the Paths Ahead

Abstract

Turning to synthetic media, this chapter documents how AI-generated sexualised deepfake industrialises TFGBV: cheap production pipelines, cross-platform markets, and victim-targeting in elections and schools. It surveys Brazil's recent cases and the overwhelming gendered pattern (nearly all sexual deepfakes target women), then analyses 2025's Deepfakes Law, which outlaws creating and sharing synthetic sexual imagery using someone's likeness and sets duties for intermediaries. It also tracks how the Supreme Court's 2025 rulings revisit the Marco Civil's liability model, articulating platform "duty of care" baselines in cases of misogyny. The chapter closes by weighing proposals to criminalise "misogyny" as such against Brazil's penal-selectivity and racial-justice critiques and by mapping non-penal levers—procedural reforms, faster removal pathways, transparency and auditing of recommender systems, resourcing of public defenders and victim services, and education. The throughline is pragmatic: technical, legal, and cultural interventions must be co-designed to reduce harm without shrinking women's expressive space.

Keywords

AI and synthetic media · Deepfakes · Duty of care and systemic risk · Penal abolitionism and antiracism · Criminalisation of misogyny

In June 2024, BBC News Brazil published an article about a Telegram group where users would commission nude pictures of women, after sending the same pictures—with the women dressed. The group had almost 2 thousand members, and while its objective was to produce the so-called *deepfakes* or *deep nudes*, the members also had deeply misogynistic conversations about women, bragging about violent acts, and consuming *gore* (Suzuki, 2024). In 2025, at least 22 female students in a private school in Belo Horizonte, capital of Minas Gerais state, reported having had pictures posted on social media manipulated by AI to create pornographic content, being disseminated and even sold in a Telegram group by another (male) student. The images were also spread in channels promoting "masturbation championships". According to the parents, the school only took responsibility after being pressured; they refer to an intern having laughed about the situation on the phone (Neves, 2025; Zuba & Gurgel, 2025).

M. Valente, *Online Misogyny in Brazil*, Sustainable Development Goals Series,
https://doi.org/10.1007/978-3-032-07727-1_6

South Korea has experienced a surge in the spread of such content. In 2024, a BBC investigation uncovered "a systematic and organised process" in which Telegram groups play a central role in large-scale production of images of girls and women across over 500 schools and universities, with police responding slowly or refusing to act (Mackenzie & Choi, 2024). The "Seoul National University Deepfake Case", also known as "SNU Nth Room", involved graduates creating and distributing fake images of at least 61 female victims on Telegram since 2019 (Park, 2024). Similar incidents have been reported in schools across different parts of Brazil (Santos, 2024), throughout the USA (Singer, 2024), in the UK (Grant, 2023)—including cases involving teachers (Wood, 2025), and in Australia (Woodall, 2025).

However, it's not just restricted to schools. Synthetic media depicting someone's likeness has been used as a political weapon against candidates, including sexualised content. During the 2024 Brazil local elections, the two only women candidates for mayor in Brazil's largest city, São Paulo, had AI-generated nude images posted on porn sites, WhatsApp, and Telegram (Macário, 2024; Borges, 2023b)). The same occurred with female candidates in other cities as well (Arsênio, 2024; Loreny, 2024; Piassi, 2024). Back in 2018, Indian journalist Rana Ayyub, who is Muslim and often reports critically about the Indian state, was targeted with a hate campaign including fabricated nude images (Ayyub, 2018). Ayyub has been a constant victim of online violence over the years (RSF, 2024). In 2024, deepfakes of superstar Taylor Swift flooded social media worldwide (Filipovic, 2024); X was criticised for an unexplained delay in blocking the content, and eventually acted by preventing any searches with Swift's name (Silberling, 2024). The case sparked calls for regulation in the USA (Rahman-Jones, 2024). When Meta's Oversight Board analysed the company's response to AI-generated nude images in the USA and India, it pointed to inconsistencies in how cases were dealt with—less promptly in India (Kira, 2024a).

Deepfakes refer to AI-produced audio or visual media that are either manipulated or primarily synthetically generated, depicting people in scenarios they were never in, aiming to appear genuine (EPRS, 2021). The term appears to have emerged in 2017 when an anonymous Reddit user, under the pseudonym "Deepfakes", used deep learning technology to swap a person's face in pornographic videos, creating realistic fake videos of women, and it began being widely covered in the media (Cole, 2017; Rana et al., 2022). While malicious deepfakes exist across various domains—such as manipulating evidence for court cases, fraud, extortion, and influencing elections—the origin of the term is closely linked to producing nude images of women. Although precise figures are difficult to determine, one industry study using open-source research estimated that 98% of all deepfake videos involve sexual content, with 99% of those targeting women. The most common victims are South Korean singers and actresses, and 84% of those featured in such videos work within the entertainment sector (Security Hero, 2023). There is a market for this material, with easily accessible "nudify apps" like ClothOff attracting millions of visitors (Hoppenstedt & Milatz, 2025), Facebook advertisements for applications offering "DeepFake FaceSwap" at 8 USD per week (Tenbarge, 2023a), websites such as Fan-Topia where such content can be purchased via credit card (Tenbarge, 2023b), and numerous stories about Telegram groups where images can be ordered (Burgess, 2024). According to reporter Samantha Cole, who uncovered the story of the "deepfakes" Reddit user in 2017, he claimed to be merely a programmer interested in machine learning: "every technology can be used with bad motivations", he said, not recognising any ethical implications of his actions (Cole, 2017).

There are currently many ongoing conceptual discussions. What should we make of deepfakes exactly? The EU AI Act, which came into force at the start of 2024 (with deferred enforcement dates), defines deepfakes as "AI-generated or manipulated image, audio or video content that resembles existing persons, objects, places, entities or events and would falsely appear to a person to be authentic or truthful". Intent is not relevant for this definition; deepfakes would then include humour-oriented parodies, art, or uses for research and medical applications (EPRS, 2021). For deepfakes depicting nudity and sexual activity, there is a wide range of terms in use: deep nudes, deepfake pornography, AI-generated image-based violence (Karagianni & Doh, 2024), and synthetic sexually explicit material (Rousay, 2023). Deepfake pornography suffers from the same limitations discussed in relation to NCII—naturalising the unconsented nature of the act. And while the conceptual discussion unfolds, it is clear this is another chapter in the use of technology to advance and amplify forms of violence rooted in sexual submission. In just a few years, technology has developed to the point where hundreds of pictures are no longer necessary to produce a convincing deepfake; currently, one is sufficient (EPRS, 2021; Rana et al., 2022; Ryan-Mosley, 2023). This makes the situation different in that the violence is seemingly even more beyond control.

6.1 The Deepfakes Law

Seemingly, we have encountered this argument before, when Google stated in 2013 that it was unable to control the appearance of NCII in its search results, which it now does routinely (see Chap. 3). Solutions can be developed on at least five fronts, based on a study published by the European Parliament Research Service: regulating the technology (actors who produce and provide this technology, mandating labelling, restrictions, and even banning malicious forms of deepfakes), the creation (the user of the system, in restricting uses and emphasising the need for labels indicating synthetic media), the circulation (social media and messaging platforms), and developing measures to protect targets institutionally and to inform and educate the audience (EPRS, 2021). It offers a clear overview of the various entry points where policy can address the ecosystem involved in the production of violence. On the voluntary or private side, there is much that platforms and AI tools can undertake (see, for example, Jankowicz et al., 2024), and organisations have been working on benchmark defensive technologies for detecting deepfakes (WITNESS, 2025), but these measures can hardly be effective without regulation of the ecosystem.

Worldwide, various approaches have been proposed to address this issue. The UK Online Safety Act introduced new criminal offences for sharing, rather than creating, sexual deepfakes (Jankowicz et al., 2024), and placed an onus on platforms to monitor illegal content, with some authors considering the rules insufficient in the case of deepfakes involving adult women (Kira, 2024b). The EU AI Act established additional transparency obligations for systems capable of generating deepfakes (Łabuz, 2023), and the EU Directive on Combating Violence Against Women and Domestic Violence, adopted in 2024, criminalises the non-consensual distribution of produced or manipulated intimate content, including the "fabrication of deepfakes"—but only if it is subsequently made accessible to the public (Jankowicz et al., 2024).

In China, the Cyberspace Administration of China (CAC) enacted the Administrative Provisions on Deep Synthesis in Internet-Based Information Services in 2023, which prohibit using "deep synthesis services" to engage in activities forbidden by laws and administrative regulations, including disrupting social and economic order, infringing on the rights and interests of others, and threatening national security and interests (Interesse, 2022). In Taiwan, legislation from 2023 penalises producing sexual materials without the depicted individual's consent with up to three years in prison, and the unauthorised distribution with sentences ranging from six months to five years and fines, with additional penalties if the act is committed for profit (Taipei Times, 2023). The Take It Down Act in the USA, introduced in 2025, is the first federal law to criminalise the distribution of non-consensual intimate images, including deepfakes (CCRI, 2025), imposing fines and imprisonment of up to two years (or three years if targeted at minors with intent to abuse or harass). It also established notice-and-takedown procedures requiring platforms to remove flagged content within 48 hours and to delete duplicates. In South Korea, a revision of the Criminal Code in 2020 criminalised the creation and distribution of "false video products", which "may cause sexual desire or shame against the will of the person who is subject to the video", regardless of intent, with punishments of up to five years' imprisonment and up to twelve years if for profit. Loopholes include that purchasing or downloading this kind of content is not targeted, content removal is very slow, and there is a lack of capacity among training and police, despite the use of AI detection tools (Park, 2024; Jankowicz et al., 2024). It also increased police powers in conducting urgent undercover investigations in these cases and tasked the state with working to remove illegal images, support victim recovery, and establish a centre dedicated to removing victims' personal information from the internet and preventing such harms (Shin, 2024).

Before the 2024 elections, the Brazilian Superior Electoral Court issued a regulation prohibiting deepfakes and requiring explicit labelling for the use of AI in electoral propaganda. The results have not yet been assessed, and the cases mentioned earlier, where women candidates were targeted with sexual deepfakes, appeared to fall outside the concept of electoral propaganda. In March 2025, after several bills had been proposed since 2018, the Brazilian Senate approved a bill aimed at criminalising the production of deepfakes. Article 147-B of the Criminal Code, added by a reform in 2021, criminalised "Psychological Violence Against Women"; Law No. 15,123 increased the penalty by half if the crime is committed using "artificial intelligence or any other technological resource that alters the victim's image or sound".

The bill had been introduced by deputy Jandira Feghali (Communist Party of Brazil, PCdoB), who, in her justification, mentioned the harms caused in a case involving girls in a school and another one involving a famous actress, Isis Valverde. In my view, sexual deep fakes were already criminalised by Lei Rose Leonel (Law No. 13,722/2018), which, as discussed, included a provision in the Criminal Code (Art. 216-B) against producing nude or sexual scenes without one's consent, including "editing a photograph, video, audio or any other record in order to include a person in a scene of nudity or an intimate sexual or libidinous act". The strategy differs, however: the Lei Rose Leonel, despite having been devised to tackle a gender-based problem, and being framed as such, is gender-neutral; the DeepFakes Law frames the issue as a psychological violence against women crime, within the chapter of Crimes Against Personal Freedom. One can argue that the text approved may be slightly inaccurate for the objective, as it is not necessarily that victim's images or sounds are altered. How this provision will be interpreted in courts is yet to be seen.

As a strategy, however, it reflects what we have extensively discussed throughout this book: criminal law being used as a message to society, without deeper conversations about its application and effectiveness. Meanwhile, despite discussions within the Federal Government about developing a proposal to address deepfakes, the current AI regulation bill being debated in Congress (Bill n. 2338/2023) includes hardly any provisions beyond labelling that could tackle this issue, and the prospects for platform regulation remain uncertain.[1] Measures for tackling the different stakeholders who have a role in creating and disseminating misogynistic content, with varying levels of direct involvement, are less developed in the debate and much less present in the policies adopted. I will come back to this shortly; first, a short detour to address an important change in how Brazil approaches platform accountability.

[1] For a full disclosure, in 2022; I was one of the members of the Brazilian Senate Commission to draft an AI Bill that resulted in the bill being discussed in Congress in 2025, which has already been amended in negotiations in the parliament to reach its present version; during the year 2025, I was also a member of a Brazilian Federal Government Working Group to devise proposals for tackling deepfakes in the legislation. While this book is being finished, the work is not yet concluded.

6.2 Marco Civil Goes to Court

As mentioned, new rules for content moderation had been under consideration, at least since the discussion of Bill 2630/20, which was dismissed in the House after four years of debate and strong opposition from the tech and conservative sectors in Brazil. In June 2025, the update was introduced through the Supreme Court.

In a landmark ruling involving questioning whether the Marco Civil article 19 rule on internet application providers' liability was constitutional, the Court struck it partially.[2] The ruling argues that, as the internet evolved, the rule no longer protected fundamental rights and democratic values adequately, and established a new general regime of notice and takedown for criminal offences or unlawful acts, meaning that the provider becomes liable once knowledge can be asserted—usually, through a private notification. In other words, the regime for NCII or copyrights starts to apply to illegal content in general. The former regime, where a judicial removal injunction followed by non-compliance confers liability, applies now only to two hypotheses: crimes against the honour (defamation, libel, or slander), to avoid that the regime is used to censor, and email, closed video or voice meeting and private messaging applications.

The Supreme Court went further. It clarified that internet service providers' liability is presumed in cases of paid advertisements and promoted posts, as well as with bots and automated accounts. Liability is *presumed* but not *strict*, as providers can still demonstrate they acted diligently and within a reasonable timeframe and escape liability. Then, there came a few transparency obligations and a new *duty of care*, or, in other words, a specific liability regime for what was defined as "systemic failure" to promptly remove content involving serious criminal offences from a list. The ruling states that this rule will not apply to individual pieces of content; a systemic failure exists when there is a lack of proper preventive or remedial measures against the identified criminal content.

And here is where it gets interesting for misogyny. The list of where platforms must adopt this duty of care includes 7 items, and one of them reads:

> (e) crimes committed against women on the basis of their sex, including content that promotes hatred or aversion toward women (Law No. 11,340/2006, Law No. 10.446/2002, Law No. 14.192/2021, and Articles 141(§3), 146-A, 147(§1), 147-A, and 147-B of the Criminal Code).

Other items include anti-democratic acts, acts of terrorism, racism, and child sexual abuse. The item on crimes against women based on their sex is broad, seeming to mean that any crime committed on these grounds *and* content that promotes hatred or aversion towards women trigger this duty of care. However, because the list of crimes that trigger the duty of care is said to be *exhaustive*, it is likely that it is interpreted over time as being specific to the legal provisions mentioned. This would mean that, in the absence of a crime of misogynistic speech, platforms would be required to carefully watch and act upon the following illegal practices, when they are committed *on the basis of women's sex*:

1. Domestic violence against women (Law no. 11,340/2006);
2. Political violence against women (Law No. 14.192/2021);
3. Crimes against the honour (defamation, libel, slander) when against a woman on the basis of her sex (Criminal Code, Article 141(§3));
4. Bullying, or systematic intimidation (Criminal Code, Article 146-A);
5. Stalking (Criminal Code, Article 147-A);
6. Psychological violence against women, particularly through AI—the deepfakes case, which I will discuss ahead (Criminal Code, 147-B);
7. Law No. 10.446/2002 is cited, which defines the attribution of the Federal Police and was changed by Lei Lola. This particular item is tricky, as, as we have seen, it includes a gen-

[2] A non-official translation done by InternetLab can be found here: https://internetlab.org.br/wp-content/uploads/2025/07/InternetLab-STF-decision-on-article--19-Translation-to-English-1-1.pdf

eral qualification of crimes that "disseminate misogynistic content", defined as those that "propagate hatred or aversion to women", but only to define police attributions.

On the one hand, this ruling changes the game in the public recognition of TFGBV, elevating it to the status of the most serious content that platforms must control. On the other hand, it is narrowed down to sex, as in previous laws, and its language leaves room for many doubts. It densifies the legal provisions against misogyny, as it mentions promoting "hatred or aversion towards women", not to generally criminalise it, but to determine that internet providers must act on it. However, such content is not criminalised per se, as the legal provisions mentioned testify. When this book is completed, the ruling may still change following clarification motions from various stakeholders; it is likely that these issues will be clarified further, and it is even possible that this item will be removed from the list.

The decision recognises a growing consensus that the regime established by Marco Civil, initially seen as promoting human rights protections, required adjustments to better cover the roles these services have developed over time in content curation, promotion, and monetisation. It also appears to address concerns about the complexities of creating a balanced model that, simultaneously, considers the rights of individuals who suffer violence and harm, while avoiding inadvertently enabling censorship by powerful entities targeting dissenting speech and diverse expressions in a country as diverse as Brazil. Naturally, it has faced criticism—for example, for using vague concepts and establishing new obligations that would necessitate an independent supervisory authority to be effective, as well as overreach into services like online encyclopaedias (Massaro & Reis, 2025). Furthermore, the provisions would be more legitimate and clearer if incorporated into legislation, and the ruling defers to Congress to draft relevant laws. These are aspects that may undergo reform. What is certain is that the Marco Civil model has evolved, and some impact on TFGBV will undoubtedly occur, even if misogyny does not remain within the duty of care. Congress might still revisit platform regulation. Everything is changing rapidly, and I recommend that the reader seek updates on the development of these issues. I hope these reflections will remain relevant for a longer time.

The arc marked by the Carolina Dieckmann Law and the DeepFakes Law is a path that, on the one hand, shows an increase in debate and understanding of the effects of violence and misogyny in the effective presence and rights of women, Black, Indigenous, and LGBTQIAP+ people in online spaces. If we go back to Chap. 2 and see how the press treated what happened to Dieckmann and how it understood the possible uses of the internet for expression, particularly of historically marginalised people and groups, we can see that progress has been phenomenal. From another perspective, however, we see how relatively limited our repertoire of legal responses still is—and how little dialogue there is between the fundamentally criminal responses and the responses that can be given in the context of regulating the internet and digital platforms, and even more specific issues involving content moderation.

These debates are fundamentally taking place in parallel, although they are increasingly overlapping due to the social movements and civil society organisations that have been forcing the door on the different aspects of the issue. For example, in March 2023, federal deputy Guilherme Boulos (Socialism and Liberty Party) proposed a bill that aimed to address online misogyny not through the lens of criminalisation—which was dominating the public debate, due to other proposals to criminalise misogyny—but by focusing on specific obligations for internet platforms. The Supreme Court has also recognised how, constitutionally, illegal misogynistic content must be treated with priority. Regardless of the details of the bill or the ruling, these are important signals, as the large majority of proposals aimed at regulating digital platforms do not even mention misogyny. This may be a result of this long process and the interaction between these multiple aspects, the threads of which I hope to have woven throughout these chapters.

6.3 Criminalising Misogyny?

In February 2023, actress and comedian Livia La Gatto made a video mocking influencer and coach Thiago Schutz, who profits from recording videos with advice for men from the Red Pill community. The term "red pill" originates from the film Matrix, where Keanu Reeves' character is presented with the choice between a blue pill and a red pill: the red pill signifies knowing the truth, while the blue pill means continuing to live in a cosy fantasy. In the redpillers' view, there is knowledge that can free men from women, who they see as self-interested and shallow. The community also propagates that women should be dominated and discarded. In some versions of the discourse, certain women have value, which is not the case with feminists.

La Gatto went viral with the video and received a message from Schutz demanding that it be removed. If she did not delete it, it would be "trial or bullet". Frightened, she publicised what had happened and obtained precautionary measures against him in court—not only that he couldn't go near her or contact her, but also the suspension of any gun possession, the seizure of his passport, and a ban on talking about Lívia on social media. La Gatto obtained the equivalent of a protective measure under the Maria da Penha Law, but no relationship between them would qualify the case as domestic violence. She also filed a police report for the threat (Tomaz, 2023).

The case sparked a significant debate in the media and on social media about misogyny on the internet. Terms such as red pill, MGTOW, and incel were referenced in various reports, podcasts, and discussions (Nery, 2023). One of the central themes that most mobilised feminist counterpublics, creating a considerable divide, was the criminalisation of misogyny.

Psychologist and professor at the University of Brasilia, Valeska Zanello, started circulating a petition for a legislative idea—which any citizen can propose if they get 20,000 signatures, forcing senators to debate the issue—to include misogyny among hate crimes. Taking advantage of the movement, MP Dandara (Workers Party, PT) and Senator Ana Paula Lobato (Brazilian Social Party, PTB) proposed a bill with similar content, each in their own legislative house. In an interview, Zanello said:

> When the case of Lívia La Gatto came up, I was very impressed by how misogyny is acceptable, especially with these "red pill" groups [macho male communities] and the attack she also suffered, a death threat. And then I thought: "Well, now is the time for us to discuss it," said the researcher.
>
> I can only think that misogyny is so normalised that it becomes invisible. Through our socialisation into womanhood, we learn to accept it. Then we learn that it's just a joke. "Oh, don't mind me, it's a dad joke", "Oh, you're the boring one, the troublemaker". So, hate speech against women is normalised, and there are many ways in which it manifests itself. (apud Borges, 2023a)

Both bills include misogyny in the list of forms of discrimination provided for in the Antiracism Law, which I have dealt with so much in this book. In the House bill, it would become a crime to practice, induce or incite misogyny, defined as "manifestation that inferiorises, degrades or dehumanises women, based on prejudice against people of the female sex or on arguments of male supremacy". In the Senate bill, misogyny is defined as "conduct that manifests hatred or aversion toward women, based on the belief in the supremacy of the male gender." In October 2025, the bill was approved in the Senate; a few days later, however, a group of ten senators requested that the matter be reconsidered by the plenary, arguing that the definition was too broad and imprecise. These developments are still unfolding as this book goes to press, and readers are encouraged to seek updated information.

Important feminists have come out in defence of the initiatives. Soraia Mendes, a lawyer and feminist researcher, wrote in the online newspaper Portal Catarinas that highlighting the misogynistic nature of the violence committed against Brazilian women since 2016 is "a requirement for getting the democratic process back on track" (Mendes, 2023). Philosopher Marcia Tiburi wrote in a leftist media, Brasil 247, that it is not possible to prosecute someone for misogyny, and that criminalising misogyny is not the same as punitivism:

> A law against misogyny may not protect women, but it does stand in the way of the patriarchy, putting limits on its misogynistic rage for symbolic and physical violence. Just as we overcame the misogynistic epistemology of "legitimate defence of honour", we won the use of the term "feminicide" and we must continue to advance against the naturalisation of hatred against women. (Tiburi, 2023)

Although these two speeches support the movement, there has been criticism that criminalisation is not the solution. Anthropologist and law professor at the University of Brasilia Débora Diniz (2023) posted on her Instagram account that women's reliance on criminal law is an illusion that reinforces patriarchal power to punish. "Criminal law was not designed to protect women, but to persecute and control them". Diniz went into exile in 2018 after being targeted by online lynch mobs and threats that extended to her family. Juliana Borges (2019), writer and sociologist, author of the book *Encarceramento em Massa* ("Mass Incarceration"), wrote on Twitter:

> Criminalising anything is not a solution for the short, medium or even long term. Strengthening the penal state is a mistake on the part of some, and a project on the part of some, which will reinforce the maintenance of inequalities based on racial hierarchies. Study and flee penal populism. (Borges, 2018)

Borges' viewpoint advocates for the abolition of criminal justice systems based on racial inequalities prevalent in the Brazilian penal system. By presenting data on the widespread presence of Black individuals in Brazilian prisons and research indicating that Black women are less protected, for instance by the Maria da Penha Law, Borges questions whether criminalisation aligns with anti-racist feminism.[3] UFRJ criminal law professor Luciana Boiteux also argued, quoting Audre Lorde, that "the master's tool will never dismantle the master's house" (Boiteux, 2023).

Despite the heated debate, the discussion of criminalising misogyny is not so new: I found at least ten bills working their way through the House of Representatives since 2016, including Bill No. 9882/2017 by Ana Perugini (Workers Party) and Bill 5944/2016 by Laura Carneiro (Brazilian Democratic Movement, PMDB). Nor is it meaningless to claim that the Antiracism Law (Law No. 7716/1989) provides for discrimination on the grounds of race, colour, ethnicity, religion and national origin, that the Supreme Court has ruled that LGBTphobia is part of this group, and misogyny is not. One wonders, indeed, what it is about misogyny that makes it so different that it has not yet been considered by the legislature or the justice system. I discussed some hypotheses in Chap. 4.

It is also true that criminal law is thought of simplistically as the first response to problems, because it appears in people's minds as the solution par excellence. And possibly because it doesn't promote structural and systemic transformations.[4] Opting for the criminalising way out also comes from an impoverished and uncritical view of conflict. Throughout this book, I have dealt with how the justice system fails in relation to racism and LGBTphobia. And I have also dealt with nine enacted laws: eight of them either create new crimes or refer to criminal law (the Lola Law). It would be unfair to simplistically say that once new crimes have been created, social mobilisation on the subject is over or that feminists are satisfied.

Decades of feminist struggles have demonstrated that these struggles are multi-situated, occurring in education, popular movements, justice systems, governments, and public policy spheres. However, it is evident that the attention given to criminalisation initiatives in the media and the public arena often outweighs all other debates, which frequently overlook the contradictions within the criminal justice system. These criminalising efforts rarely consider the experiences of the poorest women, Black women, and Indigenous women. When discussing NCII in the

[3] See also Carla Akotirene, Interseccionalidade. São Paulo: Jandaíra, 2019.

[4] According to Professor Ana Flauzina (2006): "On a more general level, we understand that the State accepts pressures from the Black movement through criminal law simply because the effects of such demands will necessarily be ineffective. They are ineffective because criminal law, unlike other branches of law, is a field of negativity and repression, not constituting a space for the promotion of emancipatory interests."

third chapter, I referenced the case study on the Top 10 involving teenagers from the outskirts of São Paulo. Local activists and educators were even reluctant to begin discussing criminalisation; for them, it was clear that they relied on the state to focus on schools and community health centres.

On this issue, I favour a middle ground. I do not believe that criminalising misogyny will directly contribute to the oppression of marginalised groups throughout history, and I also think it could address some very serious cases, such as those mentioned in this book, which are not covered by other offences like threats or defamation. There is some symbolic value in including misogyny among other forms of discrimination, but it also symbolises domination rather than reparation or overcoming. I also acknowledge the fragility, selectivity, inefficiency, and violence of the criminal justice system, and I do not believe that criminalisation will aid the most vulnerable or truly help us change the current situation. To think intersectionally is to consider whether a solution for one group might have effects on others—and often, it does. Even if we assume that criminalising misogyny alone would not reinforce violations of the rights of Black people, focusing on criminal law feeds into narratives of individual responsibility within a system that oppresses specific populations. Therefore, I do not believe that criminalising misogyny should be our primary goal or focus.

Some of the positive effects that legislation criminalising misogyny could generate include offering a clear concept and a range of dispute mechanisms to boost victims' confidence, as well as providing a basis for regulating technology based on illegal content. Civil legislation could also achieve these goals without the negative consequences associated with criminal law. For example, the Political Violence Against Women Law makes notable points by targeting political parties, and this approach could be extended further. Therefore, when exploring other solutions, why aren't we more inclined to consider legal provisions for misogyny that result in civil, monetary reparations—measures that can impact powerful individuals—or protective measures specifically tailored for the online environment? Why, similar to one of the principles underpinning the Federal Constitution's approach to racial equality (Pires, 2016), aren't we more committed to affirmative and transformative actions to combat misogyny? Why aren't we discussing restorative and reparative justice tools that move away from punishment, aiming instead to address the power imbalance between offender and victim, and to empower victims and the community? Why aren't we, like New Zealand with the creation of the Net Safe agency under its Harmful Digital Communications Act of 2015, considering educational policies against misogyny on the internet and extrajudicial dispute resolution mechanisms?[5] Or debating how the state should invest in public shelters and support services to handle this form of violence?

It's worth remembering that, on the contrary, the Bolsonaro government has proposed 94 per cent less budget for the protection network to combat violence against women than the previous government, and that several policies have been dismantled (Martello, 2022). The subsequent government increased investment, but transparency remains an issue, and feminist organisations argue that it remains inadequate (Correia, 2025). Debates on restorative justice get little attention from the legislature, and almost none from the media. The repertoire of the fight against misogyny is limited, does not consider the side effects, and does not focus on reparations for the victim and the transformation of society. For the fight against misogyny, focusing on dealing with the ghost of "gender ideology" and the silencing of gender equality debates in educational environments is more urgent than thinking about punishment.

In this context, it is also important to emphasise that the legal definition of misogyny has focused on the condition of women, without incorporating a debate that is growing in academia and civil society about misogyny as a practice against women, viewing gender as a system rather than just a cultural expression of a binary (Moschkovich, 2020). Although it makes sense to use the category of women, recognising gender as a system that functions in relationships means that we need to acknowledge that misogynistic vectors can also act in violence against other individuals,

[5] See Neris et al., 2017.

such as gay men. There is a tendency for these issues to become more prominent as the misogyny debate intensifies and grows more complex.

To find new ways of combating misogyny online, we must recognise that feminist discussions on misogyny and internet policies need to be integrated. The internet is a crucial space for women to express themselves, promote their agendas, and take centre stage, yet it remains a fertile ground for misogyny. Having worked in this field of internet rights and policies for years, it's clear how challenging it is to incorporate gender debates into discussions on freedom of expression, association, election policies, democracy, and disinformation. These issues often remain marginal, or when they do receive attention, they are quickly pushed back to the margins. For example, observe the mobilisation around potential new internet regulations in Brazil in relation to threats to democratic rule of law in 2023: misogyny and gender issues rapidly disappeared from the debate, and many key proposals—despite being longstanding threats to democracy and rights—were sidelined. Furthermore, misogynist attacks and school massacres inspired by misogynist forums have persisted even as the internet debate moved on. The same applies to antiracism, Indigenous struggles, and LGBTQIAP+ rights. Current internet rights and policies are still predominantly shaped with cis white male internet users, urban dwellers with high purchasing power, in mind. This must change.

In 2025, we can no longer accept a debate on freedom of expression that does not fully address the voices of those silenced by violence. We cannot discuss policies to fight disinformation or protect electoral integrity without making gender-based political violence central to the conversation. One of the main bills debated in recent years, Bill 2630/2020, at one point proposed immunity for parliamentarians online, driven by fears of de-platforming, as happened with Trump in the United States—without recognising the significant impact that speeches by parliamentarians have had on violence against women in Brazil in recent years, which I explore in particular in Chap. 5. What policies are required to change this situation?

Social media platform companies often have teams that are extremely skilled and well-intentioned in defending these rights and advancing content moderation policies. They prioritise the safety, well-being and rights of historically marginalised groups, but often find it difficult to get their issues prioritised internally. This is when they are not dismantled and delegitimised in times of crisis, or are the main target in the famous lay-offs that have been happening in droves in technology companies.

Social media companies do not invest enough in content moderation that considers the local context to fully understand the issues, especially in non-central economies (such as Brazil, which is relatively privileged compared to other Latin American countries). We see that internal critical perspectives are accepted only up to page two, as demonstrated by the dismissal of Timnit Gebru from Google in 2020 (Metz & Wakabayashi, 2020) and the many revelations from the Facebook Papers (Núcleo Jornalismo, 2021), as well as Meta's recent shift towards a simplistic view that content moderation for safety equals freedom of expression. No platform provides sufficiently detailed data showing the prevalence of misogyny, racism, and LGBTphobia, nor the actions they undertake. There are almost no mechanisms for participation or democratic governance in the formulation and implementation of platform policies—or in drafting the laws that regulate the internet, for that matter. Many policies are created without addressing concrete issues: for example, many social networks assume that public figures have a "thick skin" and remove less offensive content against them, without considering that misogyny constantly drives women journalists and politicians off the internet.

The present and the future point to new challenges that will require fresh research and innovative solutions. In the several years when I was working in this book, the surge in generative artificial intelligence systems, such as ChatGPT and similar platforms, erupted, bringing with it concerns about how these tools source information and represent various populations in their results. Algorithmic discrimination was already an issue, but it is beginning to take on new dimensions with the expectations surrounding these tools. Twitter's acquisition by Elon Musk and subsequent transformation into X meant that access to data became much more difficult, beyond having become a haven for an absolutist policy of freedom of expression, which has only highlighted important questions about the private power behind these platforms—in this case, concentrated in a single individual—and which demand more courageous solutions.

Researching these topics is challenging due to the lack of data, tools, and effective projects for sharing information with researchers. When it comes to regulation, there are intrinsic limits in businesses whose monetisation is based on viral content, which seeks to capture the user's attention for as long as possible and exploit micro-segmentation for targeting of content and advertisements based on personal data and the construction of profiles that crystallise and stigmatise. That is why debating the regulation of business models, data protection, regimes and rights related to content moderation, the accountability of internet platforms, transparency rules in content control policies and practices, access and diversity policies in knowledge and culture on the internet, which take into account diverse knowledge, representativeness in programming teams, rules for preventing and remedying algorithmic discrimination, and sovereignty and technological autonomy policies for marginalised populations are integral parts of the misogyny debate today. What's more, when law is the instrument, the debate does not end with the passing of laws. We have seen that implementation and institutions are a whole field of disputes. Feminism has increasingly taken on these debates, and they need to incorporate feminism in turn. Our task is to debate what rules, beyond criminal law, we need to have in place from now on to deal with misogyny on the internet.

This book concentrates on the path established by the law, without, however, relying on it to resolve the problem of misogyny. Throughout, I have emphasised the importance of culture, power, and social conflicts in manifestations of misogyny. But there is a role for the law beyond mere criminalisation. In a compelling 1987 text, brought to my attention by researchers I have been fortunate to work with over these years, Columbia University professor Patricia Williams challenges the tradition of critical legal studies, to which she belongs. In it, she rejects the idea of abandoning the discourse and language of rights, arguing that, for those who suffer from discrimination, the granting of rights is an elevation from the status of a human body to that of a social being (Williams, 1987; Neris, 2018). In other words, we cannot relinquish it. And, given everything we have experienced thus far, I would add: as women, we cannot give up the internet either.

References

Akotirene, C. (2019). *Interseccionalidade*. Jandaíra.

Arsênio, L. (2024, September 6). *Letícia Arsenio on Instagram*. https://www.instagram.com/leticiaarsenio/reel/C_l_3-oPgDg/

Ayyub, R. (2018, November 21). *I was the victim of a deepfake porn plot intended to silence me: Rana Ayyub*. HuffPost. https://www.huffpost.com/archive/in/entry/deepfake-porn_a_23595592

Boiteux, L. [@luboiteux]. (2023, March 5). *Por um feminismo antipunitivista! O caso da comediante....* [Tweet]. X. https://twitter.com/luboiteux/status/1632406538886234113

Borges, J. [@julianaborges_1]. (2018, March 5). Criminalizar qualquer coisa... [Tweet]. X (formerly Twitter). https://twitter.com/julianaborges_1/status/1632051578474569731

Borges, J. (2019). *Encarceramento em Massa*. Jandaíra.

Borges, B. (2023, March 9). *Ideia para criminalizar misoginia obtém 23 mil assinaturas em cinco dias e vira projetos na Câmara e no Senado*. G1.

Borges, J. [@JULIANABORGES_1]. (2023, March 3). *Criminalizar qualquer coisa....* [Tweet]. X. https://twitter.com/julianaborges_1/status/1632051578474569731

Burgess, M. (2024, October 15). *Millions of people are using abusive AI 'Nudify' bots on Telegram*. Wired. https://www.wired.com/story/ai-deepfake-nudify-bots-telegram/

CCRI. (2025). *Nonconsensual distribution of intimate images*. Cyber Civil Rights Initiative. https://cybercivilrights.org/nonconsensual-distribution-of-intimate-images/

Cole, S. (2017, December 11). *AI-assisted fake porn is here and we're all fucked*. VICE. https://www.vice.com/en/article/gal-gadot-fake-ai-porn/

Correia, M. (2025, March 7). Economia é coisa de mulher, mas orçamento para mulheres ainda é pouco transparente. Agência Pública. https://apublica.org/2025/03/economia-e-coisa-de-mulher-mas-orcamento-para-mulheres-ainda-e-pouco-transparente/

Diniz, D. (2023, 4 de março). *Feminismo punitivista*. Instagram. https://www.instagram.com/p/CpXM7cPuhAG

EPRS. (2021). *Tackling deepfakes in European policy (European parliamentary research service)*. European Parliament. https://www.europarl.europa.eu/thinktank/en/document/EPRS_STU(2021)690039

Filipovic, J. (2024, January 31). *Anyone could be a victim of 'deepfakes'. But there's a reason Taylor Swift is a target*. The Guardian. https://www.theguardian.com/commentisfree/2024/jan/31/taylor-swift-ai-pictures-far-right

Flauzina, A. L. P. (2006). *Corpo negro caído no chão: O sistema penal e o projeto genocida do Estado brasileiro* (Master's thesis). UnB. https://repositorio.unb.br/handle/10482/5117

Grant, H. (2023, November 27). *UK school pupils 'using AI to create indecent imagery of other children.'* The Guardian. https://www.theguardian.com/global-development/2023/nov/27/uk-school-pupils-using-ai-create-indecent-sexual-abuse-images-of-other-children

Hoppenstedt, M., & Milatz, M. (2025, July 1). *Using AI to humiliate women: The men behind deepfake pornography*. Der Spiegel. https://www.spiegel.de/international/zeitgeist/using-ai-to-humiliate-women-the-men-behind-deepfake-pornography-a-0de338f9-9cec-4ae8-a5ef-9a356b0a5bd4

Interesse, G. (2022, December 20). *China to regulate deep synthesis (Deepfake) technology from 2023*. China Briefing News. https://www.china-briefing.com/news/china-to-regulate-deep-synthesis-deepfake-technology-starting-january-2023/

Jankowicz, N., Gomez-O'Keefe, I., & Hoffman, L. (2024). *It's everyone's problem: Mainstreaming responses to technology-facilitated gender-based violence* [report]. Institute of Global Politics. https://apo.org.au/node/328240

Karagianni, A., & Doh, M. (2024). A feminist legal analysis of non-consensual sexualized deepfakes: Contextualizing its impact as AI-generated image-based violence under EU law. *Porn Studies – Special Issue: Artificial Intelligence, Pornography, and Sex Work*. https://doi.org/10.1080/23268743.2024.2408277

Kira, B. (2024a). *Deepfakes, the Weaponisation of AI against women and possible solutions*. Verfassungsblog. https://doi.org/10.59704/9987d92e2c183c7f

Kira, B. (2024b). When non-consensual intimate deepfakes go viral: The insufficiency of the UK Online Safety Act. *Computer Law & Security Review*. https://doi.org/10.1016/j.clsr.2024.106024

Łabuz, M. (2023). Regulating deep fakes in the artificial intelligence act. *Applied Cybersecurity & Internet Governance, 2*(1), 1–42. https://doi.org/10.60097/ACIG/162856

Lisboa, A. P. (2020). *Acadêmicos brasileiros se exilam por ameaças de morte*. Correio Braziliense. https://www.correiobraziliense.com.br/app/noticia/eu-estudante/ensino_ensinosuperior/2020/03/13/interna-ensinosuperior-2019,834162/academicos-brasileiros-se-exilam-por-ameacas-de-morte.shtml

Loreny. (2024, August 16). *Loreny ☼ auf Instagram: "Instagram"*. https://www.instagram.com/_eusouloreny/reel/C-vqp8ovaJP/

Núcleo Jornalismo. (2021). *Provides an overview of Brazilian media coverage on the Facebook papers, highlighting the participation of major outlets such as* Folha de S. Paulo and O Estado de S. Paulo.

Macário, C. (2024, September 24). Site pornô, WhatsApp e Telegram expõem fotos falsas de Tabata Amaral e Marina Helena nuas. Lupa. https://lupa.uol.com.br/jornalismo/2024/09/24/site-porno-whatsapp-e-telegram-expoemfotos-falsas-de-tabata-amaral-e-marina-helena-nuas

Machado, M. R. A., Lima, M., & Neris, N. (2016). Racismo e Insulto Racial na Sociedade Brasileira: Dinâmicas de Reconhecimento e Invisibilização a Partir do Direito. *Novos Estudos CEBRAP, 35*, 11–28.

Mackenzie, J., & Choi, L. (2024, September 3). *South Korea: The deepfake crisis engulfing hundreds of schools*. BBC News. https://www.bbc.com/news/articles/cpdlpj9zn9go

Martello, A. (2022, September 29). *Governo Bolsonaro propõe 94% menos de recursos no orçamento para combate à violência contra mulheres, diz levantamento*. G1.

Massaro, H., & Reis, D. (2025, October 31). Entre liberdade de expressão e dever de cuidado: Supremo Tribunal Federal redefine a responsabilidade das plataformas. InternetLab. https://internetlab.org.br/pt/opiniao/entreliberdade-de-expressao-e-dever-de-cuidado-supremo-tribunal-federal-redefine-a-responsabilidade-dasplataformas/

Mendes, S. (2023, 6 de março). *Criminalizar a misoginia não é punitivismo*. Catarinas.

Metz, C., & Wakabayashi, D. (2020, December 3). *Google researcher says she was fired over paper highlighting bias in A.I.* The New York Times. https://www.nytimes.com/2020/12/03/technology/google-researcher-timnit-gebru.html

Moschkovich, M. (2020). Notas para um materialismo bialético. *Revista Brasileira de Estudos da Homocultura, 3*(10), 109–127.

Neris, N. (2018). Um efeito alquímico: sobre o uso do discurso dos direitos pelas/os negras/os. *Revista Direito e Práxis, 9*(1), 250–275.

Neris, N., Ruiz, J. P., & Valente, M. (2017). Análise comparada de estratégias de enfrentamento a 'revenge porn' pelo mundo. *Revista Brasileira de Políticas Públicas, 7*(3), 333–347.

Nery, N. (2023). Redpill: A misoginia como lucro. *O Assunto, 912*.

Neves, G. (2025, June 4). *Alunas denunciam criação e venda de "nudes falsos" com IA em colégio tradicional de BH*. Noticias R7. https://noticias.r7.com/minas-gerais/alunas-denunciam-criacao-e-venda-de-nudes-falsos-com-ia-em-colegio-tradicional-de-bh-04062025/

Park, L. (2024, June 14). *South Korea's deepfake sex crime epidemic exposes lack of legal protections*. Korea Pro. https://koreapro.org/2024/06/south-koreas-deepfake-sex-crime-epidemic-exposes-lack-of-legal-protections/

Piassi, P. (2024). *Prefeita de Bauru registra boletim de ocorrência contra veiculação de deepfake com seu rosto sobre corpo nu*. G1. https://g1.globo.com/sp/bauru-marilia/eleicoes/2024/noticia/2024/09/19/prefeita-de-bauru-registra-boletim-de-ocorrencia-contra-veiculacao-de-deep-fakes-com-seu-rosto-sobre-corpo-nu.ghtml

Pires, T. (2016). Criminalização do racismo: Entre política de reconhecimento e meio de legitimação do controle social sobre os negros. Rio de Janeiro: Ed. PUC-Rio.

Rahman-Jones, I. (2024, January 26). *Taylor Swift deepfakes spark calls in Congress for new legislation*. BBC News. https://www.bbc.com/news/technology-68110476

Rana, M. S., Nobi, M. N., Murali, B., & Sung, A. H. (2022). Deepfake detection: A systematic literature review. *IEEE Access, 10*, 25494–25513. https://doi.org/10.1109/ACCESS.2022.3154404

Raymond, S. (2021, December 13). *Insight: Deepfake anyone? AI synthetic media tech enters perilous phase*. Reuters. https://www.reuters.com/technology/deepfake-anyone-ai-synthetic-media-tech-enters-perilous-phase-2021-12-13/

Rousay, V. (2023, August 18). *Pornhub's Deepfake deception: Yet another way the porn Giant profits from abuse*. NCOSE. https://endsexualexploitation.org/articles/pornhubs-deepfake-deception-yet-another-way-the-porn-giant-profits-from-abuse/

RSF. (2024, November 27). *Rana Ayyub, the face of India's women journalists plagued by cyber-harassment*. Reporters Without Borders. https://rsf.org/en/rana-ayyub-face-india-s-women-journalists-plagued-cyber-harassment

Ryan-Mosley, T. (2023). A *high school's deepfake porn scandal is pushing US lawmakers into action*. MIT Technology Review. https://www.technologyreview.com/2023/12/01/1084164/deepfake-porn-scandal-pushing-us-lawmakers/

Santos, E. (2024, October 11). *O que os nudes falsos em Itararé ensinam sobre o aumento de casos de deepfakes pornográficos em escolas*. G1. https://g1.globo.com/educacao/noticia/2024/10/11/o-que-os-nudes-falsos-em-itarare-ensinam-sobre-o-aumento-de-casos-de-deepfakes-pornograficos-em-escolas.ghtml

Security Hero. (2023). *2023 state of Deepfakes: Realities, threats, and impact*. https://www.securityhero.io/state-of-deepfakes/

Shin, M. (2024, September 25). *South Korea strengthens punishment for deepfake crimes involving children*. The Readable. https://thereadable.co/south-korea-strengthens-punishment-for-deepfake-crimes-involving-children/.

Silberling, A. (2024). *The Taylor swift deepfake debacle was frustratingly preventable*. TechCrunch. https://techcrunch.com/2024/01/30/the-taylor-swift-deepfake-debacle-was-frustratingly-preventable/

Singer, N. (2024, April 8). *Teen girls confront an epidemic of deepfake nudes in schools*. The New York Times. https://www.nytimes.com/2024/04/08/technology/deepfake-ai-nudes-westfield-high-school.html.

Suzuki, S. (2024, July 18). *Pornô "deepfake": O grupo brasileiro de ódio a mulheres que fabrica imagens falsas sob encomenda com IA*. BBC News Brasil. https://www.bbc.com/portuguese/articles/cv2g3wvgldlo

Taipei Times. (2023, January 8). *Bill to curb deepfake pornography clears legislature*. Taipei Times. https://www.taipeitimes.com/News/front/archives/2023/01/08/2003792190

Tenbarge, K. (2023a, March 7). *Hundreds of sexual deepfake ads using Emma Watson's face ran on Facebook and Instagram in the last two days*. NBC News. https://www.nbcnews.com/tech/social-media/emma-watson-deep-fake-scarlett-johansson-face-swap-app-rcna73624

Tenbarge, K. (2023b, March 27). *Found through Google, bought with Visa and Mastercard: Inside the deepfake porn economy*. NBC News. https://www.nbcnews.com/tech/internet/deepfake-porn-ai-mr-deep-fake-economy-google-visa-mastercard-download-rcna75071

Tiburi, M. (2023, 5 de março). *Criminalizar a misoginia é essencial e urgente*. Brasil 247.

Tomaz, K. (2023, 7 de março). *Justiça de SP concede medida cautelar, e Thiago Schutz terá de ficar 300 metros distante de Livia La Gatto e não falar com ela*. G1. https://g1.globo.com/politica/noticia/2023/03/07/justica-de-sp-concede-medida-cautelar-e-thiago-schutz-tera-de-ficar-300-metros-distante-de-livia-la-gatto-e-nao-falar-com-ela.ghtml

Williams, P. (1987). Alchemical notes: Reconstructing ideals from deconstructed rights. *Harvard Civil Rights-Civil Liberties Law Review, 22*(2), 401.

WITNESS. (2025, July 10). *New global benchmark for AI detection*. https://www.witness.org/ai-detection-global-benchmark-witness-2/

Wood, P. (2025, March 14). *Children making malicious deepfakes of their teachers*. The Telegraph. https://www.telegraph.co.uk/news/2025/03/14/children-making-malicious-deepfakes-of-their-teachers-union/

Woodall, N. (2025, February 21). *Up to 60 Melbourne students victim to "misogynistic" deepfakes, police say*. ABC News. https://www.abc.net.au/news/2025-02-21/gladstone-park-secondary-explicit-deepfakes-students/104965106

Zuba, F., & Gurgel, L. (2025, June 4). *Estudantes denunciam que tiveram imagens íntimas criadas por IA*. G1. https://g1.globo.com/mg/minas-gerais/noticia/2025/06/04/estudantes-manipulacao-vazamento-imagens-intimas-ia-colegio-bh.ghtml

Index

M. Valente, *Online Misogyny in Brazil*, Sustainable Development Goals Series,
https://doi.org/10.1007/978-3-032-07727-1

MIX
Papier aus verantwortungsvollen Quellen
Paper from responsible sources
FSC® C105338

If you have any concerns about our products,
you can contact us on
ProductSafety@springernature.com

In case Publisher is established outside the EU,
the EU authorized representative is:
Springer Nature Customer Service Center GmbH
Europaplatz 3, 69115 Heidelberg, Germany

Printed by Libri Plureos GmbH
in Hamburg, Germany